D1105241

PRESENTED TO:

_____

BY:

_____

Listen and be still

365 Reflections on God's Word

from the Pages of

TODAY

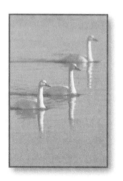

Listen and be still

365 Reflections on God's Word

from the Pages of

TODAY

This book has been compiled to be timeless. You will see no dates or months. Instead, so that you may enjoy these meditations according to your own schedule, we have provided a ribbon for you to mark your place.

The book was designed so that the reflections can be read singly as a daily devotion or thematically by section. The first two sections, entitled *Coming to Faith in Christ* and *Living the Life of Faith*, include meditations from ten different TODAY authors and can be read at any time of the year. The third section, entitled *Great Seasons of Faith*, gives special focus to the Christmas and Easter seasons.

The Road to Bethlehem offers thirty-one reflections on the birth of Jesus. If you begin this section on December 1, you will arrive in Bethlehem on December 25 in time to read "We're There at Last."

The Cross and the Risen Lord offers thirty reflections on Jesus' road to the cross and the implications of his resurrection on our life of faith. Easter Sunday's reflection, "This is the Day," is the tenth in the series, so you may want to begin this series ten days prior to Easter.

It is our prayer that each reading, in whatever order you choose, will strengthen your faith and bring you closer to our Savior, Jesus Christ.

Listen and Be Still

TABLE OF CONTENTS

The birth, life, death, resurrection, ascension, and reign of Jesus Christ changed all of human history. And these events impact our lives.

For over fifty years the Back to God Hour has been publishing a daily devotional in printed form to help readers reflect on how the events in Jesus' life are connected to our lives. From the beginning, these devotionals were written to encourage Christians to consider each day the claims of the Lord Jesus on human life.

This book is a compilation of devotions gathered around twelve themes of the Christian life. As you read them you may notice that certain passages are used by more than one author. Each pastor brings a different style and emphasis, but all of them want to bring the truth of God's Word to bear on daily life.

This book comes to you with the prayer expressed by the Apostle Paul, "I pray that out of his glorious riches he may strengthen you with power through his Spirit in your inner being, so that Christ may dwell in your hearts through faith. And I pray that you, being rooted and established in love, may have power, together with all the saints, to grasp how wide and

long and high and deep is the love of Christ, and to know this love that surpasses knowledge—that you may be filled to the measure of all the fullness of God." Ephesians 3:16-19 NIV

As you listen, in quiet stillness, may you hear God speak to your heart through these devotionals.

The Back to God Hour
2005

COMING TO FAITH IN CHRIST

THAT WE MAY BELIEVE
REV. ARTHUR J. SCHOONVELD

WITH CHRIST IN LIFE AND DEATH
DR. ALEXANDER C. DEJONG

GOD'S GLORY IN CHRIST
REV. DAVID J. FEDDES

COMING TO FAITH IN CHRIST

THAT WE MAY BELIEVE

30 MEDITATIONS AND READINGS

BY REV. ARTHUR J. SCHOONVELD

REV. ARTHUR J. SCHOONVELD

As we study the gospel of John in this series of reflections, we'll follow the Lord Jesus as he touches the lives of people around him, offering hope, healing and the gift of eternal life to all who believe in him. We'll listen to his teachings, observe his miracles, stand in awe as he gives his life for us, and be assured that we serve a risen Savior.

Our prayer is that these devotional readings may help us grow stronger in our faith, introduce people to the Lord—perhaps for the first time in their lives—and serve as an incentive for all of us to invite someone to come to know the Lord Jesus personally.

Rev. Schoonveld has been a minister in the Christian Reformed Church since 1966. He retired in 2001 after serving congregations in Michigan, California and Illinois.

You Call That Talk?

God so loved the world. . . .
JOHN 3:16

JOHN 3:16-21

Some time ago I saw a cartoon that showed two people talking to each other. One person was saying, "Talk, talk, talk. That's all religion ever is—just a lot of talk."

On the next page were drawings of a newborn baby, a cross, and an open grave. Then underneath the drawings was the question "YOU CALL THAT TALK?"

The answer to that question is found in John 3:16, where the Lord Jesus says, "God so loved the world that he gave his one and only Son, that whoever believes in him shall not perish but have eternal life."

God didn't just talk about love. God acted on it by giving his Son! The apostle John put it this way in one of his letters: "God is love. This is how God showed his love among us: He sent his one and only Son into the world that we might live through him" (1 John 4:8-9).

In case you sometimes wonder whether the Christian religion is just a lot of talk, this set of devotions is for you. Or if you have a family member, a friend, or a coworker who wonders about the Christian faith, invite that person to study the gospel of John with you as you go through these devotions.

As you look and listen, you can discover for yourself that the God of the Bible does a lot more than just talk.

PRAYER

Lord our God, help us to understand how much you love us and how much you did to give us eternal life. In the name of Jesus and in the power of the Spirit we pray. Amen.

Listen and Be Still

Children of God

He gave [them] the right to become
children of God—children. . . born of God.
JOHN 1:12-13

JOHN 1:1-14

While living in southern California several years ago, I spent a day in a commune with a religious cult called "The Children of God." During one of their Bible studies it was explained to me that to become a child of God I would have to leave my family, give up my possessions, and step down as a minister in the established church. That's how the people who were there had become "children of God": through an act of their own will and by their own choice.

Thank God it's not up to us. Thank God it's not our own will or choice that makes us true children of God. In fact, according to our text, it's not possible to become a child of God by an act of our human will. The only way to become God's child is to be born of God. Says John, "To all who received him, to those who believed in his name, he gave the right to become children of God—children born not of natural descent, nor of human decision or a husband's will, but born of God."

The greatest privilege in life is God's gift alone to give. The only thing we need to do is to simply receive him into our hearts by faith and believe in the name of the Lord Jesus Christ.

Receive the Lord Jesus, and believe in his name. And when you do, the Holy Spirit will show you how to live as a true child of God.

PRAYER

Father, give us the grace to receive the Lord Jesus as our Savior, and help us to believe in his name. Show us, we pray, by the Spirit's power, how to live as your children. Amen.

Listen and Be Still

Have You Seen Him?

The Word became flesh and made his dwelling among us. We have seen his glory. . . .
JOHN 1:14

JOHN 1:14-18

In a book called *On the Other Side*, a Dutch minister tells the story of a dying prisoner in a Japanese concentration camp during the Second World War. This is what the prisoner said: "This camp has become for me the gateway to heaven. When I came here, I knew about God, but now I have seen him." Surrounded by utter misery, the man caught a glimpse of God's presence in people for the first time in his life.

It's possible to go through life knowing about God but never really seeing God. It's possible to know about the Lord Jesus without really seeing him. It's possible to hear about the Lord without really knowing him.

Have you seen the Savior? Have you really met him?

Can you truly say that you have a personal relationship with Jesus because you have seen his glory?

If not, ask the Holy Spirit to use this study of John's gospel to help you see Jesus.

We need eyes of faith to see the Savior; we need hearts that understand who he is and what he has done. Pray that the Holy Spirit will come into your heart to help you see. Ask the Spirit to open the eyes of those around you so that together you can say with John, "We have seen his glory, the glory of the One and Only, who came from the Father, full of grace and truth."

PRAYER

Dear Lord, help us to really see you through eyes of faith so that we too can become eyewitnesses to your glory. Please also open the eyes of others around us, we pray. In Jesus, Amen.

Listen and Be Still

7

Bringing Someone to Jesus

The first thing Andrew did was to find. . . Simon and tell him, "We have found the Messiah."
JOHN 1:41

JOHN 1:35-42

In a local hospital a chaplain was explaining the way of salvation to a man who was recovering from a massive heart attack. One of the patient's coworkers was also there listening to the conversation. When the chaplain finished, the patient looked at his coworker and asked, "Did you know that?" The coworker answered, "Yes, I did." At that, the patient responded, "But why didn't you ever tell me?"

This is a crucial question: Why don't I tell that person close to me—my friend, or colleague, or coworker? Why am I withholding the most important news there is, and why don't I bother to introduce others to Jesus?

It would have been unthinkable for Andrew to keep the news about Jesus to himself. The first thing he did was to find his brother and tell him he had found the Messiah. Of course!

Only the Messiah, the Savior, can give eternal life. Only the Savior can forgive. Only Jesus saves.

Andrew understood. And that's the reason he not only told Simon about Jesus but also brought him to Jesus.

If we have met the Savior, if we believe that Jesus is the way, the truth, and the life (John 14:6), of course we'll want to tell others about him. Would we want someone to point to us someday and say, "But you never told me about Jesus"?

PRAYER

Father, forgive us for times we've failed to tell some people in our lives about you. Make it the most natural thing for us to bring others to Jesus. In his name, Amen.

Listen and Be Still

Jesus and Our Everyday Lives

Jesus and his disciples had also been invited to the wedding.
JOHN 2:2

JOHN 2:1-11

There's an old legend about a group of angels in charge of heaven's publicity. It says that shortly before Jesus began his public ministry, those angels called a special meeting to decide on the best way to introduce Jesus publicly. Together they decided that he should get everyone's attention by doing a sensational miracle in the center of Jerusalem during a major religious festival. But of course that never happened.

John tells us that Jesus performed his first miracle at a wedding in Cana in Galilee and "thus revealed his glory." Instead of a glamorous introduction before a huge crowd, Jesus chose to reveal himself at a small family wedding.

Why? Jesus does not explain. But one thing we know is that Jesus wants to be part of our everyday lives. He wants to be invited to the high points as well as the low points in our lives. Jesus wants to share in our celebrations as well as our sorrows, because he's the Savior of all of life. Jesus shows here that he came to transform all of life. He revealed his glory at an ordinary wedding, and as a result "his disciples put their faith in him."

Jesus wants to be part of your life too. Invite him to your celebrations as well as your times of sorrow. And when you do, he will transform your life, and you will see his glory.

PRAYER

Lord Jesus, we ask you to be part of our everyday lives. Please be with us in our joys and in our sorrows, and help us to see your glory. In your name we pray. Amen.

Listen and Be Still

One Thing Money Can't Buy

"I tell you the truth, no one can see the
kingdom of God unless he is born again."
JOHN 3:3

JOHN 3:1-15

The talk show host Phil Donahue once asked a guest on his cable-network show, "Let me get this straight: you mean to tell me that you have to be a born-again Christian to get to heaven?" When his guest answered by quoting John 3:3, some people in the audience were visibly annoyed. They considered it a putdown for other religions.

But whatever people might think, God says that being born again is absolutely necessary. Unless you and I are born again, we can't be saved. No matter how impressive our religious credentials or background might be, we are outside the kingdom of God unless we are born again in Christ. Nicodemus, with his impressive religious credentials, was still outside the kingdom.

For each of us, then, the most important question is *Have I been born again?* And the most important thing to know is that we can't make it happen. Parents can't do it for their children, and children can't do it for their parents. The Holy Spirit makes it happen when people begin to listen to God's Word, the Bible. As Romans 10:17 says, "Faith comes from hearing the message, and the message is heard through the word of Christ."

All we can do is place ourselves where the Holy Spirit is active: in church, which is the workshop of the Holy Spirit, and wherever else God's Word is heard.

PRAYER

Holy Spirit, work in our hearts so that we may experience new birth in Christ and become part of the kingdom of God. In Jesus' name we pray. Amen.

Listen and Be Still

Life or Death?

"Whoever believes. . . is not condemned, but whoever does not
. . . stands condemned already."
JOHN 3:18

JOHN 3:16-21

Some years ago a popular song carried these haunting lines: "I know there is no heaven, and I hope there is no hell." Millions of people go through life with that same sentiment. Many others refuse to believe in life after death altogether, and still others think that in the end everyone will go to heaven.

Whatever our wishes or opinions might be, Jesus makes clear that there is life after death and that there is a heaven and a hell. Where you or I will spend eternity is not determined by our feelings, our efforts, or our respectable lives. It all depends on whether we believe in the Son of God, Jesus Christ, as our Savior and Lord. He says, "Whoever believes in him is not condemned, but whoever does not believe stands condemned already."

Now, this isn't something we as Christians talk about flippantly. As the apostle Paul writes, "God our Savior . . . wants all men to be saved and to come to a knowledge of the truth" (1 Timothy 2:3-4). Or, as Jesus says in John 3:17, "God did not send his Son into the world to condemn the world, but to save the world through him." That's why the Bible invites us to believe, and why we in turn are called to invite others to believe. Some people have never heard. Some people don't think there's a heaven or hell. We are called to tell people what God has done to save them.

PRAYER

Father in heaven, thank you for saving us from eternal condemnation by sending your Son. Help us to believe in him through the Holy Spirit. In Jesus' name, Amen.

Listen and Be Still

No Coincidence

[Jesus] had to go through Samaria.
JOHN 4:4

JOHN 4:1-14

More than once in my work a random call to someone's house turned out to be the right thing to do at the right time. After calling to ask if I could stop by, more than once I've had someone say, "I'm so glad you called; I have to talk to someone." I think of these "random" calls as the prompting of the Holy Spirit.

Jesus knew when the Spirit was prompting him, and he obeyed. John tells us that Jesus "had to go through Samaria"— but not because there was no other way. Jesus could have done what most Jews did in those days. They traveled around Samaria to avoid any contact with Samaritans. Jesus "had to go through Samaria" because a Samaritan woman there was dying spiritually, and she desperately needed the water of life that only Jesus could offer. Meeting the Samaritan woman was no coincidence; it was divinely planned. And because of that a woman came to know about the living water of the Savior. And through her, many other Samaritans came to believe in Jesus.

It's no coincidence if you are living next door to an unbeliever. It's no coincidence if you are working near someone whose life is falling apart. It's no coincidence if you find yourself sitting next to someone who's searching for truth. God places people in our lives so that we can reach out to them in Jesus' name.

PRAYER

Lord, open our eyes and help us to understand that with you there is no coincidence. Help us to see opportunities to tell the people in our lives about Jesus. In his name, Amen.

Listen and Be Still

Would Jesus Worship in Your Church?

*"True worshipers will worship
the Father in spirit and truth. . . ."*
JOHN 4:23

ISAIAH 6:1-8

Would Jesus worship in your church?

That was the question a minister asked when preaching on Isaiah 6. He pointed out that worship that is acceptable to the Lord does not depend on style, or on the kinds of songs we sing, or on the liturgies we use. Those things, after all, are mainly a matter of our preferences, our personalities, our likes and dislikes. What matters is that we worship in spirit and in truth by standing in awe before the Lord, confessing our sins and shortcomings, and showing our gratitude for forgiveness and new life in Jesus Christ.

That's what Jesus talks about in John 4. The place of worship makes no difference to the Lord. Worship that brings praise to God is acceptable to God. Whenever God's people worship in spirit and in truth, God is honored. God the Father looks at our hearts when we come to worship. And God knows exactly what our motives are.

The question we need to ask ourselves is not "Do I like the worship style in our church?" The question should be "Is God pleased with how we worship?"

Do we worship in spirit and in truth? Does our worship lead us into the presence of our awesome God, and does it prepare us for the week ahead? In other words, would Jesus worship in our church?

PRAYER

Father in heaven, help us to worship in the right way. Keep us from sitting in church with a critical attitude, and teach us how to worship in spirit and in truth. In Jesus, Amen.

Listen and Be Still

13

New Beginnings

"Go, call your husband and come back."
"I have no husband," she replied.
John 4:16-17

John 4:13-26

Some people might have called her a five-time loser. The woman had been married five times, and now she had a live-in boyfriend. Because of her reputation, she had come to the well alone, when no one else would be there. She was an outcast and a reject as far as her people were concerned. She had tried to find purpose and meaning in life, but she had been looking in all the wrong places.

Then she met the Lord Jesus. For the first time in a long time someone reached out to her without looking for anything in return. Jesus asked her for some water, and in return he offered her the water of life. As he did so, he confronted her with the emptiness of her life—not to embarrass her, but to bring her to confession and to help her realize something: she would not find fulfillment in life until she drank of the Lord's living water.

That's Jesus: finding a person who's going through life on empty and offering her a new beginning. Today Jesus offers all of us a new beginning too. He knows about our lives, our broken dreams, our emptiness—and he invites us to come to him.

The Samaritan woman no longer saw herself as a reject or a loser. She rushed back to town to share her good news. Today the same Lord invites each one of us to drink of that living water by believing in him.

Prayer

Father, so many of us go through life on empty. Please fill us with that living water so that we in turn may share with others the water of life. In Jesus' name we pray. Amen.

Listen and Be Still

"I Have No One"

"Do you want to get well?"
"Sir. . . I have no one to help me. . . ."
JOHN 5:6-7

JOHN 5:1-15

One Saturday, while checking out a garage sale, I got acquainted with the owner. He told me that some 35 years ago, when his wife divorced him, his church had turned its back on him. In a city that prides itself on having a church on almost every street, no one had lifted a finger to reach out to him. He said, "Nobody cares about me." When I invited him to join us for Sunday dinner, he readily accepted, and before long he became a family friend.

Wherever we go, we can meet people like this person. Too often I've had people tell me that no one cared. And too often some of us walk right past people who have no one.

The Lord Jesus left the crowd to find the person at the pool. He interrupted his teaching to find the man who had no one. You and I are called to be Jesus' hands, feet, and voice. We are called to go out of our way to reach out to people who have no one.

Take a good look around. Talk to someone you don't know. On your lunch break, walk over to the person sitting by herself. Ask a neighbor over for a cup of coffee. Start a conversation with the person waiting on you. Make friends with the student who's standing alone on the playground. It can be surprising to find how God can use you to show his love.

PRAYER

Lord, open our eyes and make us willing to reach out to people who have no one. Use us to be your hands, feet, and voice to others, for your sake. In Jesus' name we pray. Amen.

Listen and Be Still

Don't Be Amazed

"A time is coming when all who are in their graves will hear [God's] voice and come out."
JOHN 5:28-29   JOHN 5:25-30

Listening to a radio talk show, I heard two professors talk about life after death. One was a Christian; the other was an atheist.

The atheist was sure that it was only wishful thinking to believe in a physical resurrection. He said, "When I die, my body will completely disintegrate and disappear, and no one will even know the difference."

Millions of people today believe what that professor believes. They see life as no more than a one-way journey to the cemetery. Other people believe that instead of a resurrection there will be a reincarnation. Still others, members of a new cult called "Clonaids," believe that human cloning is the key to eternal life.

Thank God for the good news recorded in John 5, John 11, and 1 Corinthians 15. Life for people who die in the Lord does not end in nothingness. Human cloning is not the key to eternal life. Says Jesus, "Do not be amazed at this, for a time is coming when all who are in their graves will hear [God's] voice and come out."

But I can't help being amazed. Every time I find myself standing at a grave site, I look around and marvel that someday every grave will be opened. And I know it's true because our Savior has come back to life.

PRAYER

Lord, we can't help being amazed at your power over death.
Thank you for your power and for your promise that the grave is
not the end. In your name we pray. Amen.

Listen and Be Still

Don't Be Afraid

They were terrified. But [Jesus] said to them,
"It is I; don't be afraid."

JOHN 6:16-24   JOHN 6:19-20

"Don't be afraid." It sounds so simple, but unfortunately it's not easy. Another outbreak of violence in the Middle East leaves several people dead or wounded. North Korea poses a nuclear threat. Pakistan and India continue to threaten each other. Militant religious groups claim victims in Indonesia and Africa. The war on terrorism continues. How can we possibly not be afraid?

Besides, so many other things also scare us. What if the tests show signs of cancer? What if I can't take care of myself any longer? What will I do if my spouse walks out on me? What about our children's future? What if the economy does not recover?

The only way to keep from being terrified is to listen to the Savior. Take a close look at Jesus, who tells us not to be afraid. And Jesus does more than just talk. Again and again he shows his power: feeding more than five thousand people, calming storms, walking on water, raising the dead. He is "our refuge and strength, an ever-present help in trouble" (Psalm 46:1).

Jesus doesn't promise that there will be no more waves, or storms, or wars. He makes clear that in this world we will have troubles and tribulations.

But he has overcome. The only way for us to face the future without fear is to put our hand in the hand of the one who holds all power.

PRAYER

Lord, so many things scare us. Please help us to look to you, to trust in you, and to believe that you hold this world in your hands. In your name we pray. Amen.

Listen and Be Still

What Are *You* Working for?

"Do not work for food that spoils,
but for food that endures to eternal life. . . ."
JOHN 6:27

JOHN 6:25-37

His name was George. At age 55 he was able to retire from his career as CEO of a large corporation. George's company had managed to avoid a major corporate scandal, and he had cashed in his company stock just before the stock-market slumped. But his success had come at a cost. His wife had left him, and his children barely acknowledged his existence.

Even so, he was all set to take it easy. He bought himself some toys he'd always wanted, and for the first time in many years he planned a long vacation. Then something happened. Six months into retirement, while sitting in his new fishing boat, George had a fatal heart attack. Everything he'd worked for in life had to be left behind, because he'd been working for food that spoils.

Millions of people are doing what George did—working for food that spoils. They spend their energy and efforts on things that don't last. In the process, some people sacrifice their families and even their relationship with God for things they can't keep.

The Lord Jesus warns against working for food that spoils, and he tells us to work for food that endures to eternal life. Food that spoils will someday be gone. Only the food that endures deserves our energy and effort. Make the Lord Jesus the center of your life, and let him satisfy you with the bread of life.

PRAYER

Lord, keep us from chasing after food that spoils. Teach us how to work for the food that endures to eternal life. For we know that only you can satisfy us. In your name, Amen.

Listen and Be Still

Plenty for Everyone

"If anyone is thirsty, let him
come to me and drink."
JOHN 7:37

JOHN 7:37-44

My wife and I had the privilege of spending some time in the Philippines. During one of our trips a missionary couple took us on a weekend excursion along the route of the Bataan Death March in World War II. At the place where the march ended, a monument had been set up to honor those who had died because of cruel treatment. According to one story, several people died of thirst after their guards forced them to look at water coming from an Artesian well but refused to let them drink. As one survivor put it, "Thirst was one of the major causes of death." Of course. We can't live without water.

According to the Bible, what is true for us physically is also true for us spiritually. We need the water of life more than we need anything else to survive for eternity, but millions of people don't even know it, and they don't know where to find it.

Today the Lord Jesus offers the water of life to all who will receive it. He says, "If anyone is thirsty, let him come to me and drink." Faith in the Lord Jesus Christ is the only way to quench our thirst.

Come and drink freely of the water of life Jesus offers, and invite someone else to come with you. When you believe in him, Jesus promises, "streams of living water will flow from within" you.

PRAYER

Lord Jesus, thank you for offering to us the water of life. Make us willing to drink, and help us to invite others to drink with us. In your name we pray. Amen.

Listen and Be Still

No Condemnation

"Neither do I condemn you," Jesus declared.
"Go now and leave your life of sin."
JOHN 8:11   JOHN 8:1-11

A man came to talk to me because the unthinkable had happened. He had become involved with a married woman, and they had been found out. He didn't know what to do, and he was sure that God could never forgive him. He felt his life was ruined. He was embarrassed, afraid, and filled with guilt.

What he and many others have felt was exactly what the woman in our story for today was feeling. She had been caught in the act of adultery and was dragged in front of the religious leaders, who had brought her to Jesus. Imagine her humiliation, her shame and fear. According to the law of Moses, she could be sentenced to death, and to test Jesus, the religious leaders asked him what they should do.

His answer caught everyone off guard: "If any one of you is without sin, let him be the first to throw a stone at her." In other words, he was saying, "Be careful how you judge. Don't point a finger at others unless you are without sin."

And then Jesus, the only one who was truly without sin, assured the woman that he did not condemn her.

Jesus came to save and to offer us a new beginning. If we come to him, confess, and leave our lives of sin, we can be sure that our sins have been forgiven and that he gives us a new lease on life.

PRAYER

Father in heaven, thank you for giving us a new beginning after we have fallen into sin. Give us the grace to break with sin and to serve you. In Jesus' name we pray. Amen.

Listen and Be Still

Who Sinned?

"Rabbi, who sinned, this man or his parents,
that he was born blind?"

JOHN 9:1-12   JOHN 9:2

Years ago, while I was on a summer assignment as a seminary student, I met a mother whose child was severely impaired, both mentally and physically. The mother was convinced that her child's condition was a curse for the way she'd lived when she was a teenager. She told me that God was punishing her for her sins.

Her understanding of sin and suffering was the same as that of Jesus' disciples. They had been taught that people's sufferings were caused by their sins. That's why they asked Jesus whether the man had been born blind because of his own sins or because of his parents' sins. They were sure it had to be one or the other.

This was Jesus' answer: "Neither this man nor his parents sinned, but this happened so that the work of God might be displayed in his life." In other words, don't just assume that someone's suffering is because of their sins.

Jesus doesn't deny that our sins have consequences, or that sin, in general, causes a lot of suffering in this world. But the Bible assures us again and again that God does not punish us as our sins deserve (see Psalm 103:10). If he did, none of us would stand a chance.

There are lots of reasons why people suffer. And God doesn't always tell us why. Someday we'll fully understand, but until then we have to keep from drawing wrong conclusions.

PRAYER

Lord Jesus, help us to remember that you took the punishment for our sins. And please keep us from thinking that people suffer only because of their sins. In your name, Amen.

Listen and Be Still

God Knows Our Names!

"He calls his own sheep by name. . . ."
John 10:3

John 10:1-15

One day while we were waiting to meet someone at O'Hare Airport in Chicago, we lost track of our five-year-old son. My wife and I had decided to browse around in opposite directions, and each of us thought our son was with the other. We almost panicked until we heard his name announced over the sound system and knew he was safe. Being lost in a huge, bustling crowd can be one of the scariest times in a child's life.

Today a lot of people go through life like a lost child. They feel completely lost in a vast universe with millions of people. They feel totally alone, without anyone's paying attention to them. No one seems to know or care who they are, and no one is there to keep track of them.

In John 10 the Lord Jesus assures us that in spite of what life sometimes seems like, we're never on our own. The good shepherd never loses track of his sheep. In fact, our Lord knows our names, and he keeps on calling us by name—each one of us.

"The shepherd of his sheep . . . calls his own sheep by name," says Jesus. And he adds, "I am the good shepherd; I know my sheep and my sheep know me."

That's also the theme of Psalm 139—that even in the most desperate circumstances of life, God is right there keeping track of us and calling out our names. Listen closely as the good shepherd calls out your name today.

PRAYER

Lord Jesus, sometimes we feel so lost and alone. Please keep calling our name so that we can find our way back to you. Help us to know that you always care for us. Amen.

Listen and Be Still

Is That All There Is?

*"I have come that they may have life,
and have it to the full."*

JOHN 10:7-10   JOHN 10:10

A movie titled *About Schmidt* is the story of an insurance salesman who retires and begins to wonder about the meaning of his life. As he looks back, he wonders whether all his hard work was worth the effort, and he asks the age-old question, "Is that all there is?"

Throughout the years, millions of people have been asking the same question as they look back on their lives. An Old Testament teacher gave an answer to that question when he concluded that everything in life was no more than a puff of smoke—"meaningless" (Ecclesiastes 1:2). A lot of people, including Christians, go through life discouraged and dissatisfied because life has let them down.

In John 10:10 the Lord Jesus tells us that his followers were never meant to go through life feeling unfulfilled, dissatisfied, or discouraged. He came to give his life so that you and I could live life to the full.

Jesus came to give meaning and purpose to our lives. He doesn't want us to go through life discouraged and disillusioned.

He asks us to make him the center of our lives, to follow him, and to serve him wherever we may find ourselves. And when we do, we'll never have to ask, "Is that all there is?" We'll know there's always more to come in the full life Jesus invites us to share.

PRAYER

Lord Jesus, help us to follow you so that we may find meaning and purpose in our lives. Fill each one of us with your fullness, and help us to live fully for you. Amen.

Listen and Be Still   23

Where Is God When It Hurts?

"Lord," Martha said to Jesus, "if you had
been here, my brother would not have died."
JOHN 11:21

JOHN 11:1-26

Sometimes God seems to show up when it's too late. And sometimes we feel like shouting, "God, where were you when we needed you?"

That's how Martha felt when her brother Lazarus died. She had sent word to Jesus that Lazarus was sick, but instead of coming right away, Jesus had "stayed where he was two more days." And Lazarus had died.

That's why Martha blurted out, "Lord . . . if you had been here, my brother would not have died." It was her way of saying, "Jesus, you're our friend. Where were you when we needed you?"

But Jesus had a reason for not being there. He wanted to show God's glory and to reveal his power over death. By raising Lazarus from the dead, he proved himself to be "the resurrection and the life."

But sometimes we wonder. Sometimes we wonder if God is really there. Sometimes we get the feeling that if God had only been there and stepped in when we needed him, things would have turned out differently. Sometimes God keeps us waiting, and sometimes God doesn't answer our prayers the way we want him to. Sometimes it even looks as if death has the last word.

But only the Lord of life has the last word. He proved that once and for all when he came back to life. And this risen Savior is with us always (Matthew 28:20).

PRAYER

Lord, show us your power in all of life, and give us grace to believe that you have power over death still today. You alone have the last word, O Lord. In your name, Amen.

Listen and Be Still

Jesus Wept

Jesus wept.
JOHN 11:35

JOHN 11:25-37

In one of his books Charles Swindoll tells a story about a little girl who lost her closest friend in a tragic accident. The day after the funeral the little girl went to her friend's house to visit. When she came home, her mother asked her where she had been. Her answer: "I was at my friend's house to comfort her mommy." "Well," her mother asked her, "what did you say?" "I didn't say anything," she answered. "I just sat on her lap and cried a little."

That little girl understood what it meant to comfort. She knew that if you want to show how much you care, you don't have to say anything. She understood, in the words of one author, that "90 percent of helping is just showing up." She did what Jesus did when he faced the reality of his friend's death: she wept.

When faced with death in someone else's life, we don't need a lot of words. Too often the words we speak hurt more than they help. We don't always need to quote a Bible text, or remind them that God knows what he's doing. Sometimes the best thing we can do is be with them, listen to them, and weep with them. Don't stay away from people who are grieving because you don't know what to say. Simply do what Jesus did and what Paul says in Romans 12:15: "Mourn with those who mourn." And don't ever be afraid to cry.

PRAYER

Lord, keep us from talking too much in times of sorrow. Make us sensitive to the pain of others, and teach us to weep with those who are weeping. In your name, Amen.

Listen and Be Still

The Resurrection and the Life

"I am the resurrection and the life.
He who believes in me will live. . . ."
JOHN 11:25

JOHN 11:25-26, 38-44

The first time I preached on these words of Jesus, I was conducting a memorial service for a church member killed in the Tet offensive in Vietnam. Sometime later someone asked, "How can Jesus make a claim like that? And how can you possibly repeat it when you're standing in front of the casket of a 21-year-old?" It's an important question, and it calls for an answer.

When Jesus makes that claim in John 11:25, he does not deny the reality of physical death, and he doesn't try to minimize the seriousness of death. But he wants to make clear that death does not have the last word and that life continues after death for all who die in the Lord. When Christians die, they continue to live—on a different plane and in a different place. As the apostle Paul says in Philippians 1:23, to depart from this life is to be with Christ. Physical death is a door into heaven, because Christ has come and made it possible for us to be forgiven and saved to live forever with God.

Physical death is real, and it's our "last enemy" (1 Corinthians 15:26). Death means separation, and separation causes pain. The only thing to ease the pain is the assurance that someone who dies can go to live with Jesus, who rose from the dead and will come again to raise all of us someday (John 5:28-29). You and I can have that assurance if we believe in Jesus.

PRAYER

Lord, thank you for the assurance that we will not die if we believe in you. Give us the grace to believe in you, trusting that because of you we can live with God forever. Amen.

Listen and Be Still

Love Without Limit

*Having loved his own. . . he now showed them
the full extent of his love.*

JOHN 13:1

When Jesus washed the disciples' feet, I'm sure you could
have heard a pin drop in that room. This was embarrassing for
the disciples. It was unheard of that the one they called "Lord
and Teacher" should wash their feet. Washing feet was the work
of servants and slaves, not for the Son of God.

But Jesus did what the disciples had refused to do—to show
them how much he loved them—or, as John puts it, to show
them "the full extent of his love." Jesus wanted the disciples to
know there was no limit to his love. Jesus washed the feet of
disciples who would use those feet to run from him. He washed
the feet of the person who would betray him, and of another
who would deny knowing him. In the washing of his disciples'
feet, Jesus showed how far he was willing to go to wash away
their sins.

But in doing this, Jesus also set an example for his followers.
He said, "Now that I, your Lord and Teacher, have washed your
feet, you also should wash one another's feet."

You and I are to wash each other's feet—feet that have
kicked us in the teeth, feet that were used to betray us, deny
us, or walk away from us. We are called to take the back seat,
to forgive, to be the least. Some people in our lives need us to
wash their feet.

PRAYER

Holy Spirit, make us willing to be the least and to wash the feet
of people who have wronged us. Help us to follow our Lord's
example, we pray. In his name, Amen.

Listen and Be Still

The Best Is Yet to Come

"Do not let your hearts be troubled. . . .
I am going . . . to prepare a place for you."
JOHN 14:1-2

JOHN 14:1-7

One evening many years ago in a suburban Chicago hospital, we stood around the bed of a woman in her forties who was dying of cancer. She was restless until I started reading this passage where Jesus promises to prepare a place for us.

When I had finished reading, she said, "I'm ready to go now." We prayed, and only a short time later she peacefully entered the Lord's presence. She was ready to let go because she believed Jesus' promise that the best was yet to come.

Those few minutes in that hospital room were sacred moments. We felt the presence of the Savior as he touched her and then soon took her to that place prepared for her. Of course, the rest of us were still faced with the pain of separation. We were still faced with the reality that cancer had claimed another victim. There was every reason for her husband and children to cry. But they knew she was home.

Someday all of us will face that last moment in our lives. There's much that's all wrong about death and dying. But that's precisely why we need to come to know the Lord, who alone is the way, the truth, and the life. Only then can we be sure that the best is yet to come, because only he can take us to that place prepared for us.

PRAYER

Lord Jesus, help us to believe, and help us to tell others that because of you the best is still to come. Strengthen us and help us to pass your good news along to others. In your name, Amen.

Listen and Be Still

Remaining in Christ

*"Remain in me, and I will remain in you. . . .
Apart from me you can do nothing."*
JOHN 15:4-5

JOHN 15:1-8

Shortly after we moved to southern California, someone planted a dwarf orange tree in our backyard. It was guaranteed to have oranges the very first year. A year went by without any oranges. We soon discovered why. The tree had been planted where there was no sun, with water sprinklers going full blast twice a day. We moved it into the sun and away from the sprinklers, and before long we had all kinds of oranges.

Of course! For any tree to bear fruit it has to have the right conditions. As Jesus points out in John 15, for a vine to have fruit, it needs pruning and tending and favorable conditions.

What's true for trees and vines, says Jesus, is also true for his followers. You and I were meant to bear fruit to bring glory to the Father. And as we bear fruit and show the fruit of the Spirit in our lives (see Galatians 5:22-23), the people around us will be able to see that we belong to Jesus.

To make that happen, we have to remain in Christ. Says Jesus, "Apart from me you can do nothing."

We have to stay in touch with Jesus, live close to him, talk to our Lord, and listen to him each day. We also have to ask him to remove whatever keeps us from bearing fruit. And when we do, we will bear "much fruit." It's guaranteed!

PRAYER

Lord, please keep us close to you, and help us to remain in you. Fill us with your Spirit so that we can have the fruit of the Spirit in our lives. To you be the glory! Amen.

Listen and Be Still

Never on Our Own

"Unless I go away, the Counselor will not come to you; but if I go, I will send him to you."
JOHN 16:7

JOHN 16:5-16

In his book *Secrets of the Vine* Bruce Wilkinson tells of a time in his life when he was almost ready to resign. The harder he worked, the less he seemed to accomplish. He was becoming less and less productive. His satisfaction in serving the Lord was gone. He was faced with burnout.

Through a conversation with a friend he found out the problem: while working harder, he had allowed himself to drift from the Lord. Something was missing: he was trying to do it on his own.

It happens all the time. A lot of Christians spend themselves doing ministry, but as time goes on, they find themselves becoming less and less productive, with less and less satisfaction.

Sometimes we try to do things on our own without relying on the power of the Holy Spirit. But it can't be done. Without the promised Counselor, we'll never make it.

That's why Jesus promised his disciples to send the Counselor, the Holy Spirit, so that we don't have to be on our own. Each day we have to ask the Spirit to fill us. And that's a request God is delighted to fill. As Jesus says in Luke 11:13, "If you . . . know how to give good gifts to your children, how much more will your Father in heaven give the Holy Spirit to those who ask him!"

PRAYER

Spirit of the living God, fall afresh on us. Melt us, mold us, fill us, use us. Spirit of the living God, fall afresh on us. In Jesus' name we pray. Amen.

Listen and Be Still

Famous Last Words

At that moment a rooster began to crow.
JOHN 18:27

MATTHEW 26:31-35; JOHN 18:25-27

Most of us have heard people say—and perhaps you've also said—"That will never happen to me." People blurt out these "famous last words" when they hear about what's happened to someone else, and they're positive it'll never happen to them. They mean every word they're saying. But statements like that can come back and haunt people later.

When Peter told the Lord that he would never disown him, he meant every word he said. He loved the Lord, and he believed he could not possibly deny him. Peter was ready to lay his life on the line. But the safety of the olive grove was far different from the courtyard of the high priest. Being surrounded by friends was different from standing in the dark, surrounded by Jesus' enemies. That's the reason Peter followed at a distance. That's how he came to deny his Lord.

It's much easier to preach than to practice what I preach. It's much easier to confess our faith in church than to speak up for God in the workplace. It's much easier to sing, "My Jesus, I love thee, I know thou art mine; for thee all the follies of sin I resign," than to say no to temptations.

Unless we see our own weakness and learn to depend on our Lord for strength, we'll find ourselves standing right next to Peter.

PRAYER

Father in heaven, keep me from depending on my own strength. Teach me to lean on you, and help me to resist the temptation to deny you. In Jesus' name I pray. Amen.

Listen and Be Still

The Gift of Peace

*Jesus came and stood among them
and said, "Peace be with you!"*
John 20:19

John 20:19-23

In a personal letter at the beginning of his book *The Gift of Peace*, the late Joseph Cardinal Bernardin writes that the last three years of his life were the worst of times because of false allegations of abuse against him and because of his losing battle with cancer. But those years were also the best of times, he said, because of God's gift of peace. In the book's final chapter he asks in a prayer that all his readers will find that special gift.

The gift of peace is what the Lord Jesus gave to his disciples as they were cowering behind locked doors. That's why Jesus came, to bring peace to all who are afraid, to bring peace to people who are at odds with God, to bring peace to people who are coming apart on the inside.

Peace is one of the most important gifts in all of life, and it's a gift that only the Lord can give.

Peace comes from knowing that because of Jesus Christ, our sins have been forgiven. Peace helps us to let go of everything that's not important in life. Peace also helps us to keep going in the Lord's strength even when everything seems to be falling apart.

In Philippians 4:7 we read that "the peace of God, which transcends all understanding, will guard" our hearts and minds "in Christ Jesus."

Prayer

Father in heaven, we thank you for the gift of peace, and we ask that you will give it to all who are without it. Strengthen us with your peace each day. In Jesus' name, Amen.

Listen and Be Still

Do You Love Jesus?

Jesus said to Simon Peter, "Simon son of John, do you truly love me more than these?"
JOHN 21:15

JOHN 21:15-19

One of the most beautiful professions of faith I've ever heard was in a congregation I served several years ago. A teenage girl from a local school for special-needs students wanted to make a public profession of her faith. She sat in a wheelchair, unable to walk, stand, or talk, and I asked only one question: "Lori, do you love Jesus?" She answered with a big smile, a nod, and a slight raising of her hand. That heartfelt response was more than enough for her to become a professing member of God's family in Christ.

She had answered the most important question in life. It was the same question Jesus asked Peter. Not *Why did you deny me?* Not *Do you have all the right answers?* Not *Do you have the right background?* The most important question for all of us is *Do you love Jesus?*

When all is said and done, the most important thing in life is the answer to that question. It's what Jesus wanted to know of Peter, and it's what he wants to know of us: *Do we love Jesus more than anything else in our lives?*

Jesus loves us, this we know, for the Bible tells us so. And the penetrating question to each one of us is *Do you love Jesus?* Ask yourself, your husband, your wife, your child, your parent, your friend. It's the most important question you'll ever be asked.

PRAYER

Lord Jesus, we do love you, but sometimes our love is weak and imperfect. Help us through your Spirit to love you more fully and to ask others if they love you too. Amen.

Listen and Be Still

33

God's Voice, Our Choice

These are written that you may believe that Jesus is the Christ . . . and . . . have life in his name.
JOHN 20:31

JOHN 20:24-31

In his book *A Gentle Thunder*, Max Lucado says that the gospel of John has two themes: God's voice and our choice. That, in fact, is the message of the Bible. God speaks to us, and we are called to respond.

God has spoken to us through the Gospel of John. We heard God's voice as we listened to our Lord making the claim, "I am the bread of life." And we heard his invitation to drink of the living water that only he can give. We heard Jesus' gentle urging to believe in him. We also saw him do miracles, and we stood in awe as he raised Lazarus from the dead. Then, after Jesus himself rose from the dead, he asked, "Do you love me more than these?"

If we were listening, we heard his voice.

And now he asks us to make a choice: *to believe in him, or not to believe.*

That's why God has spoken to us through the gospel of John. John sums it up in our passage for today when he says, "These are written that you may believe that Jesus is the Christ, the Son of God, and that by believing you may have life in his name."

It's up to us to respond. And once we have responded, we'll want others to hear God's voice too, so that they also can grow to follow the Savior. God wants all his children to come home.

PRAYER

Father in heaven, give us the grace to believe, and help us to reach out to others to help them believe in Jesus too. In his name we pray. Amen.

Listen and Be Still

WITH CHRIST IN LIFE AND DEATH

28 MEDITATIONS AND READINGS

BY DR. ALEXANDER C. DEJONG

COMING TO FAITH IN CHRIST

DR. ALEXANDER C. DEJONG

The apostle Paul wrote, "To me, to live is Christ and to die is gain" (Philippians 1:21). Many Bible readers have puzzled over this statement.

When you read Paul carefully, however, it becomes clear that, for him, being a Christian meant living in the closest possible communion with Christ, experiencing Christ within as the power of his life. In Galatians, Paul declares, "I have been crucified with Christ and I no longer live, but Christ lives in me. The life I live in the body, I live by faith in the Son of God, who loved me and gave himself for me" (Galatians 2:20).

These reflections explore the mystery of Christ's presence in believers. They also help us to discover that the presence of the living Christ sustains us each day and brings us to perfect fullness upon death.

Dr. De Jong (1922-2003) served churches in New Jersey, Michigan, Indiana, Colorado and Illinois. He also served as president of Trinity Christian College in Palos Heights, Illinois, and was interim Executive Director of Elim Christian School, an institution in suburban Chicago for people with disabilities. In addition, he ministered personally to many individuals suffering from various kinds of addictions.

Be Present, Lord

"If your Presence does not go with us,
do not send us up from here."
EXODUS 33:15

EXODUS 33:12-23

Moses was making a difficult journey—through a wilderness—with a willful and stubborn people. These people, our spiritual brothers and sisters, were traveling to a land they had never seen. Every day of travel had its own pains and pleasures.

Moses was educated to be a royal son, a soldier, a leader. More important, he was called to be God's special representative. He personally met God in the burning bush and saw God's mighty wonders in the ten plagues. He lived in God's presence.

Moses sought and loved God's presence and kept himself open to the working of that presence—for God made a difference, all the difference in the world. God's life and Moses' life were intertwined. Together they were to bring Israel to the promised land.

As a president or prime minister makes his or her presence felt when entering a room, God made his presence felt in Moses' life. Without that presence, Moses could not have handled the murmuring crowds, the cunning enemies, and the difficulties of travel as he led the Israelites through the wilderness.

Today and every day we must seek the wonderful reality of God's presence. We need God's presence on our life's journey, especially in the hard and painful times of sickness, doubt, and death.

PRAYER

Father of our Lord Jesus Christ, God of Abraham, Isaac, Jacob, and Moses, go with us every day, for outside your presence we lie in the midst of death. Hear us, in Immanuel's name. Amen.

Listen and Be Still

Thirsting for God

My soul finds rest in God alone;
my salvation comes from him.
Psalm 62:1

Psalm 42

Part of the delightful mystery of life is the way a person's spirit craves to inhabit a body. For example, a musician "hears" a haunting melody in his inner self, and he is restless until this music is arranged into a symphony and played—to the joy of those who hear it. Similarly, an architect discovers that he has no lasting peace until he designs a building and watches artisans construct it with stone and glass.

Life has a dynamism that expresses itself in wonderful ways. Life is a bud bursting into a flower, a bird in full song in springtime, an artist seeing his or her painting take shape on canvas. Life seeks expression! It must! That's its nature.

Actually, life for us is even more—it involves a craving for intimacy with God. That's because we are made for God; we are his expression. God "breathed into our nostrils the breath of life" (Genesis 2:7), and now we crave God's presence and companionship. Life is God's children engaging in unceasing prayer. Life is a martyr, in surrendering sacrifice, persevering to the end.

Our spirits long for God as a thirsty deer longs for fresh water, as a wandering daughter longs for her mother, or a lost son for his father. And when we willfully walk away from God, the gracious Author of our lives, he comes looking for us.

Prayer

Blessed Father, with your haunting love please seek us and stay with us so that our restless spirits may discover peace in your presence now and forever. Through Christ our Lord, Amen.

God Within

"If anyone loves me. . . my Father will love him, and we will come to him and make our home with him."
JOHN 14:23

JOHN 14:13-24

God is not far away or inaccessible. He is closer than hands or feet or even breath. When we entrust ourselves to Jesus Christ in faith, we discover God's presence at the deepest level of our consciousness.

This inner experience of God's presence is very different from the "surrender" experience of Eastern mysticism. In Yoga, for example, the "divine" is touched only when the self (the ego) dissolves or merges into some indescribable "divine ground of all life." In this experience there is no meeting with a divine Person. There is no conversation, no mutuality of love, praise, and worship. Instead of fellowship there is absorption. Instead of a call to love there is dissolution of desire.

In God's presence we discover the miracle of a seeking and gracious God. When we wander, he looks after us. When we hunger, he feeds us with food from heaven as he did with the Israelites in the wilderness. The rebellious are loved back into the ways of obedience.

Jesus pointed his puzzled disciples to the awesome reality of God's presence. To everyone who loves and keeps his words, the presence of the Father and Son and Holy Spirit is realized within. God's presence is "beyond" us as Father, "with" us as Son, and "in" us as Holy Spirit. In him we live and move and have our being as Christians.

PRAYER

Great and wonderful are your ways, O Lord. May we feel you coming to us every day as Father, Son, and Holy Spirit. In your presence today is eternal life with pleasures forevermore. Amen.

Listen and Be Still

If Jesus Were Here

"If you had been here,
my brother would not have died."
JOHN 11:21

JOHN 11:11-24

How frequently we ask Martha's question: if Jesus were here, would this have happened?

If Jesus were here, would Sam suffer so violently from the aftereffects of chemotherapy? If Jesus had stood at the street corner, would that violent smashing of cars have taken place? If Jesus were in Ethiopia or on the lonely streets of our big cities, would he not feed the hungry with miracle loaves and fish?

Now is the time to claim with fresh faith the words of Jesus: "Surely I will be with you always, to the very end of the age" (Matthew 28:20). For those who believe in him, Jesus is not far away. Right in the middle of hunger, fear, despair, suffering, he is present. Just trust him! The promise of his presence is still true, and he speaks it to us now, in our need.

Pray for an openness to Jesus' presence. As one confession of faith puts it: "With his God-head, majesty, grace and Spirit, he is at no time absent from us." Pray untiringly for contact with him. Learn from St. Augustine: "If you wish to pray without ceasing, do not cease to desire. The constancy of your desire will itself be the ceaseless voice of your prayer."

In the Lord's presence our questions about pain and suffering are gradually exchanged for childlike trust and love. We must never forget that Jesus is present.

PRAYER

Lord, when we feel left alone with only questions, we ask that we may feel your presence and hear your words of comfort and wisdom. In Jesus' name, Amen.

Listen and Be Still

Before Me, He Was!

"I tell you the truth. . . before
Abraham was born, I am!"

JOHN 8:52-59   JOHN 8:58

Christ has experienced what I live out today. As eternal God, he existed before Abraham, and as God in the flesh, he has experienced what I experience.

When I climb the upward path of physical suffering, I see Jesus' footprints. He has been there before me—in Gethsemane, on Calvary. His presence gives meaning to the times when I need medication to ease my pain. With my every step he imparts his strength, courage, and persistence. He has climbed ahead of me.

When I am disoriented by mists of sorrow, I remember his tears at Lazarus' grave. But even greater comfort is his Spirit's presence, the light touch of his hand wiping away my tears, his words "Be not afraid! I'm here! I have been here, and I know the way."

When I am tempted by the enemy, I see the sword of my Captain, who has gone before me into battle. But more heartening is his presence, which arms me and tells me that the battle is his.

When I stand at the Jordan for my final crossing, I want to recall how quietly he laid his life into his Father's hands. His resurrection life will support me. Not only was he before Abraham; he is also before me—in every experience. His life is mine. "I no longer live, but Christ lives in me" (Galatians 2:20). As I believe in him, he lives through me each day.

PRAYER

Quicken within me, Lord Jesus, a vivid sense of your presence. May I know that whatever I experience was experienced by you long ago. Help me to use all that I do today for your glory. Amen.

Listen and Be Still

Open to His Presence

Find rest, O my soul, in God alone; my hope comes from him.
PSALM 62:5

PSALM 62

In John 14:23 Jesus promises that he and the Father will come to live within those who love him and obey his teaching. How do they come to live within people? They come to those who have open hearts and seeking lives.

God comes to those who no longer need to be first or need to manage everything their own way. He comes to those who *completely, unreservedly, uncalculatingly,* and *unrestrictedly* are open to his coming—people who want nothing but his presence to control them.

Beware of calculating commercialism. Do not try to manipulate the angles of life so that personal happiness rather than God's presence takes first place. Subtly, mostly without realizing it, we look for gifts rather than for the Giver. We want blessings rather than God's presence. The sick may want the gift of healing rather than the Healer. The fearful may want courage rather than the Courageous One.

The key to a life in which the peace of God provides strength and assurance for each day is the loving presence of Jesus, the Lord of peace. But our openness to his presence must not be for the getting of a gift. It must be to make room for the Giver. Life finds its rest not in gifts, but in God.

Be open in quiet faith, and obey Jesus' teaching!

PRAYER

With the poet of long ago we lift our hearts to you, O Lord. In quiet trust we open our inner selves to experience your presence wherever we are. In Jesus' name we wait. Amen.

Listen and Be Still

Authentic Christians

The disciples were first called Christians at Antioch.
ACTS 11:26

ACTS 11:19-26

Not all people claiming the name Christian are the real thing. A real Christian is a person possessed by God. This is what caught the eye of the citizens around Antioch. They saw people possessed by the powerful Spirit of the crucified Christ, people anointed, qualified, filled, and set aside by an awesome love. A new power possessed these people.

Paul, the rabbi, was stopped, conquered, and captivated by Jesus. Ever since that moment he wanted only one reality: "I want to know Christ and the power of his resurrection and the fellowship of sharing in his sufferings, becoming like him in his death" (Philippians 3:10). Knowing Christ is vastly more than head knowledge. It is good, even necessary, for Christians to possess intellectual awareness of facts and principles, but "knowing" the Lord is something deeper. It is being caught up by his love into intimate fellowship. A real Christian, in distinction from a nominal Christian, shares the very life of Christ Jesus, much as husbands and wives share their lives.

Jesus lived his life through Paul. This happens with every real Christian. We are possessed by the Lord who saves and owns us. Can the people around you sense his presence in your attitudes and actions? Is that why you are known as a Christian?

PRAYER

Lord Jesus, display your life in ours so that others may call us Christians because they can sense your presence both in our sufferings and in our successes. In your name, Amen.

Listen and Be Still

A Worship Reminder

Neither he who plants nor he who waters is anything,
but only God, who makes things grow.
1 Corinthians 3:7

1 Corinthians 3:1-9

On Sunday we gather to worship. We sing, pray, give, make decisions, and listen to a biblically based sermon. As a minister of the gospel, I'm asking that every reader remember the preacher in personal prayer.

Every time I'm privileged to preach the gospel, I must ask for grace not to allow my preaching to become self-serving. That's because sometimes we ministers tend to look for results in terms of large crowds and large offerings.

The temptation to play "grower" is always there. It is flattering for a preacher to see other people depend on him. This perceived dependence builds up the preacher's self-esteem. Then, very subtly, there can be a shift from joyfully praising God to merely mouthing pious words. And when recognition is not given by parishioners, the preacher can turn resentful and petulant. The weed of vanity can have deep roots in the preacher as well as in anyone.

When we gather to worship, let's place the preacher in the presence of the Grower, whose Spirit ripens the harvest. It is the Grower's presence that must radiate from the most brilliant thoughts, the most precise sentences, and the most expressive illustrations. If Paul was only a seed planter and Apollos only a waterer, what must our pastor be as he ministers?

Prayer

Jesus, we pray for all God's servants, who bring your Word to your
    world. Keep them close to you so they remember that increase
comes from your grace and not from the work of mankind. Amen.

Listen and Be Still

This Is Living

*The Lord God formed man from the dust of the ground
and breathed into his nostrils the breath of life.*

GENESIS 2:7

GENESIS 2:15-25

Have you ever reflected on the phrase "This is living!"? Newlyweds on their honeymoon might say this. Others on vacation, completely relaxed and doing what they like best, might say it too.

For the believer, "living" is Jesus Christ. Experiencing and anticipating his presence is LIFE! Simple trust in Jesus, arising out of new birth in him, makes this presence real. As the Lord expresses himself to us in our daily experiences, we actually catch something of the phrase "This is living!"

The apostle Paul described real life this way: "Living to me means simply 'Christ,' and if I die I should merely gain more of him" (Philippians 1:21, J.B. Phillips).

When we read Genesis 2, we see that human life is the breath (Spirit) of God. But Adam and Eve horribly corrupted the reality of life from God and with God by eating forbidden fruit. After Adam and Eve fell into sin, shame drove them into hiding. But God went looking for them. And when he found them in their guilty shame, he promised he would undo their folly, forgive their sin, and defeat their enemy. Praise him! He did it all in Jesus Christ.

Now the presence of Jesus in a believer is a restoration of LIFE! As it was in Paradise, God's free gift of grace restores his presence within us.

PRAYER

Lord Jesus, outside of you I'm dead, so I ask in simple and obedient trust that you live in my life today and always. In your seeking love, hear my prayer. Amen.

Listen and Be Still

It Hurts God Too

Let us. . . approach the throne of grace with confidence.
HEBREWS 4:16

HEBREWS 4:12-16

God, the transcendently Holy One, dwells bodily in Jesus. And Jesus lives in us always, even in our times of hurt and suffering. This is a gospel fact!

Some Christians are rightly offended by the idea of a God who exists "way beyond the blue," out of touch with our small, smarting world. The true God is not sovereignly enthroned in apathy!

Other Christians are offended by the idea of a God who suffers. As the Almighty, he "must" be beyond and above the ability to suffer, they say. These persons have a point. God's ability to be genuinely touched by our pains does not mean he suffers the way we suffer. Much of our distress arises out of life's limitations. Our bodies sicken and decay. Our minds are restricted by limited ways of thinking. Our feelings are swayed by change. This is part of our finitude, our creatureliness.

But it is not so with God! In Jesus, he is deity made flesh. God in Christ cries, loves, wipes away tears, experiences joy, loneliness, pain, misunderstanding…everything human.

He hurts with us because he wants to be with us, in us, closer than hands and feet. He knows when we need comfort, relief, strength, or courage. Through his Holy Spirit, God is in our every experience. He is not far away. He is here, as he promised.

PRAYER

We thank you, Lord, for your abiding love, your sensitive presence, your understanding heart. Through Jesus Christ, our Savior, supply us with all we need to live to your glory. Amen.

Listen and Be Still

Genuine Faith

"Daughter, your faith has healed you. Go in peace and be freed from your suffering."
MARK 5:34

MARK 5:24-34

"Have faith!" "Just believe"! "Trust Jesus!" Common words, but what do they involve? What is authentic faith? Think about the story in Mark 5.

The woman with a bleeding problem had great need. She was frustrated, confused, financially exhausted, socially embarrassed, and afraid to meet Jesus.

She was totally empty of resources. She had nothing more to help her deal with her problem. And she was on the outer fringe of society because her blood problem made her religiously unclean. She hardly dared to touch Jesus' garment.

But she had hope. Hope can be defined as desire plus expectation. You desire some future good—in this case, healing. And you expect to receive this desired good. Without expectation, desire leads to despair, and expectation without desire produces dread.

Actually, this woman had intense desire. She determined that nothing would keep her from Jesus. No crowds, disciples, feelings of inferiority, or physical weakness would obstruct her.

This woman's genuine faith made her whole. In the same way today we are made whole, saved—if we have faith that combines need, emptiness, hope, and desire. Jesus generously gives himself, and he remains with us. Now is the time to exercise real faith.

PRAYER

Our Father in heaven, give each of us genuine faith for every trying and special situation. Watch over us on the paths of our daily lives. For Jesus' sake, Amen.

Listen and Be Still

Facing the End

"Show me, O Lord, my life's end and the number of my days; let me know how fleeting is my life."
PSALM 39:4

PSALM 39

There was a time, not very long ago, when Christians asked for time to experience a calm and conscious death. They wanted "to make a good death."

David's prayer to know about his life's end was not morbid. He wanted to know his end because he knew the brevity of life. We Christians want to say good-bye to loved ones, repair broken relationships if possible, and generally "set our house in order" before the face of God. Believers in Jesus Christ do not wish "to expire, [or] go dead unconsciously." Right up to the end we want to love, to patch up what we can, give advice when needed, enter into victory with a smile, and journey joyfully to the Lord.

David never experienced this, but his Son, our Lord Jesus, did. And he spoke clearly with a loud voice when he gave up his life to his Father. He knew victory in the middle of what looked like defeat. After taking a drink to quench his thirst, he clearly said, "It is finished." Neither the religious authorities, nor Pilate's soldiers, nor the devil took Jesus' life. He made a good death and presented his life to his Father.

The life of Christ in us enables us to do the same. We need not ignore death—or try to dress it up with cosmetics. Life is fleeting. If we face it in the Lord, we will know the victory of living and dying without fear.

PRAYER

Lord Jesus, with your resurrection life in mine, teach me to look calmly at my journey's end in order to travel confidently in your presence every day. I pray, claiming your promises. Amen.

Listen and Be Still

Paul's Flashback

I have fought the good fight, I have finished the race,
I have kept the faith.
2 TIMOTHY 4:7

2 TIMOTHY 4:1-8

Looking back often helps one look ahead with confidence. This is different from the desperate flashbacks that some people have in a near-death experience. Paul's flashback was poised, experienced in ordinary consciousness, and radiant with faith. Chained to a soldier, chilled to the bone (he had left his cloak at Carpus's house), feeling his life's energies flowing away, Paul looked back with a sense of well-being.

What did he remember? Among other things, probably his initial rejection by the apostles at Jerusalem (Acts 9:26); his passionate, painful rebuke of Peter at Antioch (Galatians 2:11); the "lions" at Ephesus (2 Timothy 4:17); his plea for stern discipline at the church in Corinth (1 Corinthians 5); his stoning at Lystra (Acts 14:19), and much more. He had fought a good fight.

His life was an obstacle course. Every day he jumped a new hurdle. Shipwreck, beatings, jail terms, church quarrels, charges of religious fanaticism, misunderstandings of every kind. All were hurdles to be cleared, obstacles to be overcome.

He kept the faith. He trusted as Jesus trusted. He taught the words of his Lord as Jesus taught the words of his Father. He agonized over his spiritual children as the Good Shepherd agonizes over his sheep.

PRAYER

Lord Jesus, we make ourselves available to you right now so that you may express your life in ours today. In your presence we wish to live, and in your name we pray. Amen.

Listen and Be Still

Life Beyond Life

[He] who raised Christ from the dead will also give life to your mortal bodies through his Spirit. . . .
ROMANS 8:11

ROMANS 8:11

Through his Holy Spirit, Jesus is alive in all Christians' lives. While his presence illuminates our lives, we reach beyond this life to a greater life beyond. This stretching hope is confident, not a weak "I hope to live beyond this life."

After all, the life beyond is not a mere continuation of life as we now experience it. Life now, before physical death, is bent toward self-centeredness. No one wants this "bentness" to continue. Self-centeredness is worth nothing but pain to the reborn self and shame to him who is our life.

If the Holy Spirit, promised by the Father, freely given by the Son, lives in us, we experience a living beyond the power of death. His life adds zest that reaches beyond every present experience, no matter how delightful those present experiences may be.

Our new life is the same resurrection life of Christ that sought out Mary Magdalene in the garden and that reinstated Peter on the shores of Galilee. This is an undying life of love.

Everything in this new life depends on the Holy Spirit's work within us as he changes doubt to certainty, fear to courage, and death to eternal life. His enabling presence is the secret of life beyond our living now. His life guarantees our life forever in glory.

PRAYER

Lord Jesus, let your life in ours be our strong comfort in sorrow, our firm hope of life forever in your presence, and our intense reaching out through your Spirit to the life beyond. Amen.

Listen and Be Still

Remain in Christ

"I am the vine; you are the branches. If a man remains in me and I in him, he will bear much fruit. . . ."

JOHN 15:5

JOHN 15:1-11

What do the phrases "in Christ," "remaining in Christ," and "abiding in Christ" really mean? Perhaps an analogy will help explain them.

Think of yourself coming home after a hard day's work and being welcomed by your loved ones. Jesus welcomes you into his presence in much the same way. Walking through the family room door, you sense an inner peace warming you. The comfortable chair, the same dishes, the stains on the rug, the familiar family photos—everything radiates the presence of people you love. Even though other family members may not be home yet, you feel their presence. Home. You feel relieved. You can relax.

Something like this happens when you "remain" or "abide" in Christ. You live in him like you live in your home. You and Christ Jesus are comfortable in each other's presence. He knows you. You know him. You feel comfortable when Jesus speaks to you in the Bible, and you respond in voiced or silent prayer. Something even more intimate and precious than this is what Jesus means when he talks about "remaining in him." As long as you stay in him, comfortable in his presence, you will bear the fruit of his Spirit: love, joy, peace, patience, kindness, goodness, faithfulness, gentleness, and self-control (Galatians 5:22–23).

PRAYER

Lord Jesus, strengthen us as we continue to abide in you. Draw us with your alluring love, and keep us daily in your presence, bearing the fruit of your Spirit for your name's sake. Amen.

Listen and Be Still

Waiting for Composure

It is good to wait quietly for the salvation of the Lord.
LAMENTATIONS 3:26

LAMENTATIONS 3:19-33

Jeremiah the prophet complained honestly and wept in frustration. He had the painful task of preaching submission to military defeat. God's people hated this messenger because of his message. No wonder Jeremiah was often sad, lonely, and bitter.

God seemed far away. Listen to these bold and bitter words: "Cursed be the day I was born! May the day my mother bore me not be blessed!…Why did I ever come out of the womb to see trouble and sorrow and to end my days in shame?" (Jeremiah 20:14,18).

The Lord's persistent love, however, kept Jeremiah going forward. Deep down, this man of God knew that if he waited patiently and trustingly, everything would work out right. His covenant God was doing something grander and greater than he could ever imagine. So he held fast to the Lord's strong but invisible hand.

It is good for us as well to wait while we question and to hope patiently in our frustrations. The affliction of weakness, the growth of cancer, the heat of fever—these are no accident. Our Lord is working deliverance even when we cannot see it or feel it. "Though he brings grief, he will show compassion, so great is his unfailing love. For he does not willingly bring affliction or grief to the children of men" (vv. 31–32). As watchmen wait for the morning, let us wait for the mercies of our Lord.

PRAYER

Heavenly Father, we ask for the Spirit of Jesus to keep us trusting and waiting hopefully and patiently for your presence to give us strength. Hear us in the name of Jesus, we pray. Amen.

A Quiet Conscience

This. . . is. . . how we set our hearts at rest. . .
whenever our hearts condemn us.
1 JOHN 3:19–20

1 JOHN 3:11-24

As a believer, you want Jesus to work through you. But often selfishness keeps this from happening, and that affects your conscience.

Each person blocks the power of the indwelling Lord. And the way you do it may not be the way another person does it, but when you feel you are standing in Christ's way, your conscience accuses you. You feel guilty, and your guilt causes anxiety that robs you of joy. A pained conscience paralyzes Christian living.

Satan, the chief accuser, latches on to your failings and hurls them at you with demonic glee, increasing your guilt load even to intolerable levels. The Roman Caesar in John's days had informers who acted something like that. Greedily they made a career out of betraying Christians to Caesar. They would use half-truths, misinformation, even confidential conversations to get Christians to trial and execution.

Satan infects our consciences. He accuses us before the Lord. But we need not worry. He has been defeated. Jesus threw him out of God's presence. Our Lord, the holder of the keys of life and death, has exclusive access to God. And his presence in us is the hedge of security and peace around our consciences. No one can lodge effective accusation against us. Christ quiets the anxious heart by his indwelling Spirit.

PRAYER

Lord Jesus, when our hearts accuse us, reassure us of your forgiving presence as we try to walk in repentance and faith. Thank you for being stronger than our fears and greater than our hearts. Amen.

Listen and Be Still

The Unforgettable Moment

"Whoever comes to me I will never drive away."
JOHN 6:37

JOHN 1:35-51

Being with Jesus means being with someone who makes a difference. The men mentioned in our Scripture reading felt the difference. When Jesus spoke, a power went forth from his words, and people followed him. Jesus made a big difference to Andrew, Philip, Nathanael, and others.

John the Baptizer, the desert preacher who preached repentance, often moved the hearts of his listeners. But he recognized his cousin Jesus as far greater than himself. "Look," he said, "the Lamb of God, who takes away the sin of the world!" Then those who were with him turned, looked, and followed after Jesus.

Another John, the gospel writer, was most likely the disciple who was with Andrew when John the Baptizer pointed to Jesus. And he never forgot his first meeting with this person who made a difference, a difference so revolutionary that he remembered the exact time it happened. It was the tenth hour. Rarely in his writings does John mention specific times. But this 4:00 p.m. was etched clearly in his memory. It was the moment of love's commitment. It was the time of decision.

How about in your life? Jesus' presence makes a difference, the difference between life and death. Go to him in prayer, repentance, and trust. Be assured of his word: "Whoever comes to me I will never drive away."

PRAYER

Lord Jesus, make a difference in our lives as we conquer temptation, experience comfort in our grief, and discover new paths of joyful service beneath your rule. In your name we pray.
Amen.

Listen and Be Still

Love That Waits

Jesus loved. . . Lazarus. Yet when he heard that Lazarus was sick, he stayed where he was two more days.

JOHN 11:5–6

MARK 5:21-43

~Did you catch something amazing, something quite unexpected, in the Scripture text above? Jesus heard that one of his best friends was sick. He received an urgent plea for help, but he deliberately waited two days to show his love. Meanwhile, Lazarus died.

Jesus displayed other surprising delays of love. Once, when in a boat with his friends, he was bone tired, so he went to sleep. One of the Sea of Galilee's sudden storms blew down upon them. Jesus kept right on sleeping. What fatigue! What trust in his Father! He allowed the waves to swamp the boat until his disciples shouted, "Teacher, don't you care if we drown?" (Mark 4:38).

He delayed with Jairus. This man was a generous, religious, godly, loving father. On his knees he pleaded with Jesus for help: "Please come and put your hands on [my daughter] so that she will be healed and live" (Mark 5:23). Jesus seemed to dawdle. He ministered to a frightened woman of faith. He waited and allowed the little girl to die. Later, though, he brought her back to life.

Our Master does not act on our schedules. He knows the end from the beginning and everything in between. But he remains totally in control, wisely and tenderly doing what he knows best.

PRAYER

Lord Jesus, when we no longer see you through eyes of faith, when we no longer sense your presence in our pain, teach us to trustingly wait for your generous help, which never fails. Amen.

Listen and Be Still

Strictly Personal

When the Lord saw her, his heart went out to her....
LUKE 7:13

LUKE 7:11-17

Grief is personal, and everyone expresses grief in his or her own way. The widow in today's story, for example, was crying while on her way to bury her only son. Other people grieve with restraint and self-control.

Jesus wants to share in the sorrows and tears of all of us; he wants to administer his comfort in a way fitted to each need. Jesus saw the widow's sorrow, and he went to the coffin, spoke, and raised the woman's dead son. The good news for the sorrowing is that the Master will deal with them in terms of who they are, very personally.

Luke used strong words to describe Jesus' love for the grieving widow. These words are translated, as above, to say "his heart went out to her," conveying deeply felt affection and sympathy. An older translation speaks of "bowels of mercy."

The Lord is here, asking for your attention and for that of all the sorrowing ones you know. Take his presence literally, though not physically. In the swirl of confusion, in the swamps of sorrow, in the fog of despair, in the shadow of death, the Lord is with you. He is present, moved with a divine compassion that expresses his perfect knowledge of your special need. Cast your cares on him. He wants to be found by everyone who asks and seeks and knocks.

PRAYER

Thank you, Great Shepherd of the sheep, that you hear our voices crying for comfort. Open our ears to hear your voice, our wills to accept your gifts, and our hearts to enjoy your love. Amen.

Listen and Be Still

Lord of Life

"I was dead, and behold I am alive for ever and ever! And I hold the keys of death and Hades."
REVELATION 1:18

REVELATION 1:1-18

Death can be pictured as a city with strong gates. Jesus holds the key to those gates. He inserted the master key into those mighty doors when he died on the cross. In order to free us from death's fearful power, he deliberately marched up to the gates of death and opened them.

Jesus went into the city of death and disarmed the devil, who had the power of death. He condemned sin and removed the sting of death forever. He walked every imaginable street within that dreadful city, chasing out of hiding everything that might torment us when we die. Whenever we think about death, we must remember that Jesus has been there.

After conquering every enemy behind the gates of death, Jesus came forth as the Victor over death and hell. Now, as the Living One, he keeps the gates open forever for anyone who belongs to him.

Some of the early Christian martyrs demonstrated in their courageous deaths that they trusted Jesus totally. Polycarp, the bishop of Smyrna, trusted the Living One. On Saturday, February 23, 155 A.D., he calmly went to be burned at the stake. Refusing to recant, he said, "Eighty and six years have I served him, and he has done me no wrong. How can I blaspheme my King, who saved me?" Today he is alive with the Living One.

PRAYER

Lord Jesus, when the shadows of death fall over me, let me see you holding the keys of death and Hades for me. In my dying let me see your life living in me forever. In your name, Amen.

Seeing Our God

This is what I seek:. . . to gaze upon the beauty of the Lord and to seek him in his temple.
PSALM 27:4   PSALM 27

We need eyes of faith to see God's presence.

Deuteronomy 32:11 tells us that the Lord is "like an eagle that stirs up its nest and hovers over its young, that spreads its wings to catch them and carries them on its pinions." This is God's presence *above* us.

Deuteronomy 33:27 says, "The eternal God is [our] refuge, and underneath are the everlasting arms." This is God's presence *below* us.

Psalm 16:8 declares, "I have set the Lord always before me. Because he is at my right hand, I will not be shaken." This is God's presence *beside* us.

Exodus 13:21 says, "The Lord went ahead of them in a pillar of cloud to guide them on their way." This is God's presence *ahead* of us.

Exodus 14:19 tells how "the angel of God, who had been traveling in front of Israel's army, withdrew and went behind them. The pillar of cloud also moved from in front and stood behind them." This is his presence *behind* us.

Psalm 125:2 says, "As the mountains surround Jerusalem, so the Lord surrounds his people." This is God's presence *surrounding* us.

Our Lord is also *in* us. Colossians 1:27 speaks of a glorious mystery: "Christ in [us], the hope of glory."

PRAYER

Father, Son, and Holy Spirit, in holiness and love grant us a sense of your abiding presence as we gather to look upon your beauty and seek you in our worship, through Christ, our Lord. Amen.

Listen and Be Still

Dying Is Giving

"Because I live, you also will live."
JOHN 14:19

JOHN 14:15-24

In both living and dying, Jesus has demonstrated that he is the pioneer and perfector of our faith. He is our example, our energy giver, and the goal of our lives.

To model Jesus, some people become his itinerant servants. They can be found where there is sickness, ignorance, and poverty. Some of these people even remain celibate like Christ. Others, like Thomas à Kempis, carry on an inner, mystical dialogue with Christ, similar to the way Jesus conversed with his Father. Thomas à Kempis's book *Imitation of Christ* remains a joy to read. Still others may be like Dietrich Bonhoeffer, who was martyred for Christ at the hands of the Nazis. Bonhoeffer wrote about "being formed with the form of Christ."

Jesus, our example and our power, was conceived by the Holy Spirit and later received the Spirit fully at his baptism. The Spirit's presence enabled him on the cross to die as an act of giving. He gave his life for God's glory and for the world's salvation!

Jesus' resurrection life is ours. When we believe in him, we receive that life as a gift. And when the time of our departure comes, we give back to God and his Christ the resurrection life he gave us, joining all who have gone on ahead, and following Jesus into greater love and unending life in his presence.

PRAYER

Lord Jesus, you are my life! In living this day, and in the final act of my dying, give me strength to give my life back to you to be cleansed, renewed, redeemed forevermore. Amen.

Death a Departure

The time has come for my departure.
2 TIMOTHY 4:6

2 CORINTHIANS 5:1-10

Paul used a picturesque word to describe his exit to the life beyond: *departure*. The word *departure* can be used to describe the releasing of tent ropes. It pictures someone breaking camp in order to travel on. Paul often did that as he crisscrossed the Mediterranean world. His personal death he saw as breaking camp, moving on to the glory beyond.

The word *departure* can also bring to mind the loosing of handcuffs or fetters of any kind. Paul saw his personal death as breaking the chains of sorrow, pain, captivity, and every other disfiguring power of this sinful world.

The word *departure* can describe, as well, the loosing of mooring lines that tie a ship to a dock. Paul sailed the Mediterranean often and was familiar with the sight of sailors untying lines, freeing ships to sail on the winds and currents of the sea. For Paul, to die was to sail into uncharted seas with Jesus as his Captain.

Finally, the word *departure* describes the untying of an animal from a plow or cart. Paul was looking forward to resting from his toil.

With Paul we may view death as a departure, casting off all the ropes that tie us to this sinful world. Death is nothing more than a safe journey with the Lord of life into the radiance of the world of God.

PRAYER

Dear Jesus, when the time of death arrives, help me to focus the eyesight of faith to see death as a departure, a journey into the glory that you received from our Father's hand. Amen.

Listen and Be Still

Well Done

"Well done, my good servant!" his master replied.
LUKE 19:17

LUKE 19:11-27

Do you remember a time when your heart expanded with joy because of a word of praise? Perhaps you cleaned up the kitchen for your mother. You heard her say, "What a beautiful job! Thank you very much!" Perhaps you heard your father say after you mowed the lawn, "Great job!"

Children, usually feeling insecure and inferior, are transformed by words of praise. Confidence replaces insecurity. Resolution takes the place of defeat. Praise enriches life, intensifying love's resolve to serve.

Praise for a life well lived and a task well done is one of the rays of heaven's glory. The Lord Jesus remembers before the throne of his Father all who have confessed his name on earth. His presence breaks through our illness and weakness at the moment of death, and his warm praise welcomes us into our Father's house.

Filled with Christ's presence, we give a cup of cold water or visit the local prison or feed the village hungry or entertain the lonely or hum a hymn in a hospital room. And someday we'll hear him say "Well done!" I'm not sure just how this will work. But remember this verse:

Our knowledge of that life is small / The eye of faith is dim.
But 'tis enough that he knows all, / And we shall be with him.

PRAYER

Blessed Lord and Master, keep us faithful as your Spirit works through us. Work your works of love through us, and may we someday hear you say "Well done!" In your name we pray. Amen.

Listen and Be Still

Like His Glorified Body

We know that when he appears, we shall be like him,
for we shall see him as he is.
1 John 3:2

1 John 3:1-6

As we grow older, our physical bodies change completely, but while these changes occur, we retain our personal identity. God made me special, and I retain my "specialness."

Eyes may require glasses, joints may swell with arthritis, shoulders may begin to sag, and the heart may hurt for more oxygen. But when things like these happen to us, we still recognize each other because the soul, the self, remains constant, hopefully mellowing and maturing in the Lord's presence.

Think of Jesus. He was different after his resurrection, yet he remained the same Jesus. He was different; at least Mary of Magdala did not recognize him immediately. But when he affectionately spoke her name, she joyfully recognized him. The same thing happened to Cleopas and his friend and to others. Jesus' body after his victory became spiritual—a real body, yet perfectly adapted to his new glory.

So it is with all who live in the presence of Christ. His body went into the grave. So do ours. But what is now a perishable body will be raised imperishable. Just like Jesus! What is now weak will be raised in power. Just like Jesus! What is now a natural body will be raised a spiritual body. Just like Jesus! We shall be like him completely when we see him as he is.

PRAYER

Lord Jesus, you are my resurrection and life. Let me be aware of your presence and help me to follow you obediently now so that I may become like you when I see you in glory. Amen.

Listen and Be Still

Our Father's House

"In my Father's house are many rooms."
JOHN 14:2

JOHN 14:1-14

Jesus called the temple his Father's "house." Every Jewish believer considered the temple the place where God lived. In the mysterious Holy of Holies, God covered and forgave sins. Because of God's presence in the temple, it was called a house of prayer.

To be sure, the eternal God "does not dwell in houses made with hands." Unlike an idol, he cannot be imprisoned within four walls. But the promise stands: God dwells among his people, enthroned on their praises. And God stays with his people.

Not only that! We dwell in God. He has "been our dwelling place throughout all generations" (Psalm 90:1). And when we take our final journey out of this life, we go home to live in God. We have a special place in our Father's house, next to our brother Jesus! Our Father's presence will give us rest. In quiet tenderness we will feel his love warm us with a fire divine. Our home is our God. We, his images, with him, the original, will experience an intimacy so beautiful that it will require unending time to experience it. We shall never weary of delighting in God's presence. Then God shall be everything to everyone.

May you hear Jesus say to you personally, "Do not let your hearts be troubled! Trust in God; trust also in me."

PRAYER

Lord God, in your presence there are pleasures without measure and without end. Lord Jesus, we ask you to stay with us every step of the way until we see you in our Father's house. Amen.

Listen and Be Still   63

The Grand Finale

I saw the Holy City, the new Jerusalem. . . prepared as a
bride beautifully dressed for her husband.
REVELATION 21:2

REVELATION 21:1-8

Transported by the Spirit, John sees the Lord's final gift to mankind. He sees a city, the bride of God. Later he sees that the city even has a garden (Revelation 22:2).

Everything shines with the radiant glory of God. The city has twelve gates, each of them a pearl inscribed with the name of one of the tribes of Israel. A wall towers fourteen hundred miles high, and inscribed on its foundation are the names of the twelve apostles. The city coming down as a gift from heaven is cubed, shaped after the pattern of perfection. Through the streets of the city flows the river of the water of life, lined on either side with trees of life whose leaves are for the healing of the nations.

This city is pictured as a bride, beautifully dressed for her husband. Suffusing everything in this picture of incredible beauty, value, and glory is love. Love triune in its radiant presence makes the city-garden a bride. In the love of Father, Son, and Holy Spirit, mankind lives perfected, fulfilled in joy eternal.

John's trance-like visions reach beyond ordinary words to express beauty and glory and grandeur that we cannot know in this life. This grand finale, though, will come in God's own time to all who persevere in faith, hope, and love till the end. Will you enjoy this precious gift?

PRAYER

We praise you, O Lamb of God, for making us your bride. Abide with us until the wedding day. Then we shall be adorned with the beauty of your eternal city. In your name we pray. Amen.

Listen and Be Still

GOD'S GLORY IN CHRIST

31 MEDITATIONS AND READINGS

BY REV. DAVID J. FEDDES

REV. DAVID J. FEDDES

God's glory shines in all that Jesus says, all that Jesus does and all that Jesus is. God loves to display his glory in Christ, and we need to see that glory. We can't thrive only on wise teaching or good rules. We need to encounter Christ, delight in his divine glory and have a relationship with him. That's the essence of eternal life.

In these reflections, then, let's explore the glory of Christ and what it means to follow him, becoming his disciples and building Christian character as the Spirit of Jesus guides us each day.

Rev. Feddes was English broadcast minister for the Back to God Hour from 1990-2005. He pastored a Christian Reformed church in Canada prior to his service at the Back to God Hour.

Come and See

"Come and see."
JOHN 1:46

JOHN 1:43-51

Would you like to meet Jesus—hear him speaking, see him in action, know his personality? Don't just depend on a religious system or on what other people say. Come and see for yourself. Go to a house where Jesus is having dinner. Hop into a boat with Jesus and his friends. Sit on a grassy hillside and listen to Jesus tell stories. Walk with him down dusty roads and see how he relates to people. Notice who likes him, and why. Notice who hates him, and why. Come and see!

How can you do that? Do you need a time machine to take you? No, you just need the Bible books of Matthew, Mark, Luke, and John. These accounts have miraculous power to carry you across time and space and into contact with Jesus. And as you go to meet him, Jesus comes to meet you in your time and place. You enter his life, and he enters yours. Come and see!

You will find that Jesus is pleased that you want to know him. You will also find that he already knows you. Like Nathanael, you might ask Jesus, "How do you know me?" And you'll discover that Jesus is the all-knowing Son of God. He saw you and sought you before you knew anything about him. When you believe in Jesus based on what you've seen so far, Jesus also promises, "You shall see greater things than that." So come and see!

PRAYER

Thank you, Lord, for knowing me and calling me into a relationship with you. Help me to walk with you and to see greater things of your glory every day. In your name, Amen.

Listen and Be Still

67

Light of the World

"I am the light of the world."
JOHN 8:12

JOHN 8:12-20

When Jesus says, "I am the light of the world," he makes an astonishing claim. He doesn't just claim to teach how to be enlightened. He declares himself to be the light. And in doing that, Jesus is saying he is God.

The Old Testament Scriptures say, "The Lord is my light and my salvation" (Psalm 27:1). So when Jesus says, "I am the light," he is saying, "I am the Lord, your light and salvation." The Old Testament also says, "My God turns my darkness into light" (Psalm 18:28). So when Jesus says, "Whoever follows me will never walk in darkness, but will have the light of life," he is saying, "I am the Lord God, who turns your darkness to light."

When the religious leaders heard Jesus' claim to be the light of the world, they immediately challenged him. And today there are still many people who challenge Jesus' claims to be the one true God. Satan "has blinded the minds of unbelievers, so that they cannot see the light of the gospel of the glory of Christ, who is the image of God" (2 Corinthians 4:4).

But some do see the light of the world, recognizing Jesus as God with us. "For God, who said, 'Let light shine out of darkness,' made his light shine in our hearts to give us the light of the knowledge of the glory of God in the face of Christ" (2 Corinthians 4:6). God reveals the light of his glory to us through Jesus!

PRAYER

"Let the light of your face shine upon us, O Lord," for "with you is the fountain of life; in your light we see light" (Psalm 4:6; 36:9). In your name we pray. Amen.

Listen and Be Still

Water to Wine

[In] this, the first of his miraculous signs. . .
he thus revealed his glory.
JOHN 2:11

JOHN 2:1-11

Jesus' first miracle was to change water into wine at a wedding banquet. Jesus did this not only to keep the party going but also to show his divine glory.

It was an amazing miracle, but it wasn't the only time the Creator changed vast amounts of water into wine. In fact, he does it all the time! It's just that most of the time he uses vines and grapes and natural processes rather than an instant miracle.

Later Jesus took a little bread and fed more than 5,000 people with it. A miracle indeed! But let's not forget that every day the Creator is taking a little grain, transforming it gradually with soil, sun, and water, and making enough bread for 6 billion people. That's a miracle too!

Psalm 104:14-15 says that God "makes grass grow for the cattle, and plants for man to cultivate—bringing forth food from the earth: wine that gladdens the heart of man . . . and bread that sustains his heart." When Jesus changed water to wine and fed thousands with bread, he showed that he is the Creator God who has always done these things for us—and keeps doing them.

Our food today is from the hand of Jesus as surely as if we were among the 5,000 people eating miracle bread (John 6:1-13). Our drink today is from the hand of Jesus as surely as if we were drinking miraculous wine at the Cana wedding feast.

PRAYER

Dear God, thank you for all you do behind the scenes as our Creator and Sustainer. Thank you also for showing yourself and revealing your glory in Jesus. Amen.

Listen and Be Still

Fighting for Freedom

"I did not come to bring peace, but a sword."
MATTHEW 10:34

Jesus does not make peace with Satan or this wicked world. Jesus brings a sword to "destroy him who holds the power of death—that is, the devil—and free those who all their lives were held in slavery by their fear of death" (Hebrews 2:14-15). "The Lord is a warrior" (Exodus 15:3). As Jesus fights, he calls us to join him in the fight for freedom from sin and Satan.

Soldiers in the military must be loyal to their commander and obey orders. If they are ordered into combat, they must go. They must be willing to give up family and friends and even their own life. This is also true in Jesus' army. If we put family and friends ahead of Christ, we can't join his army. If we value our own life more than freedom in Christ, we can't join his army.

It would be crazy to follow Jesus if he were just a religious nut who caused conflict, disrupted families, and demanded complete loyalty. But Jesus isn't a crazy guy who thinks he's God; Jesus is God. Only God has the right to call for the absolute loyalty Jesus demands.

When we enlist in the Lord's army, we become friends of freedom. If political freedom is worth celebrating and fighting for, spiritual freedom is worth far more. The cost of following Jesus may sound extreme, but the commander who calls us to give up everything for him is the same Jesus who gave up everything for us.

PRAYER

Lord Jesus, if you set us free, we are free indeed. Strengthen our hearts with complete loyalty to you, and protect us with the armor of God, we pray. In your name, Amen.

Listen and Be Still

Defeating Demons

*"With authority and power he gives orders
to evil spirits and they come out!"*

LUKE 4:31-37   LUKE 4:36

Demons are not wimps. They are rebel angels who have lost all goodness but still have terrible strength. When evil spirits take possession of someone, it's not easy to drive them out. No mere human can do it. People aren't strong enough to defeat demons.

It's astounding, then, when someone comes along who makes demons tremble and run. Evil spirits that nobody could drive away are suddenly in full retreat. When a demon-possessed man made an awful scene in a worship service, Jesus merely spoke, and the demon fled.

Another man was possessed by a whole army of demons and lived in a graveyard. He was uncontrollable, foamed at the mouth, screamed in a demonic voice, and harmed himself and others. Then Jesus gave an order. The next moment the man was in his right mind, talking with Jesus, and beaming with joy (Mark 5:1-20).

What sort of person can order demons around? Some of Jesus' enemies thought that the reason demons listened to Jesus was that Jesus himself was possessed by the chief of demons. But Jesus did so much damage to the cause of the demons that he couldn't possibly be a tool of the devil. If Jesus' power wasn't demonic or merely human, the only other possibility was that it was the power of God. "The reason the Son of God appeared was to destroy the devil's work" (1 John 3:8).

PRAYER

All glory to you, Lord Jesus, for defeating demons. "How awesome are your deeds! So great is your power that your enemies cringe before you" (Psalm 66:3). In your name, Amen.

Listen and Be Still   71

Life of the Party

"Why does he eat with tax collectors and 'sinners'?"
MARK 2:16

MARK 2:13-22

When you meet Jesus, you find that he practices what he preaches. There's nothing greedy about him. He can't be flattered or bribed or seduced. He treats women with respect and with no hint of lust. He lives each day trusting his heavenly Father for his needs, without using his fame to pile up money. Even his enemies have nothing to say when Jesus asks, "Can any of you prove me guilty of sin?" (John 8:46). Never has anyone else been so pure and perfect.

But Jesus' perfect purity isn't tied to a sour strictness. He often speaks of God's reign in terms of a huge party, and almost everywhere he goes, people are throwing parties. In fact, he's involved in so many parties that some folks criticize him for not being stern and strict enough. He has the wrong kind of friends, they say, and those people enjoy themselves far too much! But despite these kinds of complaints, Jesus keeps making friends who keep throwing parties for him.

Jesus himself is the life of the party. The sinners he befriends can't help celebrating (Mark 2:19). "I have come," explains Jesus, "that they may have life, and have it to the full" (John 10:10).

People have never been so happy as when they are with Jesus, and they keep inviting others to come and see. Will you join the party at a nearby church each Sunday?

PRAYER

Lord, you are holy, and we are sinful. Thank you for bridging the gap that divides us, so that your joy may be in us and our joy may be complete. In your name, Amen.

Listen and Be Still

Who Is This?

"Who is this who even forgives sins?"
LUKE 7:49

LUKE 7:36-50

The woman had lived a bad life, and everyone knew it. How could Jesus let such a woman touch him and kiss his feet? That was shocking—but even more shocking was what Jesus said to her: "Your sins are forgiven." The others in the room exclaimed, "Who is this who even forgives sins?" Good question!

No mere human can forgive sins committed against other people. If someone wronged you and then I came along and told that person, "I forgive you," I would be out of line. I have no right to forgive wrongs done to you. The only sins I may forgive are those that have been done against me.

So how could Jesus forgive this woman? Her immorality harmed other people's marriages and may have spread diseases. If she had had children, her lifestyle would have harmed them. Her parents and extended family were probably wounded and embarrassed. She had sinned against lots of people, but how had she ever wronged Jesus? How could he say, "Your sins are forgiven"? Jesus could say this only if he was the main one offended, the God whose law is broken and whose love is wounded in every sin. Jesus' words of forgiveness were words that only God could speak.

"Who is this who even forgives sins?"

He is God with us.

PRAYER

Lord, "who is a God like you, who pardons sin and forgives? . . . You will tread our sins underfoot and hurl [them] . . . into the depths of the sea" (Micah 7:18-19). In Jesus, Amen.

Listen and Be Still

God Alone

"Who can forgive sins but God alone?"
MARK 2:7

MARK 2:1-12

Some religious groups claim to believe the Bible, but they deny that Jesus is God. They knock on doors and tell people there's no Bible verse that proves Jesus is God. Somehow they sidestep John 1:1, which says of Jesus, "The Word was God." They dodge John 20:28, where Thomas calls Jesus, "My Lord and my God!" But even if the Bible did not state so clearly that Jesus is God, his divine glory would still shine in the way that he matches Old Testament descriptions of God.

Psalm 103:2-3, for example, says, "Praise the Lord . . . who forgives all your sins and heals all your diseases." Jesus' opponents were right in saying, "Who can forgive sins but God alone?" But they were wrong in refusing to see Jesus as God.

When Jesus said, "Son, your sins are forgiven," he was saying what only God could say. And when people objected, Jesus responded by doing what only God could do: he healed a paralyzed man. Jesus' healing work confirmed his forgiving word, and both confirmed his identity as God.

Jesus' divine glory shines not only in Bible passages that call him God but in all that Jesus says and does. If Jesus forgives sins and makes a paralyzed person dance, who can he be but "the Lord . . . who forgives all your sins and heals all your diseases"?

PRAYER

Praise to you, Lord, almighty forgiver and healer. Give me faith to recognize your divine glory and love, and help many more people to see you for who you are. Amen.

Listen and Be Still

Ruler of Wind and Waves

"Who is this? Even the wind and the waves obey him!"
MARK 4:41

MARK 4:35-41

Jesus is human, with a body like ours. During his time on earth, he could get as tired as we do. If you ever doubt whether Jesus is really human, just look at him sleeping in the stern of a boat.

But he isn't only human. If you ever doubt whether Jesus is God, just look at him giving orders to the waves and weather. Psalm 89:8-9 declares, "O Lord God Almighty, who is like you? . . . You rule over the surging sea; when its waves mount up, you still them." And Psalm 93:4 says, "Mightier than the thunder of the great waters, mightier than the breakers of the sea—the Lord on high is mighty." Only Almighty God can put a storm to sleep.

Jesus has two natures, a human nature and a divine nature. And although these two natures are joined in him, they are not mixed together into some third thing that is 50 percent human and 50 percent divine. Jesus is 100 percent human and 100 percent divine. His humanity and deity are unmixed. His divine nature didn't keep his human nature from getting tired like any other man, and his human nature didn't keep his divine nature from directing the weather, as only God can do.

As a man, Jesus knows our weakness firsthand. As Lord of all things, he has almighty power to rescue us from any storm.

PRAYER

Dear Jesus, human brother and divine Master, forgive us when our faith is too small. Help us to trust you at all times and to live in your peace. In your name, Amen.

Listen and Be Still

75

Scary Glory

"Go away from me, Lord; I am a sinful man!"
LUKE 5:8

LUKE 5:1-11

Miracles can be scary. Jesus' disciples were scared during a wild storm, but when Jesus calmed the storm, they were downright terrified (Mark 4:41). Something about Jesus was scarier than any storm.

Catching fish doesn't sound so scary. After fishing all night and catching nothing, Peter suddenly caught two boatloads of fish with Jesus' help. Why was that so scary? Peter suddenly sensed that he was a mere man in the presence of God, a sinner in the presence of the blinding holiness that angels dare not look upon.

Peter feared that he was too small and sinful to hang around with so great and holy a Lord. He said, "Go away from me, Lord; I am a sinful man!" Peter thought it would be simpler and safer if Jesus would just go away and leave him to his fishing and his sinning. But Jesus told Peter not to be afraid, and Peter ended up following Jesus into something far greater.

If you've never felt afraid of Jesus, you probably don't know him—or yourself—very well. "The fear of the Lord is the beginning of wisdom" (Proverbs 9:10). As you sense God's majesty and your own sin, humble fear is healthy. But don't let fear scare you away from Jesus. "Don't be afraid," he says; "from now on you will catch men." Jesus calls you to share in his glory and to become a partner in his mission. Will you follow him?

PRAYER

Father in heaven, thank you for showing us your glory through Jesus. Forgive my sins and calm my fears. Make me a follower of Jesus and a fisher of lost souls. Amen.

Listen and Be Still

Who Is Good?

"Why do you call me good?" Jesus answered.
"No one is good—except God alone."
MARK 10:18

MARK 10:17-31

A rich young man thinks he's good. He thinks Jesus is good too. The man is half right. When the man addresses Jesus as "good teacher," Jesus challenges him to think harder. Only God is truly good; all mere humans have sinned and fall short of God's glory. So if Jesus is not God, he is not good. But if Jesus is good, then he must be God. This forces a decision: either stop calling Jesus a good teacher, or start honoring him as God.

The young man needs to accept the truth about Jesus: if Jesus is good, he's God. The young man also needs to accept the truth about himself: he's not as good as he thinks he is. He claims that throughout his life he has kept all of God's commands. But when he actually meets God in the person of Jesus and hears the Lord's command to choose Christ over money, the young man's face falls and he walks away. He loves money more than he loves God, so he breaks God's law by not loving the Lord with all his heart.

If God alone is good and if none of us is good enough to measure up to God's standard, what hope is there? If prosperous, well-behaved, religious people who call Jesus a good teacher can't earn eternal life, we might ask, with Jesus' disciples, "Who then can be saved?" Our only comfort is Jesus' reply: "With man this is impossible, but not with God; all things are possible with God."

PRAYER

"Lord, you are more precious than silver" and "more costly than gold . . . . Nothing I desire compares with you." Do the impossible, Lord, and save me. In your name, Amen.

Listen and Be Still

Are You the One?

"Are you the one who was to come,
or should we expect someone else?"
LUKE 7:20

LUKE 7:11-23

Before Jesus came, there had never been a greater man of God than John the Baptist (Luke 7:28). But even John had his times of doubt and confusion. John prepared the way for Jesus and directed other people to Jesus, but after several months in prison, John couldn't help wondering if Jesus was really the promised one.

So John sent a message to Jesus: "Are you the one who was to come, or should we expect someone else?" John knew the words of the prophet Isaiah: "'Your God . . . will come to save you.' . . . Then will the eyes of the blind be opened and the ears of the deaf unstopped. Then will the lame leap like a deer, and the mute tongue shout for joy" (Isaiah 35:4-6).

Jesus sent back a message showing that Isaiah's words were coming true: "The blind receive sight, the lame walk, those who have leprosy are cured, the deaf hear, the dead are raised, and the good news is preached to the poor" (Luke 7:22). Everything Isaiah had predicted was coming true, and more besides.

Should we look for someone else? No. God has come. We might not know why the miracle-working Christ left John to die in prison; nor do we know why we sometimes suffer the blows of a cruel world. But we do know that our God has come; the promised signs point to him, and him alone.

PRAYER

Father in heaven, when fears and doubts attack us, help us to hear your Word afresh and to know Jesus anew as the fulfillment of all your promises. In his name, Amen.

Listen and Be Still

Equal with God

He was even calling God his own Father,
making himself equal with God.

JOHN 5:1-18   JOHN 5:18

For 38 years a man is unable to walk or take care of himself. Then along comes someone who tells him to pick up his mat and walk. The man is instantly cured, so he obeys. But the rule-makers of that day think this is a horrible sin. They have decreed that it's wrong to carry a mat on the Sabbath. They seem to think it's better to lie on the ground paralyzed than to walk in the strength of the Lord.

When religion is all rules without power to transform, all it can do is paralyze and criticize: it keeps people down and criticizes any life and vigor that doesn't fit the rules. Such religion angers Jesus (Mark 3:5).

Jesus is "Lord of the Sabbath" (Luke 6:5). Together with his Father, Jesus is the Lawgiver who commanded, "Remember the Sabbath day by keeping it holy" (Exodus 20:8). By claiming authority over the Sabbath and calling God his Father, Jesus declares himself equal with God.

That makes Jesus' enemies want to kill him. They love their dead religion that blinds them to the living God. Jesus' enemies eventually do kill him—but they can't make him stay dead.

The Lord of the Sabbath rises from the dead and makes the day of his resurrection, Sunday, into the new Lord's Day. Every Sunday is a day to celebrate the life-giving power of Jesus and to worship him as God.

PRAYER

Lord, you give movement to the paralyzed and life to the dead. Free us from dead rules to serve the living God. Fill us with your life and love. In your name, Amen.

Listen and Be Still

Arresting Words

"No one ever spoke the way this man does,"
the guards declared.
JOHN 7:46

JOHN 7:28-52

Jesus spoke with unmatched power. Even when he was only a boy, "everyone who heard him was amazed at his understanding" (Luke 2:47). As an adult, Jesus' words amazed almost everyone, whether they loved or hated him.

Jesus had astonishing insight into deep truths, yet he spoke in simple words and told gripping stories. Expert scholars tried to stump him or trick him into saying something foolish, but Jesus always had the perfect answer. The smartest people couldn't outwit him, yet the simplest people could benefit from his teaching.

People were amazed not only at Jesus' brilliance but also by the sheer authority he spoke with. He wasn't like other teachers who debated the fine points of religion and piled up quotes from other experts. Jesus often challenged expert opinion and declared the truth based on divine authority. "The crowds were amazed at his teaching, because he taught as one who had authority, and not as their teachers of the law" (Matthew 7:28-29).

Jesus' enemies sent guards to arrest him, but those tough, no-nonsense officers found themselves arrested by Jesus' words. They drank in his words and then went away without seizing him. When asked why, they said, "No one ever spoke the way this man does." That's because no one but Jesus ever spoke as God with us.

PRAYER

Father in heaven, thank you for sending your Son, your eternal Word, to speak your truth. Arrest our hearts by your Spirit, and captivate us by your wisdom. In your name, Amen.

Listen and Be Still

The Rock

"A wise man. . . built his house on the rock."
MATTHEW 7:24

MATTHEW 7:24-29

The Old Testament Scriptures often speak of God as "the Rock." "Oh, praise the greatness of our God! He is the Rock" (Deuteronomy 32:3-4). "Come, let us sing for joy to the Lord; let us shout aloud to the Rock of our salvation" (Psalm 95:1). "Trust in the Lord forever, for the Lord, the Lord, is the Rock eternal" (Isaiah 26:4).

The Old Testament also warns against building our lives on anything but God the Rock. "Is there any God besides me?" asks the Lord; "no, there is no other Rock" (Isaiah 44:8). When people don't build on the Rock, they might still try to look good and impress others, but they are just putting whitewash on a weak wall with no foundation. "Rain will come in torrents . . . and violent winds will burst forth," says God. "I will tear down the wall you have covered with whitewash and will level it to the ground" (Ezekiel 13:11,14).

When Jesus speaks of himself and his words as the Rock, he speaks with divine authority. He is not just one more teacher of Old Testament law; he is the Lord who gives the law. He is the only foundation to build on. "No one can lay any foundation other than the one already laid, which is Jesus Christ" (1 Corinthians 3:11). Without Jesus as your foundation, you collapse. But if you're built on Christ the Rock, you stand strong through every storm.

PRAYER

"When all around my soul gives way, he then is all my hope and stay. On Christ the solid rock I stand; all other ground is sinking sand." You are my Rock, O Lord. In your name, Amen.

Good Soil

*"Still other seed fell on good soil.
It came up and yielded a crop. . . ."*
LUKE 8:8

LUKE 8:4-15

If you hear God's Word but it goes in one ear and out the other, you're like hard soil. If you get excited about the Lord but later lose interest, you're like shallow soil. If you believe some things about God but your heart is crowded with worries or pleasures, you're like thorny soil. The only soil that produces a crop is good soil, "those with a noble and good heart."

What if you don't have a noble and good heart? You can get one—but only by having your heart plowed in repentance. In the Old Testament God says, "Break up your unplowed ground and do not sow among thorns" (Jeremiah 4:3). "Sow for yourselves righteousness, reap the fruit of unfailing love, and break up your unplowed ground; for it is time to seek the Lord, until he comes and showers righteousness on you" (Hosea 10:12).

Jesus brings this message afresh through his parable of the four soils. To bear a crop for the Lord, you must become good soil. The plowing of repentance loosens and softens your hard heart so that God's Word can sink in. Repentance cuts deep so that your response to Christ is not shallow but lasting. Repentance roots out weeds of worldliness so that God's Word can grow and bear fruit in you.

Has your heart been plowed in repentance? Is Jesus' Word producing fruit in you?

PRAYER

Lord, produce the fruit of your Spirit in me. Break up my unplowed ground, and give me a good and noble heart that lives by your Word. In your name I pray. Amen.

Listen and Be Still

The Singing God

"Let's have a feast and celebrate."
LUKE 15:23

LUKE 15:21-32

The Old Testament Scriptures say, "The Lord your God is with you, he is mighty to save. He will take great delight in you, he will quiet you with his love, he will rejoice over you with singing" (Zephaniah 3:17).

Jesus' parable of the lost son drives that message home. As the father in Jesus' story saved his son from ruin, God saves us from total destruction. As the father delighted to see his son return, God delights over all who come to him for help. As the father hugged his son and quieted him before the boy could offer to become a slave, God quiets us with his love and welcomes us not as slaves but as sons and daughters. As the father celebrated with music and dancing, God rejoices over his people with singing.

Can you picture God throwing a party? Can you imagine God standing up in the middle of the party, singing a happy song, and dancing for joy? Maybe you think of God as solemn, somber, and silent. Or perhaps you think God should sing only over those who deserve it.

But God's glory in Christ overflows with delight and music. In Christ we meet a glad Father who sings for joy whenever a wandering child returns home. God's glorious gladness is what every sinful younger child needs—and the same goes for every sour older brother.

PRAYER

Father, I have sinned and am not worthy to be called your son. Thank you for saving me, loving me, delighting in me, and singing over me. I love you, Lord. In Jesus, Amen.

Listen and Be Still

83

Pounding on Heaven's Door

"To him who knocks, the door will be opened."
LUKE 11:10

LUKE 11:1-13

Who would dare say that praying to God is like pounding on a door and yelling to wake someone up in the middle of the night? That sounds rash and rude, but the Lord himself urges us to pray this way.

God inspired Old Testament writers to pray, "Awake, my God; decree justice" (Psalm 7:6). "Awake, and rise to my defense!" (Psalm 35:23). "Awake, O Lord! Why do you sleep? Rouse yourself! Do not reject us forever" (Psalm 44:23). "Awaken your might; come and save us" (Psalm 80:2). God said, "You who call on the Lord, give yourselves no rest, and give him no rest" (Isaiah 62:6-7).

The Son of God, who fulfills Old Testament Scripture, compares prayer to waking up a sleepy friend at midnight. Later Jesus goes even further and compares prayer to hassling an unjust judge to uphold justice when he doesn't feel like it (Luke 18:1-8). Jesus' point is not that our Father in heaven is sleepy or unjust. It's that we should be as aggressive and persistent in prayer as we would be if we were trying to get food from a drowsy friend or get justice in a unfriendly court.

Pray aggressively for the honor of God's name, the coming of God's kingdom, and the doing of God's will. Give yourself no rest, and give God no rest. Keep pounding on heaven's door till the Lord answers with a greater outpouring of his Holy Spirit.

PRAYER

"O Thou by whom we come to God, the life, the truth, the way, the path of prayer Thyself hast trod: Lord, teach us how to pray." In your name we ask this, Lord Jesus. Amen.

Listen and Be Still

Full of Grace and Truth

"Neither do I condemn you," Jesus declared.
"Go now and leave your life of sin."
JOHN 8:11

JOHN 8:3-11

Jesus is "full of grace and truth" (John 1:14). When a sinful woman was in danger of being killed, Jesus told her accusers, "If any one of you is without sin, let him be the first to throw a stone at her." They left one by one until only Jesus remained. Only Jesus had the right to destroy her. But he said, "Neither do I condemn you." That's grace. Then he added, "Leave your life of sin." That's truth. Jesus showed her God's loving grace and told her the truth about her sin and her need to change.

Jesus' grace and truth shone even in his dealings with Pharisees, ultra-religious people who didn't really know God. Jesus was painfully truthful, calling them hypocrites, snakes, and blind guides. He warned of hell for those who didn't change. But in telling the truth, Jesus remained gracious. When the Pharisee Nicodemus wanted to talk with him, Jesus explained the way of salvation. Later, when the Pharisee Saul was killing Jesus' followers, the Lord showed him the truth about his evil deeds and about Jesus' divine lordship. Jesus also showed grace by forgiving Saul and making him a great missionary, also known as Paul.

This beautiful blend of grace and truth is nothing less than divine glory. "We have seen his glory, the glory of the One and Only, who came from the Father, full of grace and truth" (John 1:14).

PRAYER

Lord God, fountain of grace and truth, in your grace forgive our sleazy sins and our proud self-righteousness, and guide us by your truth in Christ, we pray. Amen.

Listen and Be Still

Grace and Truth United

We have seen his glory, the glory of the One and Only
. . . full of grace and truth.
JOHN 1:14   JOHN 1:1-18

Grace and truth belong together but are often separated.

Eager to be gracious, some churches lose the truth. If two people with no Christian commitment request a church wedding, the church does the ceremony. If people who don't follow Jesus want their baby baptized out of tradition or superstition, the church performs the rite. Sermons are based on "positive thinking," not the Bible. All love, no judgment. All grace, no truth.

Other churches go to the opposite extreme. Anxious for the truth, they neglect grace. They emphasize Bible knowledge and theology, with detailed rules for every situation, but grace is in short supply. The sermons are all judgment, no love. There's not much room for people who don't have "perfect" behavior and beliefs. Every few years there's another quarrel and another church split over some detail of doctrine. All truth, no grace.

Grace and truth belong together. Grace without truth isn't grace at all; it's permissiveness. And truth without grace isn't God's truth; it's legalism. What churches need, what families need, what we all need, isn't a little more grace or a little more truth. What we need is a lot more of Jesus.

"Grace and truth came through Jesus Christ" (John 1:17). If we are full of Christ, we will be full of grace and truth, and divine glory will overflow from us.

PRAYER

Father, fill us with the Spirit of Christ. Warm our hearts with the grace of Jesus, guide our minds by the truth of Jesus, and reveal your glory in us, we pray. In his name, Amen.

Listen and Be Still

Sight for the Blind

"Nobody has ever heard of opening the eyes of a man born blind."

JOHN 9:1-12, 24-41

JOHN 9:32

God has a special purpose for people with physical challenges. It's not just random chance that makes a person blind or deaf. God does. "Who makes [a person] deaf or mute? Who gives him sight or makes him blind? Is it not I, the Lord?" (Exodus 4:11).

At some point the Lord will give full physical abilities to all his people. But in the meantime God either gives or withholds hearing, sight, and other abilities. Some people might think God withholds abilities to punish people, but in fact God singles them out for a special purpose: to display God's work in their lives.

Jesus' work is God's work. When Jesus gave sight to the blind, he showed his divine glory. His enemies called him a sinner, and even some of his friends saw him only as a prophet. But Old Testament Scripture had said, "The Lord gives sight to the blind" (Psalm 146:8). So Jesus was doing work that only God could do. The man whom Jesus healed came to understand this. He said, "'Lord, I believe,' and he worshiped him."

Do you believe and worship the Lord Jesus? Blind eyes can be troublesome, but a blind soul is far worse. The Lord Jesus is the only one who can remove either kind of blindness. As the Creator of light and eyes, Jesus alone can give physical sight. As the spiritual light of the world, Jesus alone can open the eyes of our hearts.

PRAYER

Lord, save us from having blind souls and deaf hearts. Help us to hear your voice, to see your glory, and to love you as our light and salvation. In your name, Amen.

Listen and Be Still

The Good Shepherd

"I am the good shepherd. The good shepherd lays down his life for the sheep."
JOHN 10:11

JOHN 10:7-21

One of the most loved statements in the Old Testament is Psalm 23:1: "The Lord is my shepherd." Other Old Testament passages also speak of God as a shepherd: "He gathers the lambs in his arms and carries them close to his heart" (Isaiah 40:11). "The Sovereign Lord says: I myself will search for my sheep and look after them. . . . I myself will tend my sheep and have them lie down. . . . I will shepherd the flock with justice" (Ezekiel 34:11-16).

When Jesus says, "I am the good shepherd," he speaks as God. Jesus is the Lord of glory who has come to earth to be our shepherd.

Some religious leaders are thieves or hired hands, says Jesus, but the good shepherd is different. A thief rips off and ruins the sheep, but the good shepherd gives them abundant life. A hired hand is in the religion business only for the money and abandons his flock if danger threatens, but the good shepherd stays with his sheep always and is even willing to die for them.

Don't fall for phony religion. Only Jesus can bring you to green pastures, restore your soul, and guide you in paths of righteousness. Only Jesus can bring you through the valley of the shadow of death, defeat Satan and all his enemies, and give you a place in God's house forever. So trust the good shepherd, God with us.

PRAYER

Good shepherd, forgive me for all the times I wander from you. Thank you for laying down your life to save me. Lead me and keep me in your care forever. In your name, Amen.

Listen and Be Still

Hard to Believe

He had in mind to divorce her quietly.
MATTHEW 1:19

MATTHEW 1:18-25

Skeptics claim that people in the past believed in Jesus' miracles only because they were less scientific than we are. But that's nonsense. Miracles were just as hard to believe then as they are now.

When Mary got pregnant, Joseph didn't need a biology degree to know where babies came from. He figured Mary must have been with another man. It took an angel visit to convince Joseph that Mary's pregnancy was a miracle.

When Jesus' disciples were in a boat and saw Jesus walking toward them on the water, they didn't need advanced physics to know that people don't ordinarily do that. Similarly, on the first Easter, when Jesus' friends found that his tomb was empty, they didn't need modern science to know that dead people tend to stay dead. The disciples believed only after Jesus came to them and ate with them and convinced them he really was alive.

Modern science doesn't make miracles harder to believe. Miracles have always been "impossible" in comparison with ordinary patterns of nature. But what if the God who designed those patterns decides to do something different?

If you deny Jesus' miracles, it's not because you're too scientific. "You are in error because you do not know the Scriptures or the power of God" (Matthew 22:29).

PRAYER

Lord, "I . . . believe; help me overcome my unbelief" (Mark 9:24). Expand my mind to accept biblical realities, and touch my heart by your power in Christ. Amen.

Listen and Be Still

Is Faith Foolish?

*"The miracles I do in my Father's name speak for
me, but you do not believe."*
JOHN 10:25-26   JOHN 10:22-39

A man phoned our offices, reacting against one of my radio programs. He complained that I was foolish to preach Jesus' resurrection. He thought I was being terribly irrational. Then he went on to tell me that magician David Copperfield made the Statue of Liberty go away completely and then made it come back. I urged him to be serious, but he was dead serious. He knew for sure that this happened because he had seen it on television! For him, seeing was believing, and that made television the standard of truth.

Many people know enough not to believe everything they see on TV—but they still take their own ideas more seriously than God. Francis Crick won a Nobel Prize for his discoveries about the structure of DNA. After studying complex genetic codes, this brilliant scientist doubted that random evolution could ever produce DNA from scratch. So did he conclude that God was involved? No, he said that perhaps aliens from outer space put genetic material on earth. In Crick's opinion, belief in the Creator God is unscientific—but belief in aliens makes sense!

Is faith foolish? Not nearly as foolish as unbelief. If you shut your eyes to God's glory in Christ, other things become darker too. But if you believe Jesus and his miracles, you start seeing everything more clearly.

PRAYER

Dear Lord, forgive us when we feel foolish for believing in you.
Help us to believe your Word, to marvel at your miracles, and to
prize you above all else. In your name, Amen.

Listen and Be Still

The Shining Savior

*His face shone like the sun, and his
clothes became as white as the light.*

MATTHEW 17:1-13   MATTHEW 17:2

Paintings of Jesus usually make him look handsome, but Jesus looked ordinary, perhaps even homely. "He had no beauty or majesty to attract us to him, nothing in his appearance that we should desire him" (Isaiah 53:2). Living among the poor, Jesus didn't have costly clothes to look fashionable or important, either. Even Jesus' friends didn't always sense his divine majesty.

Jesus' looks were not awe-inspiring, but one day his plain face suddenly "shone like the sun." His worn, dirty clothes became "as white as the light." It lasted only a short while, but his transfiguration gave a glimpse of who Jesus was all along: the Son of the living God. It also previewed the glory that would shine from him after Jesus defeated death and ascended to heaven.

Peter never forgot what he saw and heard that day, and he wanted to tell everyone. "We were eyewitnesses of his majesty," wrote Peter. "For he received honor and glory from God the Father when the voice came to him from the Majestic Glory, saying, 'This is my Son, whom I love; with him I am well pleased.' We ourselves heard this voice that came from heaven when we were with him on the sacred mountain." Because the Bible reveals Jesus' glory, we "do well to pay attention to it, as to a light shining in a dark place, until the day dawns and the morning star rises in [our] hearts" (2 Peter 1:16-19).

PRAYER

Father in heaven, shine the light of Jesus' face into our hearts. By your Spirit speak to us of your beloved Son, that we may know your glory in him. In his name, Amen.

Listen and Be Still

The Platinum Rule

"Whatever you did for one of the least
of these brothers of mine, you did for me."
MATTHEW 25:40   MATTHEW 25:31-46

One important way God displays his glory is by standing with poor people. The Old Testament says, "The Lord secures justice for the poor and upholds the cause of the needy" (Psalm 140:12). God cares so much about poor people that he sees any action toward the poor as an action toward himself. "He who is kind to the poor lends to the Lord, and he will reward him for what he has done" (Proverbs 19:17).

When Jesus says he will judge the world on the final day, he speaks as the Lord God, who "secures justice for the poor." When Jesus says, "Whatever you did for one of the least of these . . . you did for me," he speaks as the Lord God, who identifies with the needy. Kindness to needy people is kindness to the Lord Jesus. Neglecting others is neglecting the Lord Jesus.

Jesus said, "Do to others as you would have them do to you" (Luke 6:31), and that has become known as the golden rule. If that's the golden rule, here's the platinum rule: "Do to others as you would do to Christ the Lord." As Creator and brother of the poor, Jesus takes personally everything done to his people, whether good or bad. So let's make it good.

To see God's glory in Christ, look for people who need help and can't get justice. Hidden in those suffering faces is the glory of God in the face of Christ.

PRAYER

Father in heaven, help us to see you as Father of the poor and to see Christ in the faces of the needy. Move us to show love for them and for you, we pray. In Jesus' name, Amen.

Listen and Be Still

The Lazarus Principle

*"This sickness will not end in death.
No, it is for God's glory. . . ."*

JOHN 11:1-6, 17-27, 38-44   JOHN 11:4

When Jesus was asked to come and help Lazarus, why did he stay away? Why did he let his friend suffer and die? Why did he let Mary and Martha go through the horror of burying their brother? Why does Jesus still allow dreadful things to happen to his friends?

I don't know any easy answers to such questions, but I do know the one who says, "I am the resurrection and the life." For a friend of Jesus, death is never the end. The end, the final destination, is resurrection. This was true for Lazarus, and it's true for all of Jesus' friends.

When we go through terrible times, we might wonder if Jesus cares and if he is in charge. But Jesus never stops loving his friends, and he never loses control. The Lord doesn't always keep death away, but when he allows death to come, it's not the final outcome.

A deadly illness can be "for God's glory so that God's Son may be glorified." It can also be "for your sake" (John 11:14) to increase faith and resurrection joy. Do you prize God's glory in Christ enough to say, "I eagerly expect and hope that . . . Christ will be exalted in my body, whether by life or by death" (Philippians 1:20)?

Count on the Lazarus principle: For a friend of Jesus, death is never the final outcome. The Lord, who is "the resurrection and the life," directs all things for our good and for his glory.

PRAYER

Lord of life, conqueror of death, all glory be to you. Glorify yourself in us, whether by our life or our death, we pray. Come soon and resurrect all your people. In your name, Amen.

Listen and Be Still   93

Humility and Authority

"I, your Lord and Teacher, have washed your feet."
JOHN 13:14

JOHN 13:1-17

In Jesus we meet a combination of humility and authority that we won't meet anywhere else. One moment he's cuddling babies; the next he's confronting rulers. One moment he's lying exhausted and asleep in a boat being tossed by a storm; the next he's ordering the storm around. One moment he's weeping at the grave of his friend Lazarus; the next he's ordering death itself to release his friend. One moment he's on his knees like a slave, washing his disciples' feet; the next he makes clear that he's their Lord.

Jesus feels the weakness, pain, and poverty of humanity, and at the same time he unleashes the power, healing, and abundance of God. He doesn't have even a small hut for a home, yet he strides through God's temple as though he owns the place. He doesn't have a penny to his name, yet he talks like the whole world is his. Could even the least human be humbler and more vulnerable? Could even almighty God be greater and more powerful? What else can we think except that Jesus must be completely human and at the same time fully God?

The Son of God makes us sons and daughters of God. He gives believers great authority to reign with him—and he calls us to serve with him. By the power of his Spirit we become more and more like him, spreading the light of his glory through humble acts of love.

PRAYER

Lord Jesus, bold as a lion, gentle as a lamb, make us bold with your authority and gentle with your humility. By your Spirit, display your glory in us. In your name, Amen.

Listen and Be Still

Cross of Glory

"Surely this man was the Son of God!"
MARK 15:39

MARK 15:25-39

A few days before Jesus' death, he said, "The hour has come for the Son of Man to be glorified" (John 12:23). Jesus would be glorified by being crucified. When he looked ahead to suffering and separation from his Father, he shuddered and said, "Now my heart is troubled, and what shall I say? 'Father, save me from this hour'? No, it was for this very reason I came to this hour. Father, glorify your name!" Then he heard a voice from heaven: "I have glorified it, and will glorify it again" (John 12:27-28). It may seem that God's glory was never so hidden as when Jesus suffered and died on the cross. But never did God's glory shine so brightly.

The glory of God's justice shone as the sins of the world were punished in Jesus, the representative of humanity before God. The glory of God's love shone as countless sinners were forgiven for the sake of Jesus. The glory of God's wisdom shone as God carried out a plan of salvation that amazed even the angels. God the Father was glorified in the death of his Son, and the Son was glorified in his total devotion to his Father's will and his people's salvation.

Jesus' glory shines in his miracles, in his teaching, and in his radiant personality, but the ultimate display of his divine glory is the cross. When we see how Jesus died, we can only exclaim, "Surely this is the Son of God!"

PRAYER
"To him who loves us and has freed us from our sins by his blood . . . to serve his God and Father—to him be glory and power for ever and ever!" (Revelation 1:5-6). Amen.

Listen and Be Still

"My God!"

Thomas said to him, "My Lord and my God!"
JOHN 20:28

JOHN 20:19-31

Thomas is often remembered as "doubting Thomas" because he doubted Jesus' resurrection at first. But don't forget the believing Thomas. He made the supreme statement of faith in Jesus recorded in the Bible: "My Lord and my God!"

Believing Thomas can teach us a thing or two. Sure, Thomas was hard to persuade, but once the Lord convinced him, Thomas didn't just say, "I guess Jesus really did rise after all." Thomas embraced the full meaning of what the resurrection showed about Jesus. Thomas honored the risen Christ as Lord of all things and God of the universe, and he declared his personal commitment, saying, "My Lord and my God!"

Do you adore the divine glory of Jesus and commit yourself to him? The resurrection is not just an event that happened long, long ago in a galaxy far, far away. The resurrection displays God's glory in Christ, the Lord of life. God's glory in Christ matters here and now, and you must believe, worship, and commit to the Lord Jesus here and now.

The Bible tells us of Jesus not just to give us information but to lead us into a living relationship with the living Lord right now. "These are written that you may believe that Jesus is the Christ, the Son of God, and that by believing you may have life in his name."

PRAYER

Jesus Christ, my Lord and my God, forgive my doubts, increase my faith, and fill me with love for you, for your Father, and for the blessed Holy Spirit. In your name, Amen.

Listen and Be Still

Seeing His Glory

"Father, I want those you have given me to be with me where I am, and to see my glory."
JOHN 17:24

JOHN 17:1-5, 20-26

Years after Jesus ascended to heaven, he appeared to his old friend John and gave him a glimpse of his heavenly glory. "His face was like the sun shining in all its brilliance." It was too much for John to take, and he fell at Jesus' feet as though dead. Then Jesus touched his friend and said, "Do not be afraid" (Revelation 1:16-17).

A long, direct look at the sun would blind us, and a long, direct look at the glory of Jesus would be too much for us in our present condition, since we are not yet made perfect. But someday that will change. Jesus wants his Father to give us a place in heaven so that we may see his glory and enjoy his splendor forever. The Holy Spirit promises, "They will see his face . . . . They will not need the light of a lamp or the light of the sun, for the Lord God will give them light. And they will reign for ever and ever" (Revelation 22:4-5).

I will see God's glory in Christ, and I won't have to shield my eyes. I will reign with Jesus and not feel out of place on a throne. It sounds outrageous—but this is the Father's will; this is the Holy Spirit's work; this is what Jesus wants. This will happen because God lives in me and loves me with the same love the Father has for Jesus (John 17:23, 26). God glorifies himself not by keeping glory to himself but by sharing it and making us participants "in the divine nature" (2 Peter 1:4).

PRAYER

Lord, give us faith to share in your sufferings, that we may also share in your glory. Unite us to fellow believers and to yourself in eternal love. In your name, Amen.

Listen and Be Still

LIVING THE LIFE OF FAITH

LIVING THE LIFE OF FAITH

BATTLING GIANTS

31 MEDITATIONS AND READINGS

BY REV. JERRY J. HOYTEMA

REV. JERRY J. HOYTEMA

Sometimes a Christian's walk with God seems easy and pleasant. But more often, the walk seems hard and rough. These reflections will look at some of the challenges we face in walking with God. Together we will examine several different challenges to our faith, and in each case we will look at ways in which we can battle these "giants" that obstruct our walk with the Lord.

It is our prayer that by bravely facing these challenges in the light of God's Word, we can all be assisted and walk more closely with God each day.

Rev. Hoytema is a retired pastor of the Christian Reformed Church, having served several congregations in Ontario, Canada, during his active ministry.

Battling Giants

On hearing the Philistine's words, Saul and all the Israelites were dismayed and terrified.
1 SAMUEL 17:11

1 SAMUEL 17:1-26

How well do you know Jesus Christ? My hope is that reading this group of devotions will either assist you in growing in your faith or will help you discover your need for God so that you may surrender your life to him and become a fully devoted follower of Jesus Christ.

From personal experience I know there are some things that prevent us from growing in our faith or surrendering our lives to God. In some ways these are "giants" because they can stand in the way and keep us from becoming Christians or growing as Christians.

The story of David and Goliath is one of the most familiar stories in the Bible. On the one hand there is David, a young man with no battle experience. On the other hand there is Goliath, a giant so big and powerful that the whole Israelite army cowers in fear of him. No one dares to fight against Goliath. His coat of armor weighed about 125 pounds, and his spear tip about 15 pounds. This man looked more like a tank than a soldier. But was he really invincible?

The challenges that face us may not be named "Goliath," but they may be just as big and intimidating. If we do not have God on our side, we have every reason to be dismayed and frightened. But that doesn't have to be our experience—not if we have faith in "the living God."

PRAYER

Father, help us identify some of the giants we face and discover biblical principles to defeat them. Help us, dear God, to boldly face the things that so often defeat us. In Jesus, Amen.

Listen and Be Still

The Battle Is the Lord's

*"The battle is the Lord's, and he will
give all of you into our hands."*
1 SAMUEL 17:47

1 SAMUEL 17:38-50

One biblical principle we need to alert each other to is that whatever giants we fight, the battle is the Lord's.

Goliath looked at David, and "saw that he was only a boy," a mere youth. What could this youngster do against this giant of a man? Listen to what David says: "All those gathered here will know that it is not by sword or spear that the Lord saves; for the battle is the Lord's. . . ."

Whenever we try to overcome our enemies in our own strength, we lose out.

I have a friend who is an alcoholic. He tells me that when he thinks he can handle booze on his own, he fails every time. But when he surrenders to the Lord his inability to conquer his desire to drink, he gains victory. God is the best giant killer there is.

One night my wife and I were talking about how hard it is to surrender everything to God and to his mighty power. When you are worried about your children; when you are getting older and you're alone; when you discover a lump or a tumor in your body—to leave all of that to God is hard to do.

But a child of God knows that "the battle is the Lord's." As the apostle Paul puts it in 1 Corinthians 15:57, "Thanks be to God! He gives us the victory through our Lord Jesus Christ."

PRAYER

Father, if "we in our own strength confide, our striving would be losing." Remind us daily that we can have victory only if we surrender to you. In Jesus' name, Amen.

Listen and Be Still

Facing Storms

Immediately Jesus made his disciples get into the boat. . . .
MARK 6:45

MARK 6:45-52

Did you know that the words "Don't be afraid" are stated on at least 365 different occasions in the Bible? Someone has noted that there's at least one for every day of the year.

Fear is a giant that many of us face. God knows that sometimes we get terribly afraid. As a small child, I would sometimes look under the bed, afraid that something strange might be lurking there. Some people whistle loudly in the dark because they're afraid.

In our story for today we find the disciples of Jesus in a boat on a lake in the midst of a storm, and they become afraid. What's more, they're in the boat because Jesus "made" them get into it.

It's important to note that little word "made." You see, the disciples had just seen the miraculous feeding of a huge crowd of people after Jesus had multiplied five loaves and two fishes (Mark 6:30-44). It was easy for them to follow a great miracle worker. But it became tougher to follow someone who "made" them get into a boat and ride out a storm.

We all need storms, though. Storms reveal what our life is founded on. Jesus knows that it's in the crucible of challenges that we grow in faith. John Calvin said it this way: "True piety is not fully distinguished from its counterfeit, until it comes to trial."

PRAYER

Dear God, none of us like life's storms. We sometimes worry whether our faith can stand the test. When you make us go into a storm, help us to trust in you. In Jesus, Amen.

Listen and Be Still

When You Are Terrified

They saw Jesus approaching the boat, walking
on the water; and they were terrified.
JOHN 6:19

JOHN 6:16-24

This story in John 6 is a bit different from the previous story of Jesus walking on the water. In this story, the disciples had rowed their boat for three and a half miles since evening, and now it was dark. The wind blew and the waves swept higher and higher, tossing the little boat up and down.

But then something happened that caused the disciples to be even more frightened than they already were. They saw someone walking toward them on the water. Is it any wonder that "they were terrified"?

Matthew and Mark point out that the disciples thought they were seeing a ghost (Matthew 14:26; Mark 6:49). Where can you go when you're in the middle of a lake in a frightening storm in the dark of night, and you think you see a ghost coming toward you? Have you ever been afraid like that?

There are many people who must often say, "Dear God, help me; I don't think I can make it through this day." I think of a woman who is afraid she has cancer. And there's a father who fears for his daughter who has run away. Then there are those who have just lost a spouse and who fear loneliness.

There's also fear about what the future holds in our tumultuous world. There's fear of losing one's job, and there's fear of losing one's family to divorce. Fear can grip us to the point that we can hardly breathe.

PRAYER

Lord, we can get so afraid—of the future, of what could happen in our families, of what's happening right now. Help us to know you understand, and to trust in you. Amen.

Why Do Storms Last So Long?

*During the fourth watch of the night Jesus
went out to them, walking on the lake.*
MATTHEW 14:25

MATTHEW 14:22-27

"The fourth watch" is a nautical term. There are four watches in the night. The first is from 6 p.m. to 9 p.m.; the second, from 9 p.m. to midnight; the third, from midnight to 3 a.m.; and the fourth, from 3 a.m. to 6 a.m. Jesus came to his disciples "during the fourth watch."

From around 6 p.m. that night the disciples had struggled with all their might to keep from perishing. Many of them were seasoned fishermen and had been in storms before, but now, after about nine hours, they were at their wits' end as the storm kept on.

Why did Jesus not come during the first watch? Mark, who tells the same story, writes that Jesus "saw the disciples straining at the oars, because the wind was against them" (Mark 6:48). You may think that God does not see you in the storm, that Jesus has forgotten you as you struggle. But that's not true. God sees you and knows what's happening to you all the time.

I don't know why God sometimes lets us struggle for a time. The apostle Paul describes one of his experiences this way: "We were under great pressure, far beyond our ability to endure . . . . But this happened that we might not rely on ourselves but on God, who raises the dead" (2 Corinthians 1:8-9). Sometimes Jesus lets us struggle not because he has abandoned us but to increase our dependence on him.

PRAYER

Dear God, some nights can be so long. And sometimes we wonder if you are there. Thank you for always watching over us even if you wait to rescue us. In Jesus, Amen.

Listen and Be Still

Watch Where You Look

When [Peter] saw the wind, he was afraid and,
beginning to sink, cried out, "Lord save me!"
MATTHEW 14:30

MATTHEW 14:27-32

I'm reading a book by John Ortberg with a great title: *If You Want to Walk on Water, You Have to Get Out of the Boat.* Well, Peter got out of the boat when Jesus invited him to come to him. Bravely and confidently he walked toward Jesus.

But then Peter did something that caused him to be filled with fear again. You see, the storm had not yet died down. The wind was still blowing strong, and the waves were still high. Matthew writes, "But when [Peter] saw the wind . . ." Peter took his eyes off Jesus, watched a huge wave coming toward him, and immediately began to sink.

This reading from Matthew teaches us an important principle: Keep your eyes on Jesus and do not focus on the distracting conditions around you. Peter took his eyes off Jesus and looked at the circumstances he was in. When you do that, fear will grip your soul and you'll begin to sink. That always happens when your eyes are on the storm and not on the One who has infinitely more power and can still the storm with a simple command.

The writer of Hebrews says, "Let us fix our eyes on Jesus, the author and perfecter of our faith" (Hebrews 12:2). But you know what? Even if you forget to do that sometimes and cry out, "Lord, save me!" Jesus will reach out his hand and pull you to safety.

PRAYER

Forgive us, Lord, when we focus on the storm around us and take our eyes off you. Remind us that you are far more powerful than any storm that comes along. In your name, Amen.

Do Not Be Afraid

"My peace I give you. . . . Do not let your hearts
be troubled and do not be afraid."
JOHN 14:27

JOHN 14:25-27

In the previous few meditations we have been looking at fear as a giant that stands in the way of trusting God when we face storms in life. There are three biblical principles we need to observe if we are going to slay the giant of fear.

First, Jesus is always with us, no matter what our circumstances may be. Second, we should not focus on the things in life that make us afraid, but instead we should look away from them and focus on Jesus. And, third, we should listen for the voice of Jesus in the storms that come our way. We need to hear him say, "I am with you always" (Matthew 28:20)—even in our worst storms.

What's more, sometimes storms come because we've drifted from God. C. S. Lewis once wrote, "Pain is God's megaphone to get our attention."

Here's an illustration that may help. A two-story home was engulfed in flames, and the family—father, mother, and several children—were on their way out when the smallest boy became afraid and ran back upstairs. The little boy stood in front of an open upstairs window. His father shouted up to him, "Jump, son! I'll catch you!" The boy cried out, "But, Daddy, I can't see you." "I know," his father shouted back, "but I can see you."

Jesus invites us today, "Do not let your hearts be troubled and do not be afraid." He sees us always, even if we can't see him clearly.

PRAYER

You, O Lord, are "my light and my salvation –whom shall I fear?" You are "the stronghold of my life—of whom shall I be afraid?" In Jesus' name I pray, O Lord. Amen.

Listen and Be Still

109

God's Handkerchief

"He will wipe every tear from their eyes."
REVELATION 21:4

REVELATION 21:1-4

Cornelius Plantinga, Jr., relates the story of someone who has compared the dying of a Christian to the movement of a child down a flight of stairs to a dark basement. There's an emergency at night, and all the lights have gone out. From the basement the child hears his father calling to him. The child cannot see anything. He's thoroughly afraid. He doesn't want to go down those stairs; he doesn't know what's there. Yet the child knows who is there. So, with perfect love casting out fear, the child slowly moves forward and reaches his waiting father.

It seems that every child of God that comes home to the Father has tears in his eyes. Revelation 21 teaches us that when we get to heaven, it's as if God takes a handkerchief and wipes every tear from our eyes. We never have to cry again.

On this side of heaven there are still lots of tears. Death causes rivers of tears in our world. Even Jesus wept when his friend Lazarus died; Jesus wept because he loved Lazarus (John 11:35-36).

But when we get to heaven, God will tenderly wipe the tears from our eyes. You see, death puts an end to our sinning. And sin and all the trouble it brings are what cause our tears and pain. So when we get to heaven there will be no more sin or tears again.

PRAYER

O God, many of us will shed bitter tears today. Give us the assurance that one day all of us who know Jesus as Savior and Lord will never have to cry again. In his name, Amen.

Listen and Be Still

You've Got to Run

He left his cloak in her hand and ran out of the house.
GENESIS 39:12

GENESIS 39:1-12

As we continue looking at giants that often stand between us and spiritual victory, for the next few meditations we'll look at the giant called lust.

Lust is desire that's gone out of control. In our Scripture reading for today we read about Potiphar's wife inviting Joseph to come to bed with her. The text says that she "took notice of Joseph," who "was well-built and handsome." In other words, she looked at Joseph with desire, and she was so attracted to him that she tried to tempt him "day after day."

It's a scene that's played out again and again. That attractive person at the office seems so much more understanding than your spouse. He or she really seems to care about you. And if you're a business executive away from home night after night, it's so easy to fall prey to lust. Those late-night TV movies at home can also be a trap, as you scan through channels and "just happen" to see a restricted movie. Or are you one of those who "just browse" through sensual magazines while waiting at the mall, the subway, or the airport?

Joseph recognizes the temptation of lust for what it is. He says, "How . . . could I do such a wicked thing and sin against God?"

Joseph ran away from sin as fast as he could. That's what we should do, too, when confronted by lust.

PRAYER

Lord, we thank you for the gift of sexuality. Help us to know when our expression of it becomes wicked and sinful against you, and help us to run away when we should. Amen.

Listen and Be Still

The Power of Lust

All at once he followed her like an ox
going to the slaughter. . . .
PROVERBS 7:22

PROVERBS 7:6-27

I belong to a small group that meets every week. We all need a few friends who will hold us accountable in our spiritual walk. I have an accountability card in my wallet with questions on it that trusted friends may ask me from time to time. One question reads, "Have you exposed yourself to any sexually explicit material?" Another question asks, "Have you related to a member of the opposite sex in any way that might be seen as compromising?"

Our Scripture for today talks about a man who is seduced by a prostitute. He follows her "like an ox going to the slaughter . . . little knowing it will cost him his life." For "her house is a highway to the grave, leading down to the chambers of death."

Lust is powerful and appealing. "Many are the victims she has brought down; her slain are a mighty throng," says the teacher in Proverbs. Giving in to lust can cost you your family. Giving in to lust will cost you your self-respect. The worst thing about giving in to lust is that it dishonors God, and it could even cost you your relationship with God. Lust could cost you your life.

You can defeat this giant only when you look to Jesus for strength. Pray that your heart may be filled with a deep love for God. The apostle John writes, "This is love for God: to obey his commands" (1 John 5:3).

PRAYER

Father in heaven, fill my heart with a deep love for you. Keep me from compromising my love for you. Forgive me for having impure thoughts. In your Son's name, Amen.

Listen and Be Still

It Begins in the Mind

Each one is tempted when, by his own evil desire,
he is dragged away and enticed.
JAMES 1:14

JAMES 1:13-18

Ralph Waldo Emerson wrote, "The ancestry of every action is a thought." Reflect on that statement as we focus again on the giant of lust. Every sinful action is preceded by a sinful thought or desire. Let me illustrate with two biblical examples.

You may know the story of a man called Achan in the Old Testament. He stole from the city of Jericho when the Lord had said no one was to take plunder for himself. When Achan was found out and confronted with his sin, he made this confession: "It is true! I have sinned against the Lord, the God of Israel. This is what I have done: When I saw in the plunder a beautiful robe from Babylonia, two hundred shekels of silver and a wedge of gold weighing fifty shekels, I coveted them and took them" (Joshua 7:20-21). Notice the progression? Achan saw, he coveted, and he took. That's how it always goes.

The same happened to David in his sin with Bathsheba. The story in 2 Samuel 11 tells us that David saw Bathsheba, wanted her, and then took her and sinned.

Don't let seeing lead to desiring and then taking, for it leads to death. It's true that you sometimes can't help seeing what might tempt you to sin. But with the help of the Holy Spirit you can fill your mind with the things of God and focus on Jesus.

PRAYER

Dear God, hear us as we sing, "O be careful little eyes what you see." Help us, Lord, to guard our hearts. Fill us with desire for you, and help us to focus on Jesus. In his name, Amen.

Listen and Be Still

Anger

*An angry man stirs up dissension, and a
hot-tempered one commits many sins.*
PROVERBS 29:22

PROVERBS 29:20-27

In the next few devotions let's take a look at the giant called anger. How many of us haven't faced that giant and been defeated by it again and again?

A man was in great physical shape because of the time he spent hiking. When asked why he spent so much time outdoors, he replied that he and his wife made an agreement when they were married that they would not speak angry words to each other. Instead they would cool off by going for a walk. As a result, he said, "I have spent most of my married life walking outdoors."

The Bible has a lot to say about anger, and most of it tells us that anger is a harmful emotion. Anger often gets us into trouble, harms our spiritual life, and hurts others and God. The Bible does tell us about a way of being angry without sinning, and we'll think about that later. But most of us are not very good at being angry without sinning. When we are angry, it is most often sinful anger.

Think about your own anger. Do you get angry quickly or easily? What kinds of things make you angry? Do you get angry when others don't move fast enough for you or don't agree with your ideas? Do you get angry over mistakes you've made? Whom do you need to beg for forgiveness because they have been the targets of your anger?

PRAYER

Dear God, at times we have hurt others deeply and sinned against you with outbursts of anger. Please forgive us and give us self-control, for Jesus' sake. Amen.

Listen and Be Still

What Makes You a Fool?

Do not be quickly provoked in your spirit,
for anger resides in the lap of fools.
ECCLESIASTES 7:9

ECCLESIASTES 7:1-9

The Bible minces no words when it talks about people who are hot–tempered. We all have met people who respond in anger at the slightest provocation.

Anger is most often displayed at home. I have met people who have lost all self-esteem and whose spirits are broken because they come from a home where there's been a lot of anger. In those homes a father often disciplines with angry words, and children often cower in fear because of a mother's angry voice.

In 1 Corinthians 13, often called the Bible's great chapter on love, Paul says, "Love . . . is not easily angered" (13:4-5). There will be situations and/or people that might provoke us. Our response is to be one of love, not anger. This passage on love is first of all about the way God loves us. God is patient with us. God is kind. God keeps no record of wrongs and is not easily angered. We should be so thankful that God is "slow to anger" (Psalm 86:15) and that Jesus treats us with patient mercy. We are to love others with the love of the Lord.

If we are easily angered, the Bible says that's the way of fools. So let's not be quickly provoked.

A man walked in my study and asked what I was doing. I told him I was writing about anger. "I'll be reading those meditations," he said, and then he admitted, "Oh, it's a battle!" This giant is not easily defeated.

PRAYER

Lord, forgive me when I have been quick to become angry with my spouse, my children, my parents, or my friends. May the love of Jesus be expressed through me. Amen.

Listen and Be Still

Don't Nurse Your Anger

Do not let the sun go down while you are still angry.
EPHESIANS 4:26

EPHESIANS 4:25-32

With these words the Bible is telling us we should not nurse our anger. Some people try to figure out ways to punish the person or institution that has made them angry. Others will mull over past wounds and never let go.

I know of people who haven't spoken to each other for years. Sometimes it takes a funeral to bring them together, but even then they won't speak to each other.

The well-known phrase "Never go to bed angry" is good advice, particularly if you're married. Don't keep on being angry, for you will leave havoc in your wake.

To be sure, anger is probably a part of every intimate relationship. My wife and I have rarely gone to sleep before we have settled things. There have been times when we would still be up at 3 a.m. But then our hearts would be right with each other and right with God again, and the intimacy that had been broken by angry words would return.

"Do not grieve the Holy Spirit," says Ephesians 4. Outbursts of anger cause the Spirit pain and grief. A hymn asks, "How can your pardon reach and bless the unforgiving heart that broods on wrongs and will not let old bitterness depart?" Be the first to forgive; it doesn't matter who hurt who first. You can't be at peace if you have anger in your heart.

PRAYER

"Lord, cleanse the depths within our souls and bid resentment cease. Then, bound to all in bonds of love, our lives will spread your peace." In Jesus' name we pray. Amen.

Listen and Be Still

Giving the Devil a Foothold

"In your anger do not sin" . . .
do not give the devil a foothold.
EPHESIANS 4:26-27

EPHESIANS 4:25-28

It's possible to be angry and not sin.

The Bible teaches us that God is angry with sin and wickedness. Jesus was angry when he threw money changers out of the temple (Mark 11:15-17). The Bible tempers the anger of God with these words: "The Lord, the compassionate and gracious God, slow to anger, abounding in love . . ." (Exodus 34:6).

Christians too must be angry at times. Anger should rise up within us when we see streams of refugees and hungry and displaced people in our world, or when we witness how easy it is for so many people to choose killing their unborn children. We should be angry at injustices in our world, and we should express our anger in constructive, healing ways. But it's not easy to be angry and not sin. Anger always needs to be turned into energy to address wrong. It can never simply be nursed and spit out hatefully, regardless of its cause.

Our Scripture reading teaches that anger gives the devil "a foothold." Anger allows the devil a place in your heart. When the devil finds a Christian with anger in his heart, he latches on to take up residence there.

Some people fight and argue a lot. Not only does the sun go down on their anger, but the devil is granted a foothold. Don't let that happen in your marriage or in your other relationships.

PRAYER

Forgive us, Father, when we have given the devil a foothold in our hearts, when we have cut someone down in our anger. May the love of Jesus fill our hearts, we pray. Amen.

Listen and Be Still

Get Rid of Anger

*Get rid of all bitterness, rage and anger, brawling
and slander, along with every form of malice.*
EPHESIANS 4:31

EPHESIANS 4:29-32

In Ephesians 4 the apostle Paul has been teaching that when you become a Christian, you put off the old self with its sinful practices and you put on the new self, becoming more like Jesus (vs. 22-24). It's like taking off an old coat and putting on a new one.

A radical change takes place in your life when you become a Christian. We call it conversion: making a conscious decision to turn away from sin and to turn to God in faith and repentance.

Paul makes conversion a very practical experience. He mentions a series of six ungodly attitudes and practices that must be put away. "Get rid of all bitterness, rage and anger, brawling and slander, along with every form of malice." None of these have a place in the Christian's life, and it's easy to see that anger is a root of all the others. Instead, Paul says, "Be kind and compassionate to one another, forgiving each other, just as in Christ God forgave you" (Ephesians 4:32).

Often we make a decision to be angry. We can turn it off and on. If you are angry with someone in your family and the telephone rings, for example, the moment you pick up the phone, you can change your voice so that the person calling won't even know you've been angry. Surrender your anger to the Lord and let God's love fill your heart through the Holy Spirit.

PRAYER

Lord Jesus, we thank you for the ability to see your likeness in us. In the realm of emotions, as in all others, help us to learn obedience to you. In your name we pray. Amen.

Listen and Be Still

Slow to Become Angry

Be quick to listen, slow to speak, and
slow to become angry. . . .
JAMES 1:19

JAMES 1:19-27

A radio announcer observed that we have entered the "age of rage." Road rage and shooting sprees by angry employees or ex-employees grab headlines. But in some ways this is not new. Anger has been all around us and within us for a long, long time (ever since the fall into sin). The fact that about 300 passages in the Bible deal with anger shows us that God knows we have a problem with anger.

Our Scripture reading for today teaches us that anger produces a life that's not very pleasing to God. It "does not bring about the righteous life that God desires." We all know from personal experience that anger so often results in doing wrong rather than in doing what's right.

Sometimes we might say it's not our anger that's the problem; it's the circumstances we face. But deep down we know that keeping our anger under control requires not a change of circumstances but a change of attitude. We recognize the wisdom of James's advice to be "slow to become angry."

Anger leads to an ungodly life. It results in bitterness, and it can rip apart the self-esteem and self-worth of others. Anger can even lead to hatred and murder.

One way to defeat the giant of anger is to ask God to work "the fruit of the Spirit" in our lives and to cast out "the desires of the sinful nature" (Galatians 5:16, 22).

PRAYER

Father, help me to control my tongue and my temper. Work the fruit of the Spirit into my life, and please forgive me for the ways I have hurt others in anger. In Jesus' name, Amen.

Listen and Be Still

119

Watch Out!

*"Why are you angry? . . . Sin . . . desires
to have you, but you must master it."*
GENESIS 4:6-7

GENESIS 4:1-12

The first homicide in history is recorded in the Bible's opening chapters. Adam's firstborn son, Cain, kills his brother Abel. Genesis 3 describes for us the fall into sin, and one of the first results of that fall into sin is the murder of Abel.

Can you imagine the pain of Adam and Eve as they looked upon the body of their beloved son? There lay Abel—dead! Blood seeped from his lifeless body into the earth. The grief-stricken parents must have asked, "How could you do this, Cain?"

The Bible gives us the reason. Cain was angry. God had not looked with favor on Cain's sacrifice. Even before Cain killed Abel, God asked Cain, "Why are you angry?" Then God said, "Sin is crouching at your door."

Picture in your mind what God means here. Anger is like a wild animal ready to jump out at you. The other day I saw my neighbor's cat crouching, and all at once it jumped out at a little bird and killed it.

Anger is like that. It crouches and waits; then suddenly it springs into action. It can overtake us and move us even to kill—with words if not with actions.

Each one of us needs to ask, "How many people's spirits have I wounded or killed with my anger?" We must subdue the urge to hurt others in our anger, and instead let Jesus' love flow through us.

PRAYER

Lord, there have been times when we have ripped up others with our words. We know this should not be. Help us to be kind and gentle. In Jesus' name we pray. Amen.

Listen and Be Still

The Urge to Kill

*"I tell you that anyone who is angry with
his brother will be subject to judgment."*
MATTHEW 5:22

MATTHEW 5:21-26

Children in my church are taught the Heidelberg
Catechism. It has this to say about the sixth commandment, "You
shall not murder": "By forbidding murder God teaches us that
he hates the root of murder: envy, hatred, anger, vindictiveness.
In God's sight all such are murder."

We can kill not only with a knife or a gun but also with
words. If we hurl abusive language at someone, Jesus says, we
are in danger of hellfire. When we gossip about our neighbor,
when we have hate in our heart, we can kill as surely as with a
murder weapon. When we bully someone at school, we may
well destroy that person's spirit.

I remember vividly a woman in a church I served some
years ago. Every Sunday she would sit in church like a scared
little bird. I would often ask her what was wrong, but she would
say that everything was all right. But one night my phone rang,
and a child's voice screamed, "My dad is hitting my mother!"
Then I knew what was wrong.

Do you need a new heart and attitude as you relate to
others around you? Have you been wounded, or have you been
wounding others? All of us need the good news of Jesus to
change anger to love, violence to tenderness, words that hurt to
words that heal.

PRAYER

"Lord, I want to be more loving in my heart, in my heart. Lord, I
want to be more loving in my heart." Help me to show not anger
but your love always. In Jesus' name, Amen.

Listen and Be Still

Discouragement

"Ever since I went to Pharaoh to speak in your name, he has brought trouble. . . ."
EXODUS 5:23

EXODUS 5:17-23

Another giant that often intimidates us in life is discouragement. All of God's people have had to battle this enemy at one time or another. Discouragement is one of Satan's biggest allies.

Moses had gone to Pharaoh to tell him God's message: "Let my people go." But that only made things worse for the people of Israel in their slavery in Egypt. Rather than letting up, Pharaoh increased the people's workload. And this made the people so upset that they complained bitterly to Moses, who turned around in discouragement and asked God why he had allowed it. "I went to Pharaoh to speak in your name," said Moses, ". . . and you have not rescued your people at all." In other words, "Nothing is changed, Lord; things have just gotten worse." Moses was discouraged!

Many of God's faithful servants stand on pulpits and call people to put their trust in Jesus for today and forever. Often on Sunday evening some of these preachers are discouraged because they see no fruit coming from their work; they see no change in people's circumstances, no transformation in people's lives. Work in the church can be discouraging at times.

Will you say a prayer for your church leaders today? And if you are discouraged in your work for the Lord, don't give up. God is still at work in and through you.

PRAYER

O Lord, keep discouragement from all who bring and hear your Word today. Help us to see in even the most discouraging circumstances that we can trust in you. In Jesus, Amen.

Listen and Be Still

I Wish I Were Dead

"I have had enough, Lord. . . ."
1 KINGS 19:4

1 KINGS 19:1-9

Talk about self-pity! Elijah was so discouraged that he wished he were dead. Despair and hopelessness made him feel that life was no longer worth living.

And yet, a few days earlier, things had been so different. Elijah had stood on top of Mount Carmel proclaiming that the Lord is God. He had also asked the Lord to end the drought that had lasted for three and a half years, and the rain had come pouring down. Then, in victory, he had run faster than King Ahab's chariot all the way back to town (1 Kings 18:16-46).

But then Ahab had gone home to Queen Jezebel, who was so enraged at what God had done through Elijah that she vowed to kill Elijah. So Elijah ran for his life. After a day's journey into the desert, he sat under a tree and wished he were dead. Elijah suffered from the kind of discouragement that often follows victory.

How do you handle discouragement? Notice how God ministers to his discouraged child. God lets Elijah sleep and gives him something to eat. God does not get angry with Elijah. God comes and cares for his tired prophet.

If you're down and discouraged, like Elijah, you can tell God how you feel. Then get a good night's sleep and have a meal. Remember too that Jesus says, "Come to me, all you who are weary and burdened, and I will give you rest" (Matthew 11:28).

PRAYER

Dear Lord, sometimes we're at the end of our rope. We think all is lost. Help us, we pray. Assure us of your care for us when we're tired and disheartened. In Jesus, Amen.

Listen and Be Still

Singing Hymns

Paul and Silas were praying and singing hymns to God. . .
ACTS 16:25

ACTS 16:25-34

One of the memories I have of my mother is that she liked to sing. She often said that singing keeps the devil away and lifts your spirits. I'm sure that many of God's children have found that to be true. Music can be a wonderful healer of broken and discouraged hearts.

It must not have been easy for Paul and Silas in that jail. It was midnight. Sleep would not come. The stocks they were in were painful. It may be that one looked at the other and said, "Maybe we should sing some hymns." So they sang songs of faith and hope in God.

As Paul and Silas sang and the other prisoners listened, that beautiful scene in the midst of so much pain must have made God smile. We can be sure that God also ached for these faithful followers, who were suffering for Jesus' sake. "Suddenly there was such a violent earthquake that the foundations of the prison were shaken. At once all the prison doors flew open, and everybody's chains came loose." Wow!

Maybe one of the best ways to stand up against the giant of discouragement is to sing songs of faith and praise to God, with words like these: "I will sing of the mercies of the Lord forever. . . . With my mouth will I make known your faithfulness." Or these: "I again will praise his grace for the comfort of his face; he again will show his help and favor, for he is my God and Savior."

PRAYER

Thank you, Lord, for the many songs we can sing. In our discouragement, teach us to sing songs of faith and praise. Thank you for the gift of music and song. In Jesus' name, Amen.

Listen and Be Still

Pride

There are six things the Lord hates, seven that are detestable to him: haughty eyes. . . .
PROVERBS 6:16-17

PROVERBS 6:16-19

Of all the sins that God hates, "haughty eyes" heads the list. A person with haughty eyes is someone who has a proud heart. This is a person who's been defeated by the giant of pride. Someone has said, "Pride is the ground in which all the other sins grow, and the parent from which all other sins come." Pride is the deadliest of the seven deadly sins. When you are proud, you have an unduly high opinion of yourself. Proud people say, "I am better than you."

As a child you may have tried to catch tadpoles in a pond or creek. Take a close look at a tadpole. It has a big head and a little tail. That's what proud people have: big heads. Some people are so full of themselves that they have no room for God. Pride is a difficult disease to cure.

But Jesus has a cure for pride. He calls us to live by humility and service. Jesus said once to people who were full of themselves, "Everyone who exalts himself will be humbled, and he who humbles himself will be exalted" (Luke 18:14). If you want to be great in the kingdom of God, you have to be willing to become the least and the servant of all. You have to be willing to become like a little child.

One of the things Jesus does is scatter those who are proud and lift up those who are humble (Luke 1:51-52).

PRAYER

Father, teach us to become more Christlike. Jesus, you carried a towel and washed the feet of your disciples. Make us good servants for the glory of your name. Amen.

Listen and Be Still

Loneliness

Turn to me and be gracious to me,
for I am lonely and afflicted.
PSALM 25:16

PSALM 25:15-22

There are a lot of lonely people. Maybe you are one of them. Sometimes all of us feel attacked by the giant of loneliness. "I am lonely," the psalm writer cries out. In Psalm 142:4 we find one of the saddest verses in the Bible: "No one is concerned for me. I have no refuge; no one cares for my life."

Our loneliness makes us vulnerable to substance abuse and distorted relationships. When we are lonely, we feel disconnected and not cared for. When we are lonely, we need a friend.

Jesus knew what it meant to be lonely. When he wrestled in prayer in Gethsemane, his disciples fell asleep. With pain in his voice Jesus asked, "Could you . . . not keep watch . . . for one hour?" (Matthew 26:40). Jesus knows all about our weaknesses and what it means to be human, for he was "tempted in every way, just as we are—yet was without sin" (Hebrews 4:15).

So, the first thing we need to do when we are lonely is to build a relationship with Jesus. He understands us, and he promises never to leave us alone.

We should also develop godly friends. Wrong friends just drive us deeper into loneliness. As James 4:4 says, "Anyone who chooses to be a friend of the world becomes an enemy of God." (See also Proverbs 12:26; 18:24; 19:4; Jeremiah 38:19-23; Luke 15:11-16.)

PRAYER

Dear God, sometimes I am lonely. Please put your loving arms around me and hold me in your embrace. May I be a good friend so that I will have a good friend. In Jesus' name, Amen.

Listen and Be Still

Shame

"Woman, where are they? Has no one condemned you?"
JOHN 8:10

JOHN 8:1-11

There are times when we should be ashamed of certain things we do or say. Some people seem to have lost their sense of shame in doing things that God says are wrong and sinful. But there is also a wrong kind of shame. It's the formidable giant of shame that hangs like a heavy weight around a person's neck. It's shame for what we are. It's the kind of shame that makes us say, "I am no good."

A woman came to my study and said, "I'm a failure." And I had to reassure her that although she had failed miserably, God still loved her and would forgive her.

Jesus was teaching in the temple when all at once there was a commotion. Teachers of the law, with robes flowing and fingers wagging, rushed into the temple court. They had a woman with them, and they pushed her in front of Jesus. "This woman was caught in the act of adultery," they yelled. (I wonder why they did not bring the man?) "In the law Moses commanded us to stone such women. Now what do you say?"

At first, Jesus said nothing. He began writing in the sand. (Some commentators suggest that Jesus wrote down the sins of those who had come to stone her.) When he said, "If any of you is without sin . . ." they all dropped their stones. Then Jesus forgave her, saying, "Go now and leave your life of sin."

PRAYER

Lord, your grace is amazing. When I have failed badly, thank you for not condemning me. Forgive me and make me new again by your power and through your love. Amen.

Listen and Be Still

Set Free

God did not send his Son. . . to condemn the world,
but to save the world through him.
JOHN 3:17

JOHN 3:16-21

Looking further at the story of the Pharisees and the adulterous woman, notice that Jesus says to her, "Go now and leave your life of sin" (John 8:11). But Jesus does not say, "Shame on you."

So many people are bound by the memory of their past. They think that God can never love them again because of what they have done or what was done to them.

I remember talking with someone who had been abused. "Pastor," she would say, "I have been thrown on the garbage heap of life." She felt like a dirty rag, used and thrown away. She was full of shame.

Maybe some things have happened in your life that no one else knows except you and God. You may wonder if God can ever love you again. You may say, "Pastor, you don't know what I have done and where I have been. You don't know how I feel inside." Let me just tell you that Jesus came to heal the brokenhearted and to save the crushed in spirit. Listen to the words of Jesus: "Neither do I condemn you. . . . Go now and leave your life of sin" (John 8:11).

Judgment doesn't change us; God's love and grace do. A godly pastor "is able to deal gently" with people who have sinned, "since he himself is subject to weakness" (Hebrews 5:2). And Jesus is the perfect pastor!

Is there shame in your life? Jesus came, died, and rose again to set you free from sin and shame.

PRAYER

O Jesus, out of our shameful failure and loss, we come to you.
Hold us in your loving and forgiving embrace, and free us to sin
no more. In your name we pray. Amen.

Listen and Be Still

The Last Enemy

The last enemy to be destroyed is death.
1 CORINTHIANS 15:26

1 CORINTHIANS 15:20-28

There are many more enemies we could talk about, and many more giants that we face. But there is one enemy all of us must face. It is the last enemy on this side of eternity—death.

My mother died when I was 33 years old. I remember her telling us she hoped Jesus would come back during her lifetime. When we asked her why she said that, she'd answer, "Then I won't have to die, and we won't have to say good-bye to each other; we will go together to meet the Lord."

I think my mother's feelings paralleled those of the apostle Paul when he said he "would prefer to be . . . at home with the Lord" (2 Corinthians 5:8). Paul also said he believed it was far better to be with Christ (Philippians 1:23). But he also very honestly admitted, "We do not wish to be unclothed" (2 Corinthians 5:4)—that is, separated from our bodies by death.

I think most of us are a little bit afraid of dying. Even many Christians fear death, because they don't know what it's like and they will meet the One who knows all about them. Many are also afraid of becoming a burden to their loved ones, afraid of doctors prodding everywhere, and afraid of losing dignity.

Yes, we must all face that last enemy. But in Christ we can have peace, knowing death will be destroyed.

PRAYER

Lord, remind us that we are an "Easter people"—that Jesus has conquered death by rising from the dead and that because he lives, we will live also. In his name we pray. Amen!

Listen and Be Still

The Resurrection and the Life

"I am the resurrection and the life. He who believes in me will live, even though he dies."
JOHN 11:25

JOHN 11:17-26

Mary and Martha had sent word to Jesus: "Lord, the one you love is sick" (John 11:3). Note the tenderness in these words. How many of us have not cried out similar words when a loved one was ill? But before Jesus arrives, their brother Lazarus is dead.

When Jesus gets to the home of Mary and Martha, both accuse him by saying, "Lord, if you had been here, my brother would not have died." That's almost like saying, "Lord, where were you when we needed you?" And how many of us haven't said the same thing when faced with the death of a loved one!

But then Jesus comes with these liberating words: "I am the resurrection and the life." People who believe in Jesus will live, even though they die. When you stand at the casket of a loved one who has died in the Lord, your eyes may be filled with tears and your heart filled with pain, but the one you love is not dead.

I am so thankful that Jesus weeps when he finally comes to the grave of Lazarus. The people say, "See how he loved him!" (John 11:36). Jesus knew that those who believed in him would live forever. But that does not mean death causes us no pain or grief, or that death doesn't tear apart what belongs together. Death is still an enemy. So Jesus weeps, and we weep with him—but not without hope.

PRAYER

Lord, today we pray for all who mourn the loss of a loved one, all who so keenly feel the pain of an empty place. Give them hope and comfort, Lord. In Jesus' name, Amen.

Listen and Be Still

Dressed by God

*Pray in the Spirit on all occasions with
all kinds of prayers and requests.*
EPHESIANS 6:18

EPHESIANS 6:10-20

Ephesians 6 tells us we need to put on armor that keeps us from getting killed. The Bible says, "The devil prowls around like a roaring lion looking for someone to devour" (1 Peter 5:8).

God has provided us with spiritual armor that allows us to stand against our greatest enemy, the devil. It's not armor we make ourselves; we must always remember that God provides it. God gives us a defense, and we would be foolish not to accept or use it. We should not discard any piece of this heavenly armor, for the devil will find what's missing and attack where we are most vulnerable. We should never underestimate our enemy.

We are engaged in spiritual warfare, and the only way to win the war is with spiritual weapons. So our passage for today says we must "put on the full armor of God," such as "the belt of truth" and "the breastplate of righteousness." We must also know how to use "the sword of the Spirit," which is the Bible.

But do you know what the most important piece of the Christian's battle dress is? It is prayer!

We can pray to overcome an addiction. We can pray for our families and loved ones. We can pray to overcome the giants we face—wherever Satan tries to attack. An old hymn says, "Put on the gospel armor, each piece put on with prayer." Are you fully dressed for battle?

PRAYER

Father, we thank you for the privilege of prayer. Thank you, Jesus, for teaching us to pray and for modeling a life of prayer. Protect us and keep us safe, we pray. Amen.

Listen and Be Still

Spiritual Training

*Submit yourselves, then, to God. . . . Come near
to God and. . . purify your hearts.*
JAMES 4:7-8

JAMES 4:1-10

In the province where I live, the government has established "boot camps" for young people who have been in trouble with the law. These are something like an army boot camp, where recruits are taught things that will sustain them in times of battle. They go through grueling physical exercise and discipline designed to build character. This training is crucial preparation for the future.

James's spiritual boot camp rigorously trains us in three areas to overcome our greatest enemy, the devil.

First, we must learn to submit to God. We want God to love us and forgive us, but so often we fail in the areas of obedience and commitment. Submission to authority is difficult. Yet the Bible teaches that we must be ready to obey God unconditionally.

Second, we should draw near to God. The closer we are to God, the wiser we are about the devil's schemes. We need to find time every day to spend in prayer and in God's Word, staying in tune with God.

Third, we need to wash our hands and purify our hearts. Confession and repentance result in a holy life.

Check your life today for persistent patterns of sin and areas where you are defeated, and then learn to submit to God, draw near to God, and live a life of holiness, doing as Jesus would do, in God's strength.

PRAYER

"Lord, I want to be more holy in my heart, in my heart. Lord, I want to be more holy in my heart." Help me submit to you, draw close to you, and be pure for you. In Jesus, Amen.

132  *Listen and Be Still*

God Power

I can do everything through him who gives me strength.
PHILIPPIANS 4:13

PHILIPPIANS 4:10-13

As we finish our reflections on battling giants, it's helpful to think about what we need to destroy these giants. There are three things every child of God needs to be reminded of in battling sin and temptation.

The first is, as an old confession says, "that I am not my own, but belong—body and soul, in life and in death—to my faithful Savior Jesus Christ." When I face giants, I need to remind myself that I belong to Jesus. That means I am also joined to a body of believers who hold me accountable and help me grow in faith.

Second, the cross of Jesus tells me that even though I sometimes fail, I am a person of worth who is loved incredibly by God. God sent his Son, Jesus Christ, who died for my failures and sins on the cross. His death gives me new life to live, in God's power, forever.

The third reminder is that "I can do everything through him who gives me strength." Jesus told his disciples that they would "receive power when the Holy Spirit comes" (Acts 1:8). This is power to witness for Christ and to face our enemies. With believers through the ages we can sing, "The prince of darkness grim, we tremble not for him . . . one little word shall fell him. That Word above all earthly powers—no thanks to them—abideth; the Spirit and the gifts are ours through him who with us sideth. . . . His kingdom is forever!"

PRAYER

Father in heaven, I praise you for loving me and giving me the Holy Spirit to enable me to overcome the giants I face. Help me to surrender my life to you. In Jesus' name, Amen.

Listen and Be Still

LIVING THE LIFE OF FAITH

FACING OUR FEELINGS

31 MEDITATIONS AND READINGS

BY DR. ROBERT C. HEERSPINK

DR. ROBERT C. HEERSPINK

Christians often believe their emotional lives and the doctrines of the faith have little to do with each other. But nothing is further from the truth. The powerful teachings of the gospel are healing salve for wounded souls.

Our emotional lives can become painful and unruly. Yet God's grace offers us the possibility to address our feelings. These reflections explore our emotions from a biblical perspective and investigate the resources we can use to pursue more faithful and balanced lives.

Rev. Heerspink has served Christian Reformed churches throughout western Michigan. He has also authored several publications on Christian financial stewardship.

Christ-likeness

Jesus wept.
JOHN 11:35

GENESIS 1:26-30

One of my favorite television characters was Mr. Spock in the original Star Trek series. Spock felt no emotions. He was the model of cool-headed reason.

Some of us may think Spock is a model to follow. Wouldn't it be nice to live without emotional ups and downs, as Spock seemed to do? Many of us are tired of the roller coaster our feelings create! Wouldn't it be nice to live an unemotional life?

I don't think so. People who do not experience sorrow do not experience joy. Those who can't experience despair do not experience hope. There's something missing in a life that knows no feeling.

Part of the way we image our God and Savior is as emotional beings. Christ himself enjoyed the fellowship of a wedding party. He also stood by the grave of a good friend and cried. He knew the pain of rejection as he hung on a cross. In fact, the Bible also tells us that God grieves (Genesis 6:6), becomes weary (Isaiah 1:14), and grows angry against sin (Psalm 2:12). God has created us with all of these emotions—and more—so that we can respond to life fully.

As a result, our emotions become an arena for our discipleship, because, frankly, our unruly emotions often get us into trouble. In this set of devotions, let's see how we can bring our emotions under the lordship of our Savior.

PRAYER

Lord Jesus, we thank you for the ability to see your likeness in us. In the realm of emotions, as in all others, help us to learn obedience to you. In your name we pray. Amen.

Listen and Be Still

Running on Our Feelings

While they were in the field, Cain attacked
his brother Abel and killed him.
GENESIS 4:8

GENESIS 4:1-12

Some of us make too much of our feelings. Consider the young man who said he never had a good day. And why not? Because things never went his way. And what things needed to go his way? Why, everything! His day was ruined if breakfast wasn't to his liking, if the songs on the radio weren't his favorites, or if a friend didn't pay him profuse compliments. That young man is not alone. Many people make their emotions the engine that pulls the train of life.

Scripture teaches us the danger of running on our feelings. Cain's story offers one example. He and his brother Abel each brought offerings to God. But Cain became envious and angry when his offering was not accepted. In a fit of rage, Cain killed his brother Abel.

God himself reminded Cain of his problem. Cain's envy and anger were providing an open door to evil. Like a stalking tiger, sin was "crouching at [his] door." Unwilling to master his emotions, his emotions mastered Cain. The result was tragedy.

Is your life controlled by your feelings? Do you run on feelings that wreak havoc with your relationships? Maybe it's time to break the bondage. God's grace is greater than the power of our inner emotions. God's strength helps us discipline even our emotions so that we can serve as "keepers" of others around us.

PRAYER

Father, sometimes our emotions get the upper hand. Then we regret the trouble they cause. Help us develop the discipline to help, not hurt, our neighbor. Amen.

Listen and Be Still

Feeling Stuffed?

I will remember the deeds of the Lord.
PSALM 77:11

PSALM 77

~~While some of us make too much of our feelings, others of us make too little of them. Through the years I have met Christians who want to believe that their emotions can be conveniently ignored. But bad things happen when we ignore our feelings. We stuff them down into the hidden places of our heart, only to have them burst forth in explosions of anger, or overwhelming despair, or poisonous bitterness.

Whenever I'm tempted to think that "good Christians" don't feel anger, sorrow, or pain, I'm helped by turning to the Psalms. These ancient songs of God's people are rich with emotion. In our reading for today, the poet Asaph honestly shares his inner hurt with God. His emotional distress goes so far as to include the feeling that God has rejected him.

Yet Asaph is honest with God about his emotional struggles. And this psalmist gives us a clue as to how to handle them. "'To this I will appeal . . .' I will remember the deeds of the Lord." Asaph moves toward resolving his emotional struggles by remembering the great things God has done.

The "greatest thing" God has done is to give us himself in the gift of his Son. We need to remember Christ's mercies even as we express our deepest feelings to God. By doing so, despair is conquered and hope is born.

PRAYER

Father, we often hide our hurts from you; then we wonder why you feel so distant. Help us to share ourselves with you, remembering how you've shared yourself. Amen.

Listen and Be Still

139

Running on Empty

It was not with perishable things . . . that you
were redeemed from the empty way of life.
1 PETER 1:18

1 PETER 1:13-21

T. S. Eliot, in one of his famous poems, spoke of people who are "hollow" inside.

Sometimes I feel like I'm a member of that clan. Perhaps you do too. We feel like hollow trees, weakened by what is missing at the core of our being. It's an emptiness that causes an ache deep inside, and that ache never goes away.

In these verses Peter reminds us that many people in his day tried to fill their emptiness with "perishable things such as silver or gold." Twenty centuries later, our consumerist society still wants us to think trinkets can fill the empty space in our lives. Many of us believe that the answer to our emptiness is "buy and spend." Feeling down? Master the possibilities of a materialistic lifestyle! Take a trip to Cancun! Buy a new sports car! Your emptiness will be filled!

But those remedies don't really fill the void. For it's "not with perishable things" that we are redeemed "from the empty way of life." The emptiness within us can only be filled by God, who offers to live within us through the "precious blood of Christ, a lamb without blemish or defect." Only the presence of God's Holy Spirit, received through faith in Jesus Christ, will make us whole.

If there's an emptiness inside you, your heart is calling for God.

PRAYER

King of Peace, we are restless until we rest in you. We are empty until you fill us. Through your mercy, give us your Spirit, for only you can satisfy us. In Jesus' name, Amen.

The Joy Paradox

Let us fix our eyes on Jesus . . . who for the joy
set before him endured the cross.
HEBREWS 12:2

HEBREWS 12:1-13

The idea of suffering is scary. No wonder most people think religion should offer a guarantee against suffering and pain. After all, we want to be happy. We want to have joy. And isn't suffering the great joy-killer? How can there be joy where there is pain?

Then we encounter the strange experience of Christ, "who for the joy set before him endured the cross." Hebrews dares to mention joy and suffering in the same sentence. Why?

The Bible mentions this because real joy is not attained the way most people believe it is. People today believe that a new job promotion, another rise in the stock market, or more diamond jewelry will bring happiness and joy. But the happiness from things like that is always short-lived. Deep joy eludes us.

Jesus has shown us the path of joy in sacrificial service. His death on a cross has brought the ultimate joy of knowing that his self-giving has redeemed a fallen creation. What joy!

So now, Hebrews says, let us run our race by looking to Christ as our example. Who needs your service? Maybe you're holding back because you think entering into the needs of others will kill your joy. Not so. Give yourself in service to someone for Jesus' sake, and discover the joy your Savior knows.

PRAYER

Lord, our fear of suffering can make us afraid to serve. Forgive us our fears, and help us to see beyond sacrifice to the joy our service brings. In Jesus' name, Amen.

Listen and Be Still

Ashamed of Yourself

*There is now no condemnation for those
who are in Christ Jesus.*
ROMANS 8:1

PSALM 51

Moral scandal in high places isn't new. King David wrote Psalm 51 after a moral crisis rocked his administration. He had thought no one suspected a thing, but he learned that God sees right through our cover-ups.

In this psalm David pours out his guilt before God. His heart is breaking. He feels morally dirty, in need of a spiritual bath. "Wash away all my iniquity," he prays, "and cleanse me from my sin."

Unfortunately there are many people in our culture today who think David's emotions are inappropriate. Their voices tell us guilt is unreal, so confession and forgiveness aren't needed. But those voices are wrong.

Many of us carry guilt from our past. Deep down, we know that for hurting others deeply, we deserve our guilt. We feel dirty. How can we ever be clean again?

David understood that God himself has to do the washing for us. And that's exactly what Jesus Christ came to do. Christ came to take our guilt upon himself, and one day he nailed that guilt to a cross. Christ took upon himself all of our failure so that "there is now no condemnation for those" who trust in his sacrifice to make them clean.

If there is unresolved guilt in your life, don't cover it up. Confess it to God, and claim the cleansing that God offers you in his Son.

PRAYER

Gracious God, we don't want to hide the truth from you any longer. We know you see through all of our excuses. Through Christ, forgive our sin and set us free. Amen.

Listen and Be Still

The Love Dynamic

God demonstrates his own love for us in this:
While we were still sinners, Christ died for us.
ROMANS 5:8

JOHN 15:9-17

Most of us tend to develop reciprocal relationships with others. We send a Christmas card to those who send us one. We give birthday presents to the people we receive gifts from. We entertain people who have had us over for dinner. Such exchanges are the fabric of social relationships.

That kind of dynamic also operates in the realm of love. We love those who love us. And what if someone hates us? Well, we tend to return the hate, don't we?

The gospel, however, offers a different dynamic. The energy of divine love is not a response to goodness. The energy of love springs from the Divine Lover—our Redeeming God. But this kind of love comes with an unexpected cost. "God demonstrates his own love for us in this: While we were still sinners, Christ died for us." The cost of love is the cost of sacrifice, a cost demonstrated supremely in Christ the Savior, who laid "down his life for his friends."

While we were sinners, Christ called us friends! Here is a love that doesn't operate in reciprocal relationship but creates new relationship where none existed before! If you are a Christ-friend, redeemed by his grace, then you have entered a love relationship with God. And you are empowered to break out of old patterns to love people who you thought were unlovable.

PRAYER

Father, our relationships are so ordinary. We often give to others only as they have given to us. Help us to show your love; fill us with the sacrificial giving of Christ. Amen.

Listen and Be Still

Those Loving Feelings

If I . . . have not love, I am nothing.
1 CORINTHIANS 13:3

1 CORINTHIANS 13

"Love is the feeling you feel when you feel you're going to get a feeling you've never felt before." So goes one popular definition of romantic love. Actually, that's a pretty good description of the indescribable emotion that overwhelms us when we "fall in love."

But romantic love tends to be as short-lived as it is intense. Marriages based on pure romance tend to crumble when ordinary stresses hit home. Spouses often find that they have gotten married for an ideal that does not exist. Can love survive the discovery that the one we've married is as imperfect as we are?

Yes. Paul reminds us that love is not first of all a way of feeling. Love is first of all a way of doing. "Love is patient, love is kind. It does not envy, it does not boast, it is not proud. It is not rude, it is not self-seeking, it is not easily angered, it keeps no record of wrongs." Love is a way of living that is best seen in the life of Jesus Christ.

Does that mean love as an emotion means nothing? No. But feelings of love tend to follow in the wake of loving deeds. More than one couple has discovered that deeds of loving service restore the spark of romance that once existed in their relationship.

Is there someone with whom you need to rekindle love today? What deeds of love might fan the flame?

PRAYER

Loving Lord, in a world that runs on feelings, may we follow the pattern you set. May our commitment to loving service improve our relationships for your sake. Amen.

Listen and Be Still

A Stream in the Desert

I say to God my Rock, "Why have you forgotten me?"
Psalm 42:9

Psalm 42

I admit it. The older I get, the more challenged I am to remember names. It's embarrassing to meet a former acquaintance and flip through those mental file cards, only to draw a blank. No one likes to be forgotten.

For many of us, the spiritual pain of depression lies in feeling forgotten by God. It's as though God is overlooking us in his oversight of this world. The psalmist describes this estrangement in terms of a terrible thirst. We see a deer searching desperately for water. Weary and thirsty, the animal looks for any pocket of water for relief from the heat. Such is the thirst of the psalmist searching for God.

In such a moment, the psalmist thinks back to better days, when God felt near. But those pleasant thoughts only create a nostalgia that deepens the present pain.

Then the psalmist remembers a resource that is still available: prayer. The psalmist will speak to God out of this painful experience: "I say to God my Rock, 'Why have you forgotten me?'"

Some of us are in the desert now. We thirst for God and think we have been forgotten. But the psalmist encourages us to cry out to God in the midst of our pain. Be assured that when you pray, God hears. And Christ, who is the living water (John 4:14; 7:38), makes his resources available to quench our thirst.

Prayer

Our Father, sometimes when you seem far away, it's hard to pray. Remind us that you hear even the simplest heart cry. Refresh our spirits with your living water. In Jesus, Amen.

Listen and Be Still

145

At the End of the Road

After the fire came a gentle whisper.
1 KINGS 19:12

1 KINGS 19:1-18

Elijah was a man who knew the thrill of victory. With the Lord's power, he had squared off and triumphed against the high priests of Baal (1 Kings 18). But now, only days later, Elijah huddles on a mountainside in almost total despair. What has happened?

Elijah is a victim of grandiose thinking. On Mount Carmel, facing the high priests of pagan gods, Elijah thought he had struck the final blow against the godlessness of his society. But he was wrong. The evil King Ahab remained on the throne. And the furious Queen Jezebel had issued a warrant for Elijah's arrest—dead or alive! So now Elijah huddles in the wilderness, a bitter cynic who thinks he is the only one faithful to God.

Some of us know this kind of experience. We too have had idealistic plans about the way God will use us. But the plans fall apart. With Elijah, we wonder whether anyone cares as we do about God's kingdom. We want to pout and say, "I am the only one left."

Elijah needed to learn more about God's work in the world. He expected God to work in terms of fearful, devastating events like earthquake and fire. But on the mountain Elijah learns that God works not mainly in those things but in terms of a gentle whisper.

PRAYER

Lord, when we feel we have failed, commission us again for service in your kingdom. Remind us that we join a vast community of believers already at work for you. Amen.

Listen and Be Still

Life in the Same Boat

No temptation has seized you except
what is common to man.
1 CORINTHIANS 10:13

1 CORINTHIANS 10:1-13

There's an old story about a time when all the people of the world gathered to complain to God about their problems. Each groused that his or her load was unfair. God told all the people to place their problems on a table, pick out someone else's problems, and go home. After carefully picking through the piles, each person picked up his or her own problems again and went away wiser than before.

This story is not meant to deny that some people face far greater problems than others do. But it does remind us that we often picture other people's lives as smooth sailing compared to our own. Self-pity has a corrosive effect on our spirits. It eats away our joy, makes us question God's justice, and often tempts us to compromise our obedience to Christ.

In this regard, the apostle Paul reminds us of two realities. First, a fact: "No temptation has seized you except what is common to man." We often want to believe our troubles are some exotic species of suffering that no one has even seen before. It's more likely, though, that our troubles are shared by others and have been around for years. Second, a promise: "God is faithful; he will not let you be tempted beyond what you can bear." The God who has sustained others will sustain us. That's a promise we can rely on.

PRAYER

Gracious God, we have a tendency to minimize the pain of others and to maximize our own. Keep us out of the pit of self-pity. Sustain our reliance upon you. In Jesus, Amen.

Listen and Be Still

147

Life in the Solitary

"I am with you always, to the very end of the age."
MATTHEW 28:20

MATTHEW 28:16-20

Loneliness is a strange phenomenon. Sometimes I can feel most alone when I'm surrounded by other people. I attended a conference not long ago in another state. I didn't know anyone there. Most of the people seemed to have ties with each other that went back a long way. There seemed to be an invisible wall between me and others. By the end of that long week I could feel the ache of loneliness gnawing at my soul.

Some of us are experiencing loneliness now. Loneliness can set in when we're starting a new job and we crave a familiar face. Loneliness can come when we go to a new school and have no friends to spend time with.

In the final words of Matthew's gospel, Jesus gives us both a promise and a gift to address our loneliness. He promises to be with us forever. And this gift includes the fellowship of believers in which we can find true community in Jesus' name through the Holy Spirit.

Some of us, however, have tried addressing our loneliness through the church, and we've been disappointed. The church doesn't always live up to our expectations—or to God's. Yet the church continues to offer the possibility of true community that overcomes aloneness.

There's likely a church nearby that gathers for worship. Do you join with them?

PRAYER

Lord, we thank you that you are with us always. Help us reach out to others and discover your presence in the people we meet with in your name. Amen.

Listen and Be Still

Tinged in Green

*"Saul has slain his thousands, and
David his tens of thousands."*
1 SAMUEL 18:7

1 SAMUEL 18:1-9

Have you ever noticed the way colors are associated with moods? In addition to "feeling blue," we can be "white with fear" or "red with rage." Some of us are also known to turn "green with envy."

I don't know why envy turns us green, but it seems this color was no stranger to the face of King Saul. His fiercely competitive nature allowed no equal. And when the women of Jerusalem celebrated David's triumphs above those of Saul, a cancer of suspicion and vindictiveness began to overtake him.

Some of us also turn green when others succeed. We react to our more successful neighbors with unfair criticism and devastating put-downs. We question their motives and belittle their intentions. When we do that, we actually belittle ourselves.

Saul needed to remember that neither he nor David could lay final claim to the successes of life. Each of them had a calling from God in their lives. Their achievements ultimately came as God's gifts.

It's no different for us. Each of us has a calling from God, and what matters most is not our level of outward success but the depth of our faithfulness to God's intent for our lives.

Saul's envy destroyed his ability to be of use in God's kingdom. May that not happen to us.

PRAYER

Our Father, help us to remove that tinge of green from our faces. Help us to set aside envy and pursue the callings you have for each of us. In Jesus' name, Amen.

Listen and Be Still

Reject?

Though my father and mother forsake me,
the Lord will receive me.
PSALM 27:10

PSALM 27

I often visit a bookstore connected with a major publishing house. This store sells discount books with bent pages and torn covers that cannot be sold at regular prices. These rejects make great buys.

But books aren't the only rejects we find in society. In a world in which relationships unravel easily, many of us feel as though the word "Reject" has been stamped on our foreheads.

Some of us bear the pain of a friendship that has died even after our best attempts to hold things together. Some of us have been rejected and divorced by a spouse. Others of us know the pain of being released by our employer after decades of faithful service.

The psalmist in our Scripture for today knows what it means to feel orphaned by society. But this psalmist shows that it's possible to bear the pain because he's embraced by another family, the family of God: "Though my father and mother forsake me, the Lord will receive me."

Those of us who have known rejection need to know that Jesus Christ is our elder brother who welcomes us into the family of God. Within that family we find a divine acceptance created by God's grace. The welcoming arms of God are strong medicine for anyone who knows what it's like to be forsaken.

PRAYER

Our Father, we thank you that those who trust your Son find a warm welcome in your arms. Heal our wounds of rejection by the accepting grace of your love. In Jesus, Amen.

Listen and Be Still

No Fear

When I am afraid, I will trust in you.
PSALM 56:3

MATTHEW 14:22-36

When my nephew was a toddler, he had no fear of heights. His father once found him climbing the ladder of a 10-story silo. His mother once found him playing on the porch roof after crawling out the window of his second-story bedroom. In his case, a little fear would have been a healthy response to danger.

But not all fear is healthy. Some of us struggle with fears that have messed with us and limited our obedience to Christ. Unseen terrors have robbed us of joy.

In our Scripture for today we encounter a terrified disciple. Peter is out on the waters of life. He is there because Jesus invited him to come. But while he's out there, he begins to wonder what he's gotten himself into. Losing his focus on the Lord, he feels himself sinking into the cold waters.

Then Peter feels a strong hand reaching out to him. It's the hand of his Lord, who has already told the disciples, "Take courage! It is I. Don't be afraid." God in Christ—the "I am who I am"—is on the waters of Galilee to be with a fearful Peter.

Christ continues to find disciples who are sure the waters of life are getting the upper hand. He continues to extend his strong arm to keep us from going under. Feel his hand around your wrist today. Hear him say to you, "Take courage! It is I. Don't be afraid."

PRAYER

No fear? Sometimes that doesn't seem possible, Lord. But then we feel Jesus' strong hand grip our own. And we know that all is well. In his name we pray. Amen.

Listen and Be Still

Just Plain Angry

Do not let the sun go down while you are still angry.
EPHESIANS 4:26

EPHESIANS 4:17-32

For many of us, the emotional skeleton in our closet is anger. We pound the table and glare at people we care about while we shout, "I am not angry!" For some reason, no one believes us.

I don't like to admit my anger. I tell people I'm frustrated or a bit "put-out." It's so hard for me to own up to the fact that I'm just plain angry.

Why do we get angry? We like to think our anger is always justified—even righteous! But, frankly, very little of our anger is born of noble intentions. The root of most of our anger is self-centeredness. We want life to go our way. We want people to cooperate with our plans and intentions. And when these things don't happen, the flames of anger shoot high.

In Ephesians, Paul is very honest about anger. He recognizes that anger is inevitable. All of us get angry sometimes. But Paul also recognizes that anger must be identified and dealt with quickly. Allowing anger to fester for more than a day allows the devil to gain a foothold against us.

I tell couples I counsel that if they allow their anger to fester beyond nightfall, they are opening themselves to grief. When was the last time you turned out the lights and were still angry at someone in your life? It's time to deal with the anger, time to extinguish the flames.

PRAYER

Lord, our anger is seldom healthy. Mean-spirited words and actions often inflict deep wounds. Please forgive us. Give us courage also to ask the forgiveness of others. Amen.

Listen and Be Still

Grief and Grace

We do not want you. . . to grieve like the rest of men, who have no hope.
1 Thessalonians 4:13

1 thessalonians 4:13-18

On my bookshelf is a thin volume that contains the lame comments people tend to make when they visit people who are bereaved: *Big boys don't cry. You should be over this by now. You can always find someone worse off than yourself.* Many of us have heard comments like these in the presence of the grieving.

Why do people say such things? Perhaps they're trying to deny the uncomfortable presence of sorrow. Or, in the case of some Christians, maybe they have the notion that real Christians do not grieve.

Paul would disagree. Grief is a natural response to a sense of loss. Grief comes because our loved one or friend was an important part of our life. In the face of such loss, Paul says frankly, "We . . . grieve."

But Paul also qualifies the kind of grief a Christian experiences. We grieve, he says, but not like people who "have no hope." Ours is an expectant grief, even an optimistic grief. How can this be? Because the emptiness our grief creates is filled by the presence of the One whose very name is Resurrection and Life. Christ's triumph over the grave fills grief with grace.

If you are grieving, I invite you to fill the emptiness of your heart with the presence of Christ. He comes to you today with the promise that all who mourn can find comfort in his love.

Prayer

God of all comfort, seek out all who sorrow. In the face of death, grant us a hope founded on the One who stepped alive from the tomb on Easter morning. In his name, Amen.

Listen and Be Still

153

Worried Sick?

*"Seek first his kingdom and his righteousness,
and all these things will be given to you as well."*
MATTHEW 6:33

MATTHEW 6:25-34

We live a in a worried culture. In the months following the events of September 11, 2001, even a bit of talcum powder left behind in a hotel bathroom became a reason to call in bioterrorism experts.

What does worry do to us? It has a way of turning us in on ourselves. We stew over our safety, our health, our finances. In our anxiety our reason and energy slip away. At its worst, worry so paralyzes us that we can barely function.

How do we cope? Some people try a rational approach. One chronic worrier analyzed his worries and discovered that only 8 percent were legitimate concerns over which he could have some control. His rational approach suppressed his worry by 92 percent!

But that approach doesn't work for me. My worries tend to go beyond reason. The same may be true for you. That's because the real answer to worry doesn't lie in reason. It lies in a relationship with God. People who know they have a heavenly Father know they can count on divine care. God's assurance is the gift for those who believe in the Father's Incarnate Son, Jesus Christ.

With a heavenly Father who cares for us, we can focus on the things that count. Amazingly, even as we focus on God's reign and righteousness, God focuses on providing us the care we truly need each day.

PRAYER

Father, as we seek your kingdom, may we know that you are seeking our good. May our anxieties be left behind as we search for more ways to serve Jesus today. Amen.

Listen and Be Still

The Bitter Dregs

See to it that. . . no bitter root grows up
to cause trouble and defile many.
HEBREWS 12:15

LUKE 6:27-36

I have often sat and listened to people who have been severely hurt by others. I've noticed that some of these folks seem to have inside them a tape recorder that plays the story of their hurt again and again. Every time they play the tape of their pain, they are assaulted once more. Every time their tape plays, their bitterness increases.

Why don't we discard those tapes if they are so painful? Maybe it's because our bitterness is a form of revenge. Oddly, we can gain energy from our hatred. Bitterness feeds our own sense of self-righteousness. As someone once said to me, "If I let go of my bitterness, I'll have nothing left to live for."

But what does bitterness deliver? Bitterness is a root that bears all kinds of troubling and defiling fruit. Bitterness hurts us and the people we love most.

Jesus offers a word of advice to bitter people. He says, "Pray for those who mistreat you." This is strong medicine and can only be taken along with a large dose of divine grace. The truth is, I don't want to pray for people I don't like—not to mention those who deliberately do me wrong. But Jesus knows that the antidote to my bitterness is a Christ-like concern for the person who has wronged me. Is there anyone who has wronged you and whom you should pray for today?

PRAYER

Father, from his cross your Son prayed for his executioners. He conquered the bitterness that tempted his own soul. Help us trace that pattern in our own lives. In Jesus' name, Amen.

Listen and Be Still

155

Feeling Lost?

"Rejoice with me; I have found my lost sheep."
LUKE 15:6

LUKE 15:1-7

A wife says to her husband, "We're lost." Her spouse grumbles, "No we're not. We just don't know where we are." More than one couple has had this kind of exchange while driving through unfamiliar territory.

It's one thing to be momentarily confused about whether to turn left or right at an intersection. But how do we handle our confusion on the road of life?

The truth is, many of us have been traveling life's road for decades, and we still don't know where we are. Life befuddles us. We aren't sure of our ultimate destination. And we don't know what principles should guide our choices when we come to the next crossroad. We are lost, but we don't want to admit it.

Here's the good news: Someone out there is looking for the lost. He is the good shepherd, Jesus Christ.

A shepherd in Israel never gave up on a lost sheep. He would track for miles across the roughest terrain to search out a sheep that had strayed. And when he found it, he would carry that sheep on his shoulders back to the safety of the fold.

Perhaps you are hearing footsteps behind you on life's journey. Turn and see who is there. The good shepherd may be tracking you down. Stop resisting his care. Let him pick you up in his strong arms. Discover your identity as a sheep of the Lord's sheepfold.

PRAYER

Father, we give thanks for the persistence of the good shepherd. Give us joy in knowing that today the Shepherd has again carried lost sheep to safety. In his name, Amen.

Listen and Be Still

When Friends Don't Come Through

The Lord stood at my side and gave me strength. . . .
2 TIMOTHY 4:17

2 TIMOTHY 4:9-18

"I love humanity. It's people I can't stand." Do you share the cynicism behind this comment by Linus of the Peanuts comic strip? People often disappoint us. We lean on the dependability of others, and then what we need so desperately isn't delivered.

Paul had that experience. During his ministry, Paul had led Demas to Christ. The enthusiastic Demas had signed on with Paul's mission team. When Paul was first imprisoned, Demas had been among his colleagues in Rome. Letters written to the Colossian church and to Philemon during that time include greetings from Demas (Colossians 4:14; Philemon 24).

But now Paul is imprisoned again in Rome, and Demas is not there. Writing to his young friend Timothy, Paul expresses his sense of betrayal. "Demas, because he loved this world, has deserted me and has gone to Thessalonica." And Demas is not the only one whose commitment has crumbled. Paul adds, "At my first defense, no one came to my support . . . ."

Disappointment is one of life's cruel realities. But Paul reminds us that there is One on whom we can rely: "The Lord stood at my side and gave me strength." During Paul's hearing there was one Friend with him in the courtroom—the Lord Jesus Christ. In him we too can trust and never be disappointed (see Psalm 22:5).

PRAYER

Lord Jesus, help us to forgive the failures of others. Please also assure us that in our need you are the Friend who will never let us down. In your name we pray. Amen.

Listen and Be Still

157

Undoing the Past

"Yes, Lord," [Peter] said, "you know that I love you."
JOHN 21:15

LUKE 22:54-62

〰️Do you have regrets? I do. I love music. More than once I have wondered why I didn't have the discipline to learn to play the music that inspires me.

But that's a pretty minor regret. Many of my regrets are deeper and more painful. Maybe yours are too. Some of us regret the lack of investment we've made in our marriage. Others of us regret the opportunities we've passed by to spend time with our children. Still others of us regret the years we've wasted by failing to nurture our faith relationship with Christ.

When it comes to regret, few of us can outdo Peter. When he was cornered and asked about his relationship to Jesus, his courage collapsed. Afterward Peter broke down and couldn't stop the tears from flowing.

But only a few days later, he experienced a miracle of forgiveness. The Christ whom Peter had denied restored him to service.

Peter's story had a different ending from that of another disciple, who also had regrets. The regrets of Judas, Jesus' betrayer, drove him to take his own life (Matthew 27:3-5). For some of us, the pain of the past may be so great that we think the only solution is to do as Judas did. But the grace of Jesus is so amazing that it can forgive and restore us to serve in God's kingdom, just as it did for Peter.

PRAYER

The past cannot be undone, Lord. But the past can be forgiven.
Please forgive our lost opportunities for obedience. Renew us to
serve faithfully in your kingdom. Amen.

Listen and Be Still

When the Energy Tank Hits Empty

Moses' father-in-law replied,
"What you are doing is not good."
EXODUS 18:17

EXODUS 18:13-27

I'm a type-A person. When people make demands on my time, I struggle to say no. There seem to be such good reasons to say yes. Saying yes makes people happy. Saying yes makes me feel needed, productive, useful.

But saying yes to every demand opens me to the danger of burnout. God did not design me to run continually at full throttle. Emotional exhaustion sets in. I become weary and unproductive.

That's why I relate to Moses, the ultimate biblical example of burnout. Moses had become the personal caregiver to the entire nation of Israel! He spent his days settling squabbles and making judgments. When Moses' father-in-law came for a visit, however, he quickly sized up the situation: "What you are doing is not good."

Jethro gave Moses some wise advice. Even a divinely appointed leader like Moses is only one person. The work of ministry needs to be shared with others.

Some of us need to learn that lesson. We are frazzled and exhausted. Our energy tank has long ago hit empty, and yet we keep pushing harder. We need to develop a sense of balance, doing some things but not all things. Other people are called to work with us in God's kingdom. So we all need to ask, What work is God giving me to do? And what might God be asking of others?

PRAYER

Lord, keep us from thinking we are indispensable. Help us to be willing to share your work with others. Then help us to serve you with all our heart, soul, and mind. In Jesus, Amen.

Listen and Be Still

Beyond Failure

*I consider everything a loss compared to
the surpassing greatness of knowing Christ. . . .*
Philippians 3:8

Philippians 3:1–11

What do you fear the most? For many of us, failure is our greatest fear. We're afraid that if we ever fail, we will be destroyed. And then failure comes our way, and to our amazement we find that we survive it. But we do not survive untouched. We usually learn that some things we thought were very important are not so important after all.

Paul experienced the pain of failure when he discovered that his personal successes amounted to nothing. He'd had a faultless family pedigree, but then he found that genetics weren't the basis for being included in God's family. He'd obeyed all the rules, but then he found that good works couldn't save him. Paul had also persecuted the church, but then he found that he was trying to destroy not heretics but the redeemed people of God.

Talk about failure! Paul had made a mess of his life at every turn! But from the mud hole of failure Paul learned the lesson of grace. There is mercy at the bottom of the pit of disgrace. There is hope at the bottom of the well of hopelessness. Paul learned to throw away his false piety and to pin his hope on a Savior who turned the apparent failure of a cross to resurrection victory.

If you are in the pit of failure, look to the hand of Christ reaching out to you. Failed lives are the very ones he came to save.

Prayer

Lord Jesus, we thank you that you accept us, even when our failures make it hard for us to accept ourselves. May the lessons we learn from failure make us useful to you. Amen.

Listen and Be Still

Beyond Wishes

*We have this hope as an anchor
for the soul, firm and secure.*
HEBREWS 6:19

HEBREWS 6:13-20

Someone sat in my office the other day. He had been hammered again and again by failure and tragedy. "I don't know, Pastor," he said; "I'm not sure I can keep going. I've lost hope that things will ever be different."

Hope is a disappearing commodity in our world. Many people have lived for years with the hope that technology would deliver a brighter future. Now they aren't so sure. Many had also hoped that medical research would create a new world. Now we face troubling questions like this one: Could cloning offer a scientific form of "everlasting life"?

For many of us, hope has become little more than a wish. We "hope against hope" that things will turn out for the best. But inwardly we don't believe that anymore. We feel like a ship that has lost its mooring.

Our lives do not need to be set adrift. We can have a sure and steadfast anchor for the soul. That anchor is Christ's redeeming work for our sake. By his death on a cross, Christ has prepared a way for us into the very presence of God. Our Lord Jesus has gone ahead of us as our great High Priest, our representative to secure the path into God's presence.

Our hope is not a wish. Our hope is based on the way things are. When we're anchored in Christ, no wind, wave, or current can move us from our mooring.

PRAYER

Father, please keep us from drifting through life. Help us, through faith in Christ, to be anchored in his saving work always. Move us by your Spirit to serve faithfully. Amen.

Listen and Be Still

An Awe-Filled Life

"Holy, holy, holy is the Lord God Almighty,
who was, and is, and is to come."
REVELATION 4:8

REVELATION 4

I learned of awe while visiting the Canadian Rockies. It was early evening in Waterton National Park, and I was sitting on the shore of a lake, watching the sun disappear over the mountains. As the sky changed to a canvas of reds, yellows, and crimsons, I was transfixed. It was as though I was experiencing a little bit of heaven on earth. In my own life I realized the psalmist's words, "The heavens declare the glory of God" (Psalm 19:1).

Many of us have had experiences like that while enjoying the world of nature. God's creation inspires us to a sense of awe at the greatness of our Maker. And that's just a taste of the wonder we will experience one day as we stand before the throne of our Redeemer God. In a vision, the apostle John saw the creation symbolized in the four living creatures, and he saw the church symbolized in the 24 elders. Together church and creation join to sing, "Holy, holy, holy" to the Lord Almighty.

What a glorious experience! And for all who know Jesus, that experience isn't just a future event. Nor do we have to go to the Rockies to learn of awe. Our worship as the church is a foretaste of our ultimate praise.

There's probably a church near you that gathers for worship each Sunday. Be sure to join with them and experience the awe that comes to all who stand in adoration before the throne of the King.

PRAYER

Lord, we thank you that in worship we can join with the church of all ages in praise of you. Give us a vision of your glory and grace as we confess your name. In Jesus, Amen.

Listen and Be Still

Who Am I?

I no longer live, but Christ lives in me.
GALATIANS 2:20

GALATIANS 2:11-21

"What am I worth?"

Ask that question of an employer, and the answer will often be given in terms of productivity and the dollar value a person adds to the company. A lot of people are impressed by that kind of answer. They define their worth by how much they accomplish and how much they earn. But, frankly, defining a person's worth that way isn't too impressive.

If you ask the Lord about your worth, God will tell you it's not centered in what you do but in who you are. If you are a Christian, your worth is found in your identity as a temple of the living God. By the Holy Spirit, Christ the Lord lives in you.

Consider the worth of the White House. It's not the most impressive home in the United States. But it is by far the most valuable. Why? Because of who lives there. The value of the White House lies in its being the home of the president of the United States.

The same is true of me. I gain my worth by being the dwelling place of God's Spirit. What an exhilarating truth! Honestly, you and I will never have enough wealth or gather enough awards to really "feel good" about ourselves. We don't need to. Our value comes from sharing Paul's great confession: "It is no longer I who live, but it is Christ who lives in me" (TEV).

PRAYER

Lord, forgive us for thinking that our worth is tied to our work or our bank accounts. Help us to live out the amazing identity of being a home to your Spirit. In Jesus, Amen.

Listen and Be Still

The Power of Community

They devoted themselves to the apostles'
teaching and to the fellowship. . . .
ACTS 2:42

ACTS 2:42-47

I meet regularly with a group of pastors for a brown-bag lunch. We have devotions together and pray together. We also share with each other the hurts and joys of our ministries and our private lives. In these ways we care for each other in the name of Jesus.

I am always surprised by the number of people who think they don't need that kind of community. As a pastor, I often strike up conversations with strangers. When I tell them I'm a minister of the gospel, I often hear the response "I'm a Christian too."

"Great!" I say. "What church fellowship do you belong to?" "Oh," comes the reply, "I'm between churches right now." I suspect that many people have been "between churches" for years.

My spiritual health would be seriously affected if I never gathered with other believers. I need the accountability that other Christians provide. I also need their encouragement, support, and prayers.

The first believers in Christ needed all these things. They devoted themselves to "the fellowship." This was a community life that added significantly to their joy in having faith in Christ.

Do you gather with a group of Christians to share your hurts and joys? If not, I encourage you to do so. It's a place where you will experience the care of Christ.

PRAYER

Father, often we think we can "go it alone" as Christians. But that's a mistake. We need others. Give us the courage to seek real Christian community in our lives. In Jesus, Amen.

Listen and Be Still

What's in a Name

*Barnabas took [Saul] and
brought him to the apostles.*
ACTS 9:27

ACTS 9:19b-31

I've always been fascinated by the meaning of names, yet I often find that a name doesn't describe the one who bears it. My name, Robert, means "bright with fame." But I am hardly a celebrity.

It's different in Scripture, where names often describe their bearers. Consider the character of the man who was named Barnabas.

Barnabas literally means "son of encouragement." Barnabas lived out the meaning of his name. We first meet him in Acts 4 as he offers a generous gift of money to help meet the needs of others. And later we discover that Barnabas plays a key role in the life of Paul (Saul). Before his conversion, Paul had been the point man in an effort to destroy the church by force. Who could blame the apostles if they wondered whether Paul's conversion to the Christian faith was real? But Barnabas discerned the integrity of Paul's conversion and became Paul's advocate to the leaders in Jerusalem. At this critical moment in Paul's ministry, no one offered him more encouragement than Barnabas did.

I find it interesting that Paul's good friend had not been given the name Barnabas at birth. His given name was Joseph. But the apostles called him Barnabas because that name matched his personality. Is there anyone to whom you need to be a Barnabas today?

PRAYER

Lord, there are people around me who are going through all kinds of struggles. They need encouragement. Make me a Barnabas to a hurting person today. In Jesus' name, Amen.

Listen and Be Still

Weeping and Rejoicing

Rejoice with those who rejoice;
mourn with those who mourn.
ROMANS 12:15

ROMANS 12:9-21

In a previous devotional we thought about our need to become Barnabas people. In Romans 12 Paul helps us explain what that means in a practical way. He says, "Rejoice with those who rejoice; mourn with those who mourn." Paul invites us to practice a sense of empathy with the people around us. We need to enter into the lives of others and allow them to share their deepest feelings.

Many of us have been doing that for years. When people around us go through tough times, we make ourselves available to share their hurts. But what strikes me about Paul's invitation is not so much that he invites us to "mourn with those who mourn." He also asks us to "rejoice with those who rejoice."

Empathizing with people in grief is hard work. But in some ways it may be even more difficult to enter into the joys of others. It's hard to celebrate with the colleague whose career is soaring to new heights while your own career remains mired in the doldrums. It's hard to rejoice with the friend whose children are gathering honor after honor at school while your own kids struggle to get passing grades.

But our effectiveness to minister in times of hurt is shaped by our willingness to celebrate in times of joy. If you are a Barnabas person, you will be involved in both of these Christlike activities.

PRAYER

Lord, help us to put aside our envy and enter into the joy of others today. In doing so, may we build strong friendships for future ministry in your name. Amen.

Listen and Be Still

Our Only Comfort

Praise be to. . . the God of all comfort,
who comforts us in all our troubles. . . .
2 CORINTHIANS 1:3-4

2 CORINTHIANS 1:1-7

One summary of Christian belief begins with the question, "What is your only comfort in life and in death?" At first it may seem there are more important questions to ask than that one. But the Heidelberg Catechism isn't asking about a comfort that merely makes life "comfortable" or "cozy." The word comfort literally means "with strength." The question is asking where we will find the strength to bear up under the pressures of life.

The apostle Paul understood the importance of such comfort. He had gone through some tough times. Yet he confessed that as his troubles increased, so did the comfort of his Savior.

Why was that comfort available? In John 14:16-17 Jesus explains that the great Counselor, or Comforter, given to us forever is "the Spirit of truth." Comfort comes to those who have received the Holy Spirit of Christ in faith. No wonder the catechism answers the question of comfort by saying, "I am not my own, but belong . . . to my faithful Savior, Jesus Christ."

Many of us have spent a long time trying to get comfortable in life. Perhaps we have forgotten comfort's real definition. Life's only real "comfort zone" is found in a faith relationship with Jesus Christ. Have you confessed Christ as your Lord? Do you belong to him?

PRAYER

Lord, only if we belong to you can we handle life's pressures. We place ourselves in your care, knowing that nothing in life or in death can separate us from your love. Amen.

Listen and Be Still

LIVING THE LIFE OF FAITH

The Habit of Prayer

31 Meditations and Readings

by Dr. Joel H. Nederhood

THE HABIT OF PRAYER

DR. JOEL H. NEDERHOOD

An old catechism states that "prayer is the most important part of the thankfulness God requires of us." But what, really, is prayer, and how do we pray?

These reflections lead us to focus on the value of prayer in the life of a Christian, and help us to remember how important it is to be in prayer with God throughout our days.

Dr. Nederhood served for many years as Director of Ministries and as a radio and TV minister in the English language for the Back to God Hour. He retired in 1996 and has continued writing, teaching, and preaching regularly.

Our Prayer Book

God created man in his own image. . . .
GENESIS 1:27

GENESIS 1:26-27

Practically everything about the Christian religion can be discussed in terms of prayer. This is why it's so important for Christians to think about prayer—and then actually to pray. It's in terms of our prayers that we reveal how well we understand our Christianity.

For Christians, the Bible itself is a prayer book; everything about it has something to do with prayer. It reveals to us the true God, who actually prays himself. And, in the Bible, we find invitations to pray, promises about the effectiveness of prayer, examples of prayers, and all conditions that make prayer desirable and possible. Christians who love the Bible love to pray.

Prayer is possible because we are imagebearers of God. This means we can talk with God because we are like him. And God wants us to talk with him. Because we are like God, something inside us makes us want to express our feelings and tell him what's on our minds. It's like being on an elevator with someone you want to start a conversation with.

This makes Christianity different from all other religions. Christianity says that God has created human beings to be something like himself. Now I know why I want to talk with God so eagerly and why I want to converse with him better than I do. Now I know why God has done so much to communicate with me.

PRAYER

Triune God, Creator of all, we worship you. We are overwhelmed by the mystery of your being. Thank you for speaking to us and for being patient as we try to respond. In Christ, Amen.

Listen and Be Still

171

Prayer in the Morning

In the morning I lay my requests
before you and wait in expectation.
PSALM 5:3

PSALM 5

Praying people are naturally drawn to the book of Psalms, for it is full of prayers. Some are prayers of adoration, but most are prayers that pour from the lips of a person who is surrounded by oppressive threats.

The psalms depict a dangerous and treacherous world, where evil lurks not only in nature's storm and wind but also in hatreds that boil within the human soul. The world of the psalms is one of hatred, suspicion, attack, and even murder. In other words, it's a world much like our own. So the prayers of the psalms fit into our current lives.

And what a way to start the day when living in such a world! One of the graces we experience as God's children is that we simply approach God with our requests, lay them at his feet, and wait with expectation to see how he will answer. Sometimes we are embarrassed to come so often, but our requests are not ignored, even though they are frequently the same.

Notice, now, how Psalm 5 establishes a connection between prayer and the house of God. The house of God has always had special meaning. Every morning we pray as individuals, and on Sunday we gather with the people of God and encourage one another to continue bringing requests to God. Prayer encouraged by the body of believers—what a way to start the day!

PRAYER

Use the church, O God, to encourage your people to bring their requests to you each morning. Thank you for the hope we may have as we wait for your answers. In Christ, Amen.

Listen and Be Still

"Come to Me"

*"Come to me, all you who are weary and
burdened, and I will give you rest."*
MATTHEW 11:28

MATTHEW 11:25-30

If only there were someone to talk to. No, if only there were someone to cry with. Everyone is so busy. Where can you go when your heart is broken?

Sometimes we get caught in a trap of our own making. We make many mistakes, and each mistake builds on another—and when we try to get help, we have to admit how much we have failed, and that's so hard.

"Come to me," Jesus says. "When you are in trouble, come to me." The Gospels in the Bible encourage us to turn to Jesus when people don't understand, when we are nearly paralyzed by guilt, or when life itself seems unworthy of our efforts.

Jesus understands. He is serious when he says to all of us prodigal sons and prostitutes and greedy people, "Come to me." Where are you now? What has happened to you? You have made decisions that seemed so good at one time, but you have plunged deeper and deeper into failure. And now there is no one to help you, no one to turn to.

"Come to me," Jesus says. "Don't be afraid to bare your inmost feelings. I understand. I will pay for your sin and help you put your life back together. I love you."

We need Jesus' love. And we must simply come, no matter what we've done, no matter how far we have strayed away.

PRAYER

"Out of my bondage, sorrow and night . . . Jesus, I come; Into thy freedom, gladness and light, Jesus, I come to thee." Thank you, Jesus, for loving us so much. In your name, Amen.

Listen and Be Still

In His Name

*"The Father will give you
whatever you ask in my name."*
JOHN 15:16

JOHN 15:9-17

"Who let you in here? Why are you talking to me this way?" God would be justified in asking us these questions when we come to him, because two things disqualify us: we are small, and we are sinners.

But we pray in the name of Jesus. That changes everything. "You may ask me for anything in my name, and I will do it," says Jesus in John 14:14. And in chapter 15 he says his Father will do the same.

We must always remember to pray in Jesus' name, for we have no right to talk to God on our own. Using Jesus' name, we call on God to remember Jesus' perfect life and sacrifice; we ask him to listen to us as if he is listening to his Son. Because Jesus has saved us, we can approach God with the confidence that Jesus' blood covers our sins.

And when we are conscious that we must always pray in Jesus' name, we realize we must pray appropriately. We cannot pray for trivial things or for anything that opposes God's kingdom. Praying in his name, we, like Jesus, submit our will to God's.

The assurances Jesus gives are absolute. If we could understand perfectly what it means to pray in his name, we could unravel the mystery of prayer and of how God answers it, and we could pray perfectly. Meanwhile, we do our best . . . in Jesus' name.

PRAYER

O God, there's so much about prayer that we don't understand.
But we hear the assurance that has come to us today. Bind us
closer to you through your Spirit, we pray. In Jesus' name, Amen.

Listen and Be Still

Heart to Heart

Pour out your hearts to him. . . .
PSALM 62:8

PSALM 62

Life is so tender. We are so fragile. Our bodies disappoint us. Our emotions overwhelm us. Sometimes all we feel like doing is crying.

No, we are not depressed in the clinical sense. We are just overwhelmed by sorrow, loss, and pain. Some who feel this way are elderly and weak. But, surprisingly, many who feel this way are young people. The heart—that mysterious center of our being—can suddenly be plunged into despair.

Psalm 62 is for the brokenhearted. It is a marvelous description of God as our shield, our protection, our ultimate and perfect resource. In it we find a declaration that we should carry with us every moment: Our God is strong, and he is loving (62:11-12).

The Bible invites us to pour our hearts out to God. And the comfort God has for us does not consist of his writing down little statements about his love and power so that we, reading them, will be encouraged. Our God has a heart, as do we. And God's heart is full of love. Heart to heart—this is the way it is when the anguished Christian approaches God.

What if bad goes to worse in your life? What can you do then? You can pour out your heart to God. In your anguish you can struggle into God's presence and bring your broken heart near to his.

PRAYER

Sometimes, Lord, our broken hearts threaten to engulf our consciousness with paralyzing anguish. The pain is almost too much to bear. Hear us, O loving God. In Jesus, Amen.

Listen and Be Still

The Unbeliever's Prayer

"Help me overcome my unbelief!"
MARK 9:24

MARK 9:14-27

Faith and unbelief usually exist side by side and mixed together within us. This was true of the father who presented his demon-possessed son to Jesus. This is true of the most hardened unbeliever, who sometimes doubts his or her unbelief. This is also true of the most fervent believer, who sometimes shudders as wisps of doubt chill his or her soul.

Do you really want to believe in Christ more than you do now? I ask you this if you have never surrendered your life to him, if you wander where there is only faithlessness. I also ask you this if you are someone who believes, or perhaps "has believed," but has lost the zest of living by Christ's Spirit—you pray little, read the Bible even less, and seldom join in public worship.

We can pray for faith. The father in Mark 9 did that. But how can we pray for faith when prayer itself takes faith? There's something here that goes beyond our ability to think things through logically. Yet it is true: if you want to believe, you must ask God to overcome the unbelief that clutches you so strongly.

Jesus did not turn aside the father's prayer. He performed a miracle of great release for the father's beloved son. He will not ignore the most earnest plea of any of us who on this day, feeling weak and empty, earnestly ask for stronger faith.

PRAYER

O God who knows our hearts perfectly, you know that only you can overcome our unbelief. Please do that now, and make our faith strong. In Jesus' name we pray. Amen.

Listen and Be Still

Hearing and Praying

If anyone turns a deaf ear to the law,
even his prayers are detestable.
PROVERBS 28:9

PSALM 119:33-40

God detests the prayers of people who don't listen to him. He speaks clearly in Scripture, and whenever God's people come together in worship, his Word is proclaimed. But some people are deaf to it all. Usually they merely arrange their lives so that they never hear God's will for them. And when they pray, God says, "Aren't you forgetting something? You never listen to me; why do you expect me to listen to you?"

Psalm 119 is a glorious song of praise that honors God's law and rejoices about the life we can experience living according to this law. And sentences of prayer are scattered throughout: "Praise be to you, O LORD; teach me your decrees." "Teach me, O LORD, to follow your decrees; then I will keep them to the end. Give me understanding, and I will keep your law and obey it with all my heart. Direct me in the path of your commands, for there I find delight" (119:12, 33-35).

One of the most important prayers we utter is that God will take away our natural deafness and enable us to hear his will for our lives. If we don't listen to his Word, the Bible, we will slip into ways that will separate us from him. Then we will find that if we feel compelled to pray only when crises upset our lives, there is no one there to hear us. And that's frightening.

But God is merciful . . . so let's listen to him.

PRAYER

Lord, open our ears to your life-giving law. By nature we are deaf, and we avoid listening to you whenever we can. Forgive us for being so stubborn. In Christ we pray. Amen.

Listen and Be Still

Prayer Posture

Peter . . . got down on his knees and prayed.
Acts 9:40

Acts 9:32-43

Posture is important. If you don't sit properly at your workstation, for example, you'll pay with backaches and headaches and drowsiness.

Posture is important in prayer also. And there are several postures we can assume. One evening Ezra prayed on his knees with his hands spread out and his head bowed (Ezra 9:5-6), and when he really began wrestling with the Lord, he threw himself, weeping, to the ground (10:1). Peter was once alone in a room with a woman's corpse, praying on his knees for her resurrection (Acts 9:40). He was following the example of Jesus, who had often knelt in prayer.

When the people of God are deeply moved and have to wrestle with their heavenly Father, it seems only natural for them to fall to their knees. The apostle Paul knelt with the Ephesians as he was about to leave them, never to see them again in this world (Acts 20:36). When we're grieved or deeply concerned, we kneel.

In prayer we recognize God's glory and confess our smallness. And it helps to express these things in a humble posture on bended knees. When we slip to our knees, perhaps by our bed at the end of the day or at any time, we join a multitude of millions of believers who today and throughout the centuries have knelt in prayer to God.

PRAYER

Teach us to kneel, O Lord. Overcome our pride, overrule our intricate theologies, take us by the hand, and gently help us bend our knees before you, our glorious Savior. Amen.

Listen and Be Still

Our Special Devotion

Devote yourselves to prayer. . . .
COLOSSIANS 4:2

COLOSSIANS 4:2-6

One thing that should make us think twice about becoming a Christian, if we aren't one yet, is that we will have to make sure we arrange time for prayer and for gathering with God's people for prayer and worship. All Christians should make time for worship and prayer.

No, prayer isn't just for some who have a special calling. It's for all Christians. In Colossians 4 we learn that we should pray for the church and its members. And the apostle Paul asks the Colossians to remember him and his important work in prayer. He assumes that the members of the church will spend time going over their prayer lists while they pray, adding to those lists the names of people with special needs.

The truth today is that many members of the church—busy wage-earners, some with responsible work that is always on their minds—find it hard to pray as much as they would like. There's so much to do that it's hard to devote oneself to prayer. This problem causes a never-ending tension for the serious Christian.

I've never heard anyone say, "I'm looking forward to retirement, because then I will have more time for prayer." But I have heard sick people say, "Now that I'm laid up, I feel that God has given me the special task of prayer." Indeed, God often arranges our lives so that we can devote ourselves to prayer.

PRAYER

Bring us close to you, O God, and help us see that, if we are truly your children, we will pray often. Help us to use every opportunity you give for this task. In Jesus' name, Amen.

Listen and Be Still

Prayer in the First Degree

"When you pray, go into your room. . . ."
MATTHEW 6:6

When we think about prayer, we might think first about public prayer. Sometimes prayers are offered at public events—a banking association I know of, for example, opens meetings at its conventions with prayer. And worship services, of course, include prayer.

In Matthew 6, though, Jesus shows us that when we think about prayer, we should think first about private prayer. We should view such prayer as "prayer in the first degree" because it can be the most pure and the most effective. Try as we might, there are always elements that can slip into our public prayers and diminish them. Any prayer expressed in someone else's presence tends to be different from what we pray when we are all alone with God.

It's encouraging to know that private prayer is so important, that there are no barriers between ourselves and God when we converse privately with him. And God is right there with us when we pray. God pays special attention to what we say when he hears us praying all by ourselves, for we are not trying to impress anyone; we are just opening our hearts to God.

The place of private prayer is the most beautiful place in the world—for each of us. May we earnestly cultivate the habit of going into our room, closing the door, and praying in secret to our heavenly Father.

PRAYER

Lord, use what we have discussed here, use even this prayer,
to prepare our hearts for a private place. Help us to feel your
presence when we close the door and pray. For Jesus' sake, Amen.

Listen and Be Still

Moving Mountains

"If you believe, you will receive whatever you ask for in prayer."
MATTHEW 21:22

MATTHEW 21:18-22

Some things in this Scripture reading from Matthew may puzzle us. For example, some of us might rather hear Jesus' prayer-promise here in connection with a more attractive miracle. The cursing and withering of the fig tree bothers us. We'd rather think of the power of prayer in connection with positive miracles and events, not negative ones.

But Jesus was talking to people who would become the foundation of his church, and, like it or not, the church would face fierce enemies and wage bitter battles. He knew that his followers would have to call God at times to wield his almighty power against those who were bent on destroying his people. So he challenged them to believe that prayer would move mountains.

Our greatest puzzlement comes in trying to comprehend just what it might mean to tell a mountain to throw itself into the sea. Jesus was using a figure of speech here, obviously. Telling mountains to toss themselves around is an exaggeration of the impossible, isn't it? Jesus was simply telling us here to pray that impossible circumstances be changed.

Many of our problems, for example, are as big as mountains. And how miserable they can make us sometimes! But we must believe and pray and wait to see how God will solve them.

PRAYER

Lord, you see the mountains of problems we have. We believe what you have said, but at times we hardly dare to pray about them. Help us to trust your power. In Jesus' name, Amen.

Listen and Be Still

Prayer and Forgiveness

"If you hold anything against anyone, forgive him, so that your Father . . . may forgive you your sins."
MARK 11:25

MARK 11:20-25

We are astonished at Jesus' description of the power of prayer here. As we noted when looking at a similar passage from Matthew in the previous devotional, prayer can move mountains—that is, God's power can help us solve impossible problems. But there are conditions.

In Mark the conditions are described more fully than in Matthew. Again faith is mentioned. But there's also another condition: as we come before the Lord and ask him to do the impossible, we must examine ourselves and be sure we don't harbor hatred for anyone. We must forgive those who have wronged us. Otherwise God won't listen to us.

This brings us up short. We wouldn't think that our relationships with our spouses, children, coworkers, and others would have anything to do with the effectiveness of our prayers. But they do. Our willingness to forgive those who have hurt us is the measure of how well we understand God's forgiving love.

Right here is a clue as to why so many of us are ineffective "pray-ers." We harbor grudges. We are unwilling to make adjustments to smooth things out. But we must—to understand the fullness of God's love.

The first word of our prayers won't get through to God unless he first forgives us. And he will not move mountains for people who refuse to forgive others.

PRAYER

Lord, before we ask you to move any mountains for us, help us to realize we need your forgiveness and we need to forgive. Help us repair our broken relationships. In Jesus, Amen.

Listen and Be Still

Without Letup

Pray continually.
1 THESSALONIANS 5:17

1 THESSALONIANS 5:12-28

There are, of course, many times of prayer. There are prayers in church and other public places, private prayers, prayers upon rising in the morning, prayers at mealtimes, prayers upon retiring at night. On special occasions, too, we may feel we ought to pray, either by ourselves or with others.

But prayer without letup—what is that? Well, we might say, for example, that we should be sure not to neglect the times of prayer we just noted. Or we might say that prayer is appropriate at all times—times of celebration and times of sadness. That would be true. But the apostle means more here. He's saying that prayer should be something like breathing, not eating. For we eat at certain times, but we breathe always.

This doesn't mean we should continuously mutter prayers, possibly disturbing those who may be next to us, or setting aside all the other things we need to do. It means we should try to cultivate the habit of praying at some level of consciousness all the time. It's possible, after all, to be doing more than one thing at once—for example, I can drive my car and listen to the radio at the same time. So we should ask God to help us "pray continually." I cannot fully explain this. I cannot claim that I do it. But the command is there for all to see. May God show us more about what this means.

PRAYER

Lord, teach us to pray so that something in our consciousness is speaking with you all the time. Forgive us for overlooking this possibility. In Jesus' name we pray. Amen.

Listen and Be Still

He's So Close

The LORD our God is near us
whenever we pray to him. . . .
DEUTERONOMY 4:7

DEUTERONOMY 4:1-8

When we're puzzled about the idea of praying continually, it can be helpful to remember that God is "near us whenever we pray to him."

Deuteronomy 4 helps us understand what it might mean to pray without letup. Notice that prayer and God's nearness are connected with the fact that God gave his people decrees and laws that no other nation possessed. These gave the people a way of life—if they were obedient to God's law, they would live. And God's law was with them always. Now, God's presence was made real in his revelation of the law, so God's nearness, too, was with them always. As a result, his people could always pray to God; God was always right there.

Surely this means that one way for us to pray is to earnestly try to relate everything we do in life to the way of God's law, which the Lord has revealed for us. Doing so, we show that we realize the reality and the nearness of God. All who want to experience the full richness of prayer, in fact, must study God's Word and learn to live by its teachings.

Praying without letup seems strange until we remember that God is so close to us. He is right here . . . at your elbow . . . at mine—in our hearts and in his Word to us in the Bible. When someone is so close, it's only natural to talk with him all the time.

PRAYER

Thank you, God, for revealing yourself to us in your Word, which shows us the way of life. Help us to feel your nearness and to speak to you naturally all the time. In Christ, Amen.

Listen and Be Still

Please Teach Us

"Lord, teach us to pray. . . ."
LUKE 11:1

LUKE 11:1-4

In spite of all the good things we can say about prayer, the simple fact is that prayer is a problem. So many barriers in our lives are erected with the result that the last thing we get around to is prayer.

Lack of faith is our biggest problem. When it comes to having a life of prayer, it's not enough to have a vague notion about the existence of God or even of the person of Jesus. What we need is a living relationship with God. And prayer is hard work; lazy Christians don't tend to do much of it.

Eric Alexander, speaking to students gathered at a missionary conference some years ago, declared that prayer is the hardest work Christians ever do and that, because everyone does their easy things first, prayer is put last.

Time—not having enough of it—is also a barrier. And when we do begin to pray, our inability to keep at it, with concentration, is difficult. Yes, these are some of our problems with prayer. But what is the solution?

The solution is the same as the solution for any other problem we may have: we must go to Christ in prayer and ask him to help us. If we don't have time for prayer, we should ask him to help us find it. If we find we can't concentrate, we should ask for help with that.

PRAYER

Hear us, O Lord, as we ask for the ability to pray. Then everything else in our lives will fall into place. So we join your disciples and ask what they asked for. In Jesus' name, Amen.

Listen and Be Still

This Is How

"This . . . is how you should pray. . . ."
MATTHEW 6:9

Sometimes people say that when we think about prayer, we shouldn't just think about it as asking for things. It should also be praise and worship, they say. That's true. But let's never forget that when Jesus taught the perfect prayer, he told us to ask for things. And that's what prayer is, to a large extent—simply asking God and asking God . . . without end.

The perfect prayer tells us to ask for things that many people would never think of asking for: Father, let everyone everywhere honor your name; Father, grant that the earth will become like heaven, with everyone doing your will; Father, please give us food . . . and shelter and all the ordinary things we need to live; Father, forgive us poor sinners, and teach us to be forgiving; Father, arrange our lives so that we don't meet a test we cannot handle; and, Father, keep us safe from the evil one, who keeps prowling nearby.

As people grow in faith, as they live closer and closer to the heart of God, they pray for the things God wants. Their wills and God's will come closer together. They learn to look at their lives and the events of the world in the same way Jesus and his Father do. They grow more and more capable of praying according to God's will, and they are increasingly astonished by the marvelous way their prayers are answered.

PRAYER

Lord Jesus, thank you for the model prayer you have given us. Use it to encourage us to ask for what we need and to help us develop concerns that are like yours. In your name, Amen.

Listen and Be Still

Penitence

*Against you, you only, have I sinned
and done what is evil in your sight. . . .*

PSALM 51:4

PSALM 51

A major element of our prayers is our confession of sin. Psalm 51 stands out in the Bible as one of the most moving, personal confessions of sin. It is usually viewed as David's expression of penitence, spoken after his sins of adultery and murder.

The depth of David's fall is unexplainable. But so is the depth of human sin today; think of the genocides and holocausts that have taken place in only recent history. The depth of the sin each of us harbors in his or her heart is also unexplainable.

We are all sinners, and we realize this when we stop comparing ourselves with others, when we stop justifying ourselves. We see it as soon as we see our lives in the light of God's holiness. David's confession arose out of his understanding that he had sinned against God—not just against Uriah, whom he had murdered, and not just against Bathsheba, whom he had violated.

The reason we are what we are and do what we do is that our hearts are wicked. This is the emphasis in Psalm 51. In this prayer psalm David asks for a new heart and a steadfast spirit. His external sins, he realized, were the fruit of an inner corruption.

Sins of attitude, envy, resentment, bitterness, and lust— all these are in us too. When you pray, don't forget to ask for forgiveness and renewal.

PRAYER

"Hide your face from my sins and blot out all my iniquity. Create in me a pure heart, O God, and renew a steadfast spirit within me." Help us all to pray this way. In Jesus, Amen.

Listen and Be Still

His Tearful Prayers

During. . . Jesus' life on earth, he offered up
prayers and petitions with loud cries and tears.
HEBREWS 5:7

HEBREWS 5:7-10

When I mentioned in a previous meditation that God actually prays himself, I was thinking of the way Jesus Christ, the Second Person of the Trinity, prayed while on earth. God the Son prayed to God the Father—"the one who could save him from death."

Jesus' prayers to his Father, though generally private, are nonetheless described for us. Hebrews 5 says that Jesus prayed to his Father "with loud cries and tears." One might have expected that Jesus' divinity and his closeness to the Father would have made their communications rather cool progress reports. But no. The Son of God immersed himself totally in human life, and his prayers were often accompanied by cries and tears.

So it often is with prayer. Instinctively we feel that our most fervent prayers have been those we have spoken between clenched teeth, with tears flowing freely—prayers we have uttered when afraid or confronted with tragedy. The stark reality of death, for example, draws prayers from the depths of our souls.

Possibly we are often reluctant to pray because we do not wish to open ourselves to hurt and pain. We prefer to pray coolly, with great self-control. But we have a God who prayed entirely differently. And we must not hesitate to follow him into the fullness of human anguish, when the time comes, in prayer.

PRAYER

Thank you for coming to us, O Jesus, and for crying our cries and weeping our tears. May we not be afraid to enter the deepest trials and follow your example totally. In your name, Amen.

Listen and Be Still

His Will and Ours

"Not my will, but yours be done."
LUKE 22:42

LUKE 22:39-44

The description of Jesus' cries and tears in the previous meditation tells us that obedience is very important in the context of prayer. Hebrews 5:8 emphasizes that "although [Jesus] was a son, he learned obedience from what he suffered." And Luke 22 shows us that Jesus, in his most anguished prayer, on the night before his death, stressed more than anything else that he wanted to do his Father's will.

Confronted by the horror of the cross, Jesus, in his humanity, recoiled. He saw things in his coming suffering that we are not even capable of seeing. He was to receive the full force of God's wrath against sin. No wonder he flinched and cried out for reprieve. In the same moment, however, he affirmed the importance of doing the will of his Father in heaven. That will is supreme, and it is good.

Our prayers become what they should be as we grow more and more willing to obey God. When we pray, then, we must always purge our hearts of selfishness. Even when the circumstances from which we want to be delivered are repulsive, we must ask God to give us the Spirit of obedience and sacrifice. For his will is good, and ours is flawed.

Surely God wants us to express our desires urgently, clearly, and *obediently*.

PRAYER

Almighty God, loving Father of our Lord Jesus, as you heard your Son's prayer in the garden, hear ours as well. And through your Spirit make us obedient, as he was. In his name, Amen.

Listen and Be Still

189

How He Spends His Time

He always lives to intercede. . . .
HEBREWS 7:25

HEBREWS 7:23-25

Some Christians talk about a Bible teaching called "the perseverance of the saints." By that they mean that once a person is saved, he will always be saved. Other Christians point out that this makes believers careless. "The idea of 'Once saved, always saved' leads to complacency," they say.

There is eternal safety for those who believe in Jesus, but this teaching cannot be reduced to the simple formula "Once saved, always saved." Anyone who thinks he or she was "saved" once and now has nothing to worry about has not understood the Bible's teaching.

Those who believe in Jesus will most surely be brought through temptations and afflictions in this life, and they will endure them. But not because they "accepted Jesus" and thus guaranteed their glorious future. They will endure because of the perseverance of Christ, who prays continuously for his people.

We must recognize that prayers are being uttered in heaven for us at this very moment by no other than the Lord Jesus Christ. Think of it! Jesus came into this world and lived for his people. He died for us. And now he prays for us continuously.

Our prayers are important—but his are infinitely more important. Because of them, we who believe will make it through to glory.

PRAYER

Thank you, Jesus, for praying for us every moment of every day. Assure us that nothing will be able to separate us from your prayerful love. We pray in your name. Amen.

Listen and Be Still

Your Perfect Prayer

*He who searches our hearts knows
the mind of the Spirit. . . .*
ROMANS 8:27

ROMANS 8:26-27

Suppose you were told that you could bring a perfect prayer before God. Would you believe it? Most of us know that with something as holy as prayer we often don't do very well.

But perfect prayers do originate from those who believe in Jesus. Believers should know, however, that although their prayers come from their hearts, they are not the author. The Holy Spirit, who lives in them, brings perfect prayers to God on their behalf.

Romans 8 talks about this in connection with a very distressing problem: not knowing exactly what to pray. There are times when we experience this problem, aren't there? The apostle Paul, for example, told the people in Philippi that he was torn between desire and duty—he wanted to go and be with Christ, yet he felt a duty to go on serving the church (Philippians 1:23).

Sometimes we pray and seem to receive no answer. We pray for success in business. We pray that we will be able to marry a certain person. But what we ask for may not be best for us. So the Holy Spirit within us overrides our ignorance, and when God searches our hearts, he hears the Spirit's groans—he hears a prayer perfectly in tune with his will.

What a mystery this is! God himself prays within us. Praise the Lord!

PRAYER

Holy Spirit, as we think about the way you pray for us, we realize how dependent we are on you. Comfort us with the assurance that your prayers are always heard. In Jesus, Amen.

Listen and Be Still

Just like Elijah

Elijah was a man just like us.
JAMES 5:17

JAMES 5:13-18

Do you have to be someone special to be able to pray and receive answers? No. James encourages believers in Jesus to pray earnestly in faith for what they need.

Remember Elijah, James says. Elijah was just like we are. In 1 Kings 17-18 we find the record of Elijah praying for drought and rain. God used Elijah's prayers to create circumstances that changed the nation of Israel. But what kind of a man was he? Why, he was just like you and me.

The book of 1 Kings tells us this about Elijah: he was despondent (18:42), suicidal (19:4), and had a poor self-image (19:4). That's just part of the picture of this man's life. When I look at Elijah, it seems almost as if I am looking into a mirror. Don't you feel the same way?

But the prayers of this man were astonishingly effective. No, we don't have to wait until we reach some peak of moral perfection before we pray in all circumstances. I can pray, and when I am sick, I can call ordinary people just like myself and ask them to pray for me. We all can just go right ahead and pray—we who are people like Elijah.

If Elijah's prayers were effective in the Old Testament, think how effective ours can be now, when we, poor and imperfect men and women, sinners, come to God in the name of Jesus!

PRAYER

Lord, it's encouraging to know that you honored the prayers of Elijah years ago. We are like him in so many ways. Encourage us to bring our every need to you. In Christ, Amen.

Listen and Be Still

Hearing Hezekiah

*"I have heard your prayer
and seen your tears. . . ."*

ISAIAH 38:5

ISAIAH 38:1-8

God's prophet Isaiah finally had to tell Hezekiah the bad news: he would not recover. Hezekiah was crushed. When you are used to being king, as Hezekiah was, and having everyone do what you say, it's frustrating to encounter something you cannot handle.

So Hezekiah prayed. And he wept. He turned his face to the wall and wailed. He clenched his fists and summoned all his strength, and through his sobs he said to God, "Please reconsider." He used the only argument he knew how to use: "I have worshiped you and served you. You can't do this to me."

So Isaiah came back. And his message was simple: God would give Hezekiah fifteen more years. Isn't that awesome? Here was a man wailing in his bed, crying out to God, and God was right there listening to him.

That's the way it is with us. Often when we think about prayer, we think about the distance between ourselves and God. Where is he? By what mysterious power can our prayers be carried from our sickbed to that distant realm where God is living?

But God does not live in a distant realm. He was right there with Hezekiah, listening and watching, and he is right here with us whenever we pray. We must not forget this. We pray, and we weep, and God hears and sees. Pray and discover this for yourself.

PRAYER

O God who listened to Hezekiah centuries ago, hear us as we pray to you now. And see our tears. Please protect us, heal us, and save us, we pray. Through Jesus, Amen.

Listen and Be Still

Prayer and the State

I urge, then. . . that requests, prayers
. . . be made. . . for kings. . . .
1 TIMOTHY 2:1-2

1 TIMOTHY 2:1-8

The state gets very nervous about prayer. Prayer in the public school is an explosive issue; in some cases, student Bible study and prayer groups are being kept from using public buildings. Even so, there is no question that believers should pray for those who govern.

The state changes its attitude in times of special need, such as when the nation's leader gets cancer or when astronauts have trouble in space. Believers earnestly pray at times like these; they understand that praying for their government is a never-ending obligation. They do it even when their prayers are not requested.

Believers pray for their government because they know that the government does not have ultimate power but operates under the control of the Lord. Prayers are their highest and most effective civic duty.

Christians are to pray for government in terms of its primary role. As 1 Timothy 2 says, government must maintain peace so that we can have the tranquillity necessary for living holy lives. Peacetime allows for the full development of church life and missions.

In this age of violence and widespread disobedience, believers' prayers for their rulers must be fervent and intense. If the truth were known, we would all see that only these prayers explain why our nation, our culture, our civilization has not yet collapsed.

PRAYER

We pray for our leaders, Lord. Give them health and wisdom.
Also give them faith so that they will want to serve you above all.
Give us all the desire to honor you. In Jesus, Amen.

Listen and Be Still

The Wisest Thing to Do

If any of you lacks wisdom, he should
ask God, who gives generously. . . .

JAMES 1:5

JAMES 1:1-8

These days it seems that most of us lack wisdom. Yes, in this high-tech, modern age in which knowledge continues to increase exponentially, wisdom is often as scarce as hen's teeth. We can tell this is true by all the people-problems around us. To mention one example: the way marriages are breaking up shows that something has gone fundamentally wrong with the way people treat each other.

On another level, think of the many thousands of megatons of nuclear weapons stored in the world's arsenals—the equivalent of thousands of World War IIs just sitting there, waiting to be used. Surely this says something about how unwise the human race has become.

Wisdom is God's gift. It is different from knowledge. It is different from technical competence. It is rooted in a proper understanding of oneself and a proper appreciation of others. It is a form of love, exercised in the awareness of God's claim on us all.

The wisest thing anyone ever does is pray for wisdom. Lack of wisdom is caused by lack of prayer. And there is so little wisdom these days because there is so little faith and prayer. Those of us who on this day stare at problems of our own making, caused by our own foolishness, must ask God for wisdom. This is the wisest thing we ever do.

PRAYER

O God, we are ashamed of so much that we have done. And all these things have been caused by our impetuousness and stubbornness. Please give us wisdom. In Christ, Amen.

Listen and Be Still

195

Prayer and Marriage

Husbands. . . be considerate. . . with your wives
. . . so that nothing will hinder your prayers.
1 PETER 3:7

1 PETER 3:1-7

If a married couple really understands what the Bible says in 1 Peter 3, and if they really live by it, their marriage will be as solid as the rock of Gibraltar. But few people understand this, and that's why many marriages are as flimsy as cotton candy.

Good marriages result in a good prayer life. I can think of at least two reasons why this is so. First, resenting, punishing, and quarreling with one another does not create internal feelings that go well with prayer. When a couple isn't getting along, it's hard for them to try to get along with God. When they're mad at each other, it's hard for them to pray for each other.

Second, a good marriage takes a lot of what good prayers are made of. It takes a lot of forgiving. In 1 Peter husbands are told to be considerate with their wives. Of course, this holds true for wives as well. The only way two people can live together in marriage with mutual advantage is that they know how to forgive again and again. Only sinners who know that God has forgiven them are able to forgive one another fully.

God hears the prayers of marriage partners who know they are forgiven and who know how to forgive. For, as Jesus says in Mark 11:25, "When . . . praying, if you hold anything against anyone, forgive him, so that your Father in heaven may forgive you your sins."

PRAYER

Lord, help those who are having marriage troubles. Take away their animosity and give them a spirit of forgiveness. Help them to pray—privately and together. In Jesus, Amen.

Listen and Be Still

Prayer and Rejection

"Far be it from me that I should sin against the LORD by failing to pray for you."

1 SAMUEL 12:23

1 SAMUEL 12:20-25

Samuel's heart was heavy as he talked to the people . . . for the last time as their leader. He was the final judge in a long line of judges who had managed to keep the people of Israel together under God. God had saved the best for last; Samuel was conscientious, God-fearing, incorruptible, untiring—he was everything a judge was supposed to be. But—irony of ironies—when he was judge, the people requested a king, and God said to him, "Go ahead, give them one—they are rejecting me, not you."

Now Samuel was about to turn the people over to King Saul. He could not conceal his disappointment. He was ashamed because he realized that his disgraceful sons were not fit to succeed him (1 Samuel 8:1-3). "But," said the brokenhearted judge, "I will pray for you . . . always." Through his disappointment, Samuel sensed the measure of his obligation. He realized that it is a sin to stop praying for those who have disappointed you, disagreed with you, possibly even disgraced you.

Do you have someone whom you have stopped praying for because something has spoiled your relationship? Like Samuel, we must remember those who still need our prayers, though circumstances may have brought separation. To fail them when we are on our knees is a sin . . . against God!

PRAYER

Many of us, like Samuel, have experienced rejection, O God, and we have been hurt by people who need our prayers now more than ever. Help us to pray for them. In Jesus, Amen.

Listen and Be Still

Prayer for Children

"Perhaps my children have sinned. . . ."
JOB 1:5

JOB 1:1-5

It's one thing to pray for your children when they are young and you can tuck them into bed at night. But Job's children were not young anymore.

Job was rich, and his children had grown up and taken their places in his vast, prosperous enterprise. They had their own lands, their own cattle. His seven sons and three daughters would get together every once in a while and have a party. Job would not be invited. When the parties were over, he would pray for them, in the only way he knew how—the smoke of his burnt offering would ascend heavenward, and he would gaze upward and say to God: "This is for them. I know how easy it is to sin, and possibly in their festivities, maybe when the wine confused them, they cursed you in their hearts. O God, please forgive."

Parents who know Christ and who know the way the world is and the way their adult children are will surely pray as Job did. Sometimes, when others see the children of such parents, those children look no different from other people. But they are different. Their lives are surrounded by the prayers of faith-filled parents. And parents who can no longer tuck their children safely into bed at night are at least comforted to know that God will not abandon them and that he will forgive their sins as they ask him to forgive.

PRAYER
Lord, you know that many of us as parents long to tuck our children into bed, but we never will again. Take them and care for them and be their heavenly Father. In Jesus, Amen.

Listen and Be Still

Prayer and Peace

In everything, by prayer and petition, with thanksgiving, present your requests to God.
PHILIPPIANS 4:6

PHILIPPIANS 4:2-7

"How can you go on?" the man asked his friend. "With all that's happening to you, how can you continue your work? I could never do what you are doing. When things happen to me like what's happening to you, my emotions take over, and I can't do anything."

A long silence followed. Then the answer came, haltingly: "I really don't know how I can go on. Sometimes my troubles nearly overwhelm me. But I guess it's true—it really works. I pray about what's happening to me, and God calms my soul and gives me peace."

This conversation really took place. The man who asked his friend how he could go on was not really a believer—he had a very thin faith at best, and he didn't pray much. So when troubles entered his life, he would become paralyzed. Sometimes his life would stand still for six months. He stared at his friend after his friend told him about the way prayer brings peace. I wish I could tell you that he prays more now. I don't know if he does or not.

But it does work: we simply have to bring our troubles to the Lord. Family problems and marriage problems can often be so dreadfully complex. And physical problems can terrify us.

But prayer displaces crippling anxiety. The peace of God will come. I know of no other way.

PRAYER

We thank you, merciful Father, that when we pray, we receive peace. Help those who are bewildered and sick with fear—help them to pray and to find your peace. In Christ, Amen.

Listen and Be Still

Never Give Up

Jesus told his disciples. . . that they
should always pray and not give up.
LUKE 18:1

LUKE 18:1-8

"Never give up"—you've heard people say this. Maybe people have said it to you. But how can one keep praying over and over again, when it seems as if there aren't going to be any results?

Jesus' story about the persistent widow impresses us with the usefulness of continual prayer. And he makes his point by means of a contrast. The widow who needed justice had no claim whatsoever on the judge. Widows in that society didn't have any rights. And the judge was not one bit interested in her problem. But he gave in because she finally wore him down.

"It's the same when one of God's chosen ones keeps calling night and day," Jesus says. The widow was a nobody, but one of God's chosen is a Somebody—with a capital S—no, with all capitals: SOMEBODY! And each chosen one prays to the God described in Psalm 103:11: "As high as the heavens are above the earth, so great is his love for those who fear him."

The great "pray-er" George Meuller prayed for years for the salvation of a friend, but that friend was never converted . . . until the day Meuller died. That friend attended Meuller's funeral with a testimony to God's grace in his heart. And I've heard of a minister who prayed for his son's conversion for years but who died before it happened. Today that son is praising God.

PRAYER

Lord, it's hard to keep praying when everything seems hopeless. But you know more about prayer than we do, and you say, "Keep on praying." So please help us. In Jesus, Amen.

200 *Listen and Be Still*

Prayer and Sleep

I will lie down and sleep in peace. . . .
PSALM 4:8

PSALM 4

When the nurse entered the room, she found him staring off into space, dressed in street clothes, unwilling to put on the hospital gown and admit that he was a patient. His open Bible was on the table beside him. She gave last-minute instructions about his operation, scheduled first thing in the morning.

She looked at him intently. "You're really uptight, aren't you?" she asked. He didn't have to admit it; she could see it. She nodded toward the Bible. "Be sure to read Psalm 4. It will help you."

When she left, he read Psalm 4, the evening prayer, a good prayer the night before an operation: "Answer me when I call to you, O my righteous God. Give me relief from my distress; be merciful to me and hear my prayer." The patient sensed the urgency of the man who wrote it. He felt the same. What would his life be like after tomorrow? What if he had cancer?

The questions tumbled over each other. Then he read the last verse: "I will lie down and sleep in peace, for you alone, O Lord, make me dwell in safety." Not the doctors, but the Lord would provide safety, whatever was to happen. Now he could lie down and sleep. "I will remember Psalm 4 tomorrow," he promised himself. "Words to fall asleep with, words to be anesthetized with, words to remember when I die."

PRAYER

God of the night before a frightening tomorrow, thank you for coming to us in our agitation and assuring us of the safety you give all who trust in you through Jesus. Amen.

Listen and Be Still

THE CHRISTIAN FAMILY

31 MEDITATIONS AND READINGS

BY DR. PETER H. ELDERSVELD

DR. PETER H. ELDERSVELD

Scripture tells us that Christians are to love God with all their heart. And parents are told to talk about God "when you sit at home and when you walk along the road, when you lie down and when you get up" (Deuteronomy 6:7). Fathers are urged to bring children up "in the training and instruction of the Lord" (Ephesians 6:4).

But how do people establish a Christian home? And how do parents teach their children to know and love the Lord? May God use these meditations to provide answers to these questions, to bless you as his children and to help you grow in Christ.

Early in the ministry of the Back to God Hour, the Family Altar, now known as TODAY, was developed to provide part of the follow-up to radio-sermon broadcasts and to assist believers in their daily devotional life. This series of reflections on The Christian Home was first published in 1965.

Dr. Eldersveld pastored churches in Iowa and Illinois before he became the first Radio Minister of the Back to God Hour in 1946. He served the Back to God Hour until his death in 1965.

Listen and Be Still

The Family Pattern

They will become one flesh.
GENESIS 2:24

GENESIS 2:18-25

We often say that the most important institution on this earth is the home. But why do we say that? Not merely for secular reasons; nor because the sociologist says so; nor because we are sentimental and romantic about the home. There's a deeper reason, found only in the Word of God—and that makes the home a good subject for meditation in our family worship.

In a sense, the home is the masterpiece of God's creation. When God had finished making everything else, he united the first man and woman in holy marriage. Human history began with a wedding. Then God told that first family to take possession of his new creation. It was given to a husband and wife together—to be a home. You might say we live in a "family universe." It was made along family lines. This was the pattern of creation, "each according to its kind" (Genesis 1:24).

Distinct from all other creatures, and yet like them, is the human family. Its distinction is that it was made in the image of God and given dominion over all things.

The home became God's principal point of contact with his world. No one can really understand human civilization or address its problems intelligently if he or she fails to see the theological significance of this basic institution. "There's no place like home"—simply because within it is the heart and the hope of humanity.

PRAYER

Great God, use our home to serve your purpose in this world. Fill it with your Spirit, save it by your grace, and rule it with your love. In Jesus' name we pray. Amen.

Listen and Be Still

Where Sin Began

When the woman saw. . .
she took some and ate it.
GENESIS 3:6

GENESIS 3:1-13

The home was God's main point of contact with his world, but it also became the door through which the devil entered God's world.

In fact, there was no other way for the devil to get in. God had given his new creation to that first family. They were in charge of it. Whatever they did with it would determine its future course. History began in that home. And, under God, the whole universe was dependent upon it. The goodness of God's creation was in the hands of that husband and wife. If they remained faithful to God, his creation would remain good. The only way to bring sin into the world was through the door of Adam and Eve's home.

Notice the "togetherness" of that first sin. The Word of God goes out of its way to point out that Adam and Eve were in this thing together. The world was not plunged into sin because a man sinned, nor because a woman sinned, but because they both sinned. All the evil in this world began in that home God had made out of the man and woman created in his own image.

So the best institution on earth became, in a sense, the worst. The home became the source of sin and death. It is now the place where all children of all generations are conceived and born in sin, and where they make their first contact with sinful people—their own parents.

PRAYER

O God, we confess the sins of our home. We plead for your mercy in Christ, for both parents and children. Forgive us and cleanse us, we pray. For his sake, Amen.

Listen and Be Still

The First Gospel

*"He will crush your head, and
you will strike his heel."*
GENESIS 3:15

GENESIS 3:14-24

The gospel ("good news") we hear in our churches has a long history behind it. It came into the world through the first home, the same home through which sin had entered the world. Yes, the church began in a home, a sinful home.

God was there—to preach the first gospel sermon. The devil was there—to be condemned forever. And the sinners were there—to be saved from their sin by the grace of God. All the basic elements of a real worship service were right there in that home: the Word of God, the judgment of sin, and the gospel of salvation.

No, God did not abandon the family pattern he had established, even though it had turned against him. Instead, he began to use it as the pattern of redemption. After all, it was his point of contact with humankind.

So the good news God preached was a "family gospel." God promised to bring a Savior out of that same home in which sin began. The Son of God would come into this world—not the way angels enter it, but through the portals of human flesh. He would be born into it, the Son of Adam and Eve, one of their descendants—and yet without their sin. Today we know the gospel promise has been fulfilled, for Christ has come, and he has crushed the head of Satan while he himself was "crushed for our iniquities" (Isaiah 53:5).

PRAYER

Lord Jesus, we thank you for the ability to see your likeness in us. In the realm of emotions, as in all others, help us to learn obedience to you. In your name we pray. Amen.

Listen and Be Still

Perserving the Promise

*Noah found favor in the
eyes of the Lord.*
GENESIS 6:8

GENESIS 6:5-13

It was a long way from the first gospel promise to the fulfillment of that promise—from the family in Paradise where it was given, to the family in Bethlehem where Christ was born. At least four thousand years of history separated those two events.

How was that promise kept alive in a sinful world? The first man and his wife believed it, and were saved. But their first son, Cain, despised it and even killed his brother Abel, who believed it. So in the very first home the lines were drawn immediately— for and against the gospel. Every family inherited the sin of that first family, but not every family inherited the gospel promise that God had given to that first family. And as human beings multiplied, the problem of preserving the promise became more critical—for the opposition grew, while the believers became a dwindling minority.

But God himself had made the promise; it was a divine covenant. Though the minority had been reduced to just one godly home, that was enough to keep the promise alive. Noah found favor with God.

Notice how God used Noah's family to preach the gospel to a world that mocked it. The people who perished in the flood could not say they "never had a chance." For more than 100 years everyone lived in the light of the gospel coming to them from someone who believed God's promises.

PRAYER

Lord Jesus, we thank you for the ability to see your likeness in
us. In the realm of emotions, as in all others, help us to learn
obedience to you. In your name we pray. Amen.

Listen and Be Still

The Chosen Family

*"All peoples on earth will be
blessed through you."*
GENESIS 12:3

GENESIS 12:1-9

Saving Noah's family was not a permanent solution to the problem of preserving the gospel promise in a wicked world. Most of Noah's descendants were no better than their ancestors. Again the overwhelming majority despised the promise and threatened to extinguish it.

God chose not to keep on destroying the world every time it got to that point. To keep the gospel promise alive in a world of sinners, he would follow the same familiar family pattern. For the home was still God's main point of contact with his world.

God chose the family of Abram and proceeded to build a great nation out of it. To that nation he would commit his promise. It would be a nation set apart from all others, to guard the treasure of grace and to pass it along to successive generations.

Was God discriminating against other nations, excluding them arbitrarily? No. For he said to Abram, "All peoples on earth will be blessed through you." And today in Christ we can see that all nations have been blessed through that one chosen family.

But in spite of its favored place in history, the nation that grew out of Abram's family became the first to reject the gospel promise when it was finally fulfilled in Christ (John 1:11)! In the end that nation lost the treasure they had preserved for others.

PRAYER

Lord, keep us from sinning against our privileges. Dwell in our home with your Spirit, so that we may share in your salvation. In Jesus' name we pray. Amen.

Listen and Be Still

The Covenant Nation

*"I will establish my covenant. . . to be your God
and the God of your descendants after you."*
GENESIS 17:7

GENESIS 17:1-9

A nation is only as strong as its homes. They determine its character, its social structure, its politics, its place in history. This was particularly true of the nation God chose to carry the gospel promise that culminated in the coming of the Son of God as the world's Savior. It was a nation born of a family with whom God formally established his covenant of grace.

What was the secret of their strength? Not superior wisdom or greater virtue. They were not better than other nations, and in some respects they were even worse. Repeatedly they rebelled against God, and repeatedly he punished them. How they sinned against their privileges! They proved themselves altogether unworthy of the favor they enjoyed.

The secret of their survival was simply that God established his covenant with them. God had promised to be their God. And he kept that promise until it was finally fulfilled in Christ. Even when the people forsook him, God did not forsake them. He remembered his covenant with their father Abraham.

That promise made all the difference in the history of this world. For it produced the Savior of the world, the Son of God and the seed of Abraham. For that purpose the nation was preserved, even though many of its people perished in unbelief along the way.

PRAYER

O God, forbid that we should miss the great blessings of the gospel you preserved throughout history. May we believe it and live in the light of it. In Jesus, Amen.

Listen and Be Still

A God-Filled Home

The Lord blessed him and
his entire household.
2 SAMUEL 6:11

2 SAMUEL 6:9-15

Many families among God's Old Testament people sinned against their covenant privileges. But others kept the faith in true devotion. Some of them were outstanding, like Obed-Edom's family. This family is given honorable mention in the Bible—no doubt because one of the most remarkable things about it was that the ark of the covenant was in that home for three whole months.

The ark was the sacred symbol of God's presence among his people. It was a beautiful chest made of acacia wood, overlaid with gold, and decorated with figures of angels. Among other things it contained the stone tablets on which God had written the Ten Commandments. The ark was to be kept in the Most Holy Place in the tabernacle and later in the temple. No human hand was permitted to touch it directly. It had to be carried on poles inserted through rings at the four lower corners. Only the high priest was to enter the holy place where the ark was kept, and then only once a year, to make atonement for the sins of the people.

How, then, did the ark get into the house of Obed-Edom? Well, that's a long, dramatic story that we will look into in the next several readings. It will help us to answer the question *What makes a God-filled home, like the one of Obed-Edom?* This question is certainly a crucial one for us today.

PRAYER

God of grace, thank you for the examples of godly homes given to us in Scripture. Our homes are not always like them. Forgive our family sins, we pray. For Jesus' sake, Amen.

Listen and Be Still

The Journey of the Ark

Instead, he took it aside to
the house of Obed-Edom. . . .
2 SAMUEL 6:10

2 SAMUEL 6:9-12

In the previous reading we asked how the ark of the covenant got into the house of Obed-Edom. Many years earlier the ark was taken out of the Most Holy Place in the tabernacle and carried into battle with the Philistines. What a terrible mistake! The Israelites suffered a crushing defeat, and they lost the ark to the Philistines, who were afflicted with a deadly plague until they sent the ark back to the land of Israel. Then many of the people of Beth Shemesh, who received the ark from the Philistines, died. So they sent the ark on to Kiriath Jearim, where it was put in the house of a man named Abinidab. There it remained for many long years of sorrow and shame for Israel, culminating in the horrible defeat and death of their first king, Saul. (See 1 Samuel 4-31.)

When David became king, he decided to bring the ark back to the tabernacle, where it belonged. But tragedy struck again. One of the drivers of the cart carrying the ark was killed when he touched it. David didn't dare to move the ark further, so he put it in the house of Obed-Edom, which was nearby. No one else wanted it.

But notice what happened next. God "blessed...Obed-Edom and everything he [had], because of the ark." Wherever the ark had gone, only misery had followed, except in the house of Obed-Edom. Why? The answer is in the story itself; let us study it carefully.

PRAYER

Our Father, help us to understand this story so that we may build Christian homes where the rich blessings of your presence abound, through Christ our Lord. Amen.

Listen and Be Still

Using the Almighty

*"The glory has departed from Israel,
for the ark of God has been captured."*
1 SAMUEL 4:22

1 SAMUEL 4:5-11

You cannot build a God-honoring home if you do what the leaders of Israel did when they took the ark of the covenant into battle. They thought they could use God when they were desperate, even though they had broken every one of his commandments without conscience and without repentance.

They acted out of sheer superstition. But you will find the same thing in many homes today. People think they can summon God to serve them, like some butler or bellhop, in an emergency. For years they trample on his law, ignore his church, and profane his Word. But when trouble strikes, they think God must come and deliver them—quick! They have no real sorrow for their sins, and no real intention of repenting.

No, God cannot be used. To be sure, he says, "Call upon me in the day of trouble; I will deliver you" (Psalm 50:15). But he says that only to penitent people, to those who forsake their sins and beg for his mercy when they call on him for help. The unrepentant sinner will not be heard when he or she calls for help.

The Christian home is a place where confession of sin is a daily practice and where the saving grace of God abounds, through faith in Christ—which is what makes it a God-filled home, the only kind that can really call upon the Lord in times of trouble.

PRAYER

We need you in our home every day, O Lord. Forgive our sins, and help us to forsake them. Be merciful to us in all our needs. May we serve you, in Jesus' name. Amen.

Listen and Be Still

Only One God

*"The ark of the god of Israel
must not stay here with us."*
1 SAMUEL 5:7

1 SAMUEL 5:7

You cannot expect God to bless your home if you try to do with God what the Philistines did with the ark when they captured it. They took it into the temple of their god, Dagon, a dumb idol. They thought they could have both! But Dagon fell in pieces before the ark, and the people were punished with a frightful plague.

Many people today think they can have all the gods of this world in their homes—plus the only true God. Most of their worship goes to the gadgets and comforts and pleasures that have the love of their hearts. But, still, they feel they ought to have some place for God too. So they say family prayers now and then, do a bit of Bible reading perhaps, and become members of a church for the benefit of religious status.

Of course, when these families participate in their church and when they attend worship services, they take their gods with them—at least in spirit. After all, they are still the same people at heart. And that's how churches become secular and worldly, preferring the word of humankind to the Word of God. They ignore the first commandment of God's law, which says, "You shall have no other gods before me" (Exodus 20:3). Such families are like temples of Dagon—with God added.

No, you can't have a God-filled home, or a God-filled church, if you don't have the only true God—alone.

PRAYER

Dear Lord, help us to keep the gods of this world out of our home and out of our church. Give us the grace to worship you—and you alone. In Jesus' name, Amen.

Listen and Be Still

The Curse of Curiosity

God struck down some of the
men of Beth Shemesh.
1 SAMUEL 6:19

1 SAMUEL 6:10-21

Some of the people of Beth Shemesh were intrigued by the ark of God. Their first reaction, when they saw the ark coming, was a good one. They built an altar and made a sacrifice to the Lord. But then they became curious. Someone said, "I wonder what's in it. Let's take a look." So they lifted the lid and peeked inside. No one was permitted to do that. God had threatened punishment on anyone who did. And that punishment fell heavily on them.

Today many people are merely curious about God. This is the way they approach the Bible, the church, and even the deepest mysteries of the Christian faith. Nothing is sacred to them. They have no sense of holy reverence when they deal with holy things. The Word of God is subjected to inquisitive scrutiny merely for scientific speculation. People flip through the pages of holy Scripture as though it were some novelty book. They speculate about it. Bible courses in some schools become mere academic studies. God becomes an item of investigation in which he must answer all the little questions of our tiny minds.

The curse of religious curiosity is a dreadful thing. If you want a God-filled home, you must worship when you read God's Word, approach it with holy awe, and surrender your heart in humble faith.

PRAYER

O God, we approach you with fear and trembling, for we are sinners in your sight. We come with many questions; give us the one answer we need: Jesus, our Lord. Amen.

Listen and Be Still

The Forgotten God

It was a long time. . . that the ark remained at Kiriath Jearim.
1 SAMUEL 7:2

1 SAMUEL 7:1-6

The people of Kiriath Jearim were not very impressed by the presence of the ark. Apparently they were only taking it off the hands of the Beth Shemites, who were afraid of it. So they just put it in away the house of Abinidab, and it seems that the people simply forgot about it for many years.

Meanwhile, some terrible things happened in Israel. The people rebelled against the prophet Samuel, which was really rebellion against God. They demanded a king, who led them down the pathway to ruin (1 Samuel 8-31). It was a dark chapter in the history of God's people—while the ark lay forgotten in Abinadab's house.

Perhaps the people in Abinidab's household paid attention to the ark and to the God it symbolized. After all, Eleazar was consecrated to guard it. But imagine—throughout most of the "house" of Israel, the sacred symbol of God's presence was simply forgotten.

Many homes are like that today. God may have a place in them—but not a very conspicuous place. You'd never know he was there if someone didn't tell you. It doesn't look as if God has anything to do with what goes on in that house; let him stay in his place, out of the way. Such families pay God the compliment of recognition, but he must not bother them as they live their lives without him. Is your home like that in any way?

PRAYER

Deliver us, Lord, from the sins of modern worldliness, and begin right in our homes. Take the central place there, we pray, and help us to be faithful. In Jesus' name, Amen.

Listen and Be Still

The Penalty of Presumption

He died there beside the ark of God.
2 SAMUEL 6:7

2 SAMUEL 6:1-8

If you want to come home again, don't make the mistake Uzzah made. He took hold of the ark because he thought it was going to fall from the cart. To us, it may look as though his punishment was too severe. After all, he meant well; he was only trying to help. But he made a fundamental and fatal mistake in his thinking about God. He thought God needed him!

God had expressly commanded that no one's hand should ever touch the sacred ark. Uzzah knew that. He may have acted on impulse when he took hold of the ark, but it was a very revealing impulse. It betrayed the presumption that God is dependent upon people.

John Newton once said, "If you see the ark of God toppling, you can be perfectly certain it is due to a swimming in your head." In other words, if you think God needs you, there is something radically wrong with your idea of God.

Instead, you need God! It's an infinite condescension on God's part that he will live with you in your home. And although your hand must always be ready to serve God, don't ever think he can't get along without it. Remember, the ark never did fall from that cart. Uzzah was the one who fell. Presumption in our relationship with God is a deadly sin. For it denies the basic fact in this universe—that God is really *God!*

PRAYER

We confess, Lord, that we do not always recognize your sovereignty in our lives and in our world. Be merciful to us and forgive our presumption! In Jesus' name, Amen.

Listen and Be Still

A Home for God

"The Lord has blessed the household of Obed-Edom. . . ."
2 SAMUEL 6:12

PSALM 128

Now that we've reviewed the story of the ark, we know some things we must not do if we want a home that is truly blessed by God. We must not think we can summon God to serve us; nor must we put him in competition with other gods. We may not subject God to idle curiosity; nor may we live in indifference to him.

What made the house of Obed-Edom different? Why did the ark bring only blessing there? Because God was at home there!

Just imagine what Obed-Edom said when he was told that the ark was coming to his house. He probably said to his family, "Think of it! Our house is going to be the Most Holy Place, the innermost sanctuary of the whole nation! The sacred symbol of God's promise is coming here—the hope of salvation!"

And we can be sure that he and his family began to clean house and rearrange everything, not only to make room for the ark, but to give it the central place, where it would be the heart of the home. Wherever you went in that house, you could surely say, "God is here!"

For three whole months that house was the spiritual heart of Israel—the Most Holy Place of the kingdom of God! The Lord's gospel promise found its finest expression there: a truly God-filled home; a family who believed the promise and honored God faithfully!

PRAYER

Help us to learn from the example of the family of Obed-Edom, Lord, and thus to share in the blessings you wish to shower upon us also. For Jesus' sake, Amen.

Listen and Be Still

A Picture of Peace

The Lord blessed him and
his entire household.
2 SAMUEL 6:11

PSALM 127

An unknown poet has given us this rather imaginative picture of the house of Obed-Edom:

The house of Obed-Edom, where safe the ark abode,
while there were wars and fightings on every mountain road,
while men engaged in battle in every valley fair,
the house of Obed-Edom had peace beyond compare.
With famine on the border and fury in the camp,
with starving children huddled in the black night's shivering
    damp;
with mothers crying sadly, and every moan a prayer—
in the house of Obed-Edom, was neither want nor care.
The fields of Obed-Edom, no foemen trod them down;
the towers of Obed-Edom were like a fortress'd town;
and only grace and gladness came daily down the road
to the house of Obed-Edom, where the ark of God abode.
The kin of Obed-Edom are on the earth today.
In a house of Obed-Edom your family too may stay;
if, more than all the treasures for which men toil and plod,
you prize the covenant blessing, the ark, the Christ of God.

PRAYER

Eternal God, we know how important the homes of your people
are. May ours be useful in your service, to communicate your
promise of salvation in Jesus. Amen.

Listen and Be Still

The Ark Goes Home

David…brought up the ark of God. . .
to the City of David with rejoicing.
2 SAMUEL 6:12

2 SAMUEL 6:12-19

The ark of the covenant, the sacred symbol of God's presence among his people, could not remain indefinitely in one family's house, even though that was a godly home. Eventually the ark had to be brought back to the Most Holy Place in the tabernacle, from which it had been taken many years before.

But notice that no one dared to bring the ark back to the tabernacle until after it had brought so much blessing in the house of Obed-Edom. Everyone remembered the trail of misery the ark had left, wherever it went. But when King David and his people saw what happened in the house of Obed-Edom, they were no longer afraid of the ark. They decided it was safe to bring the ark back where it belonged.

The home of Obed-Edom taught the whole nation a very important lesson. It demonstrated the kind of faith that ought to have been in every home. Its spiritual character undoubtedly became a subject of conversation, as well as a pattern for others to follow. And, of course, everybody wanted the blessings that were showered on that home. The people probably thought, "Well, if the ark can do so much good in the house of Obed-Edom, why can't it do the same for all of us?"

The whole nation was given a new spiritual perspective because of the faith of one God-filled home.

PRAYER

Heavenly Father, help us to see more clearly how important our homes are within our nation. Teach us to set the kind of example that others may imitate, to your glory. Amen.

Listen and Be Still

The Church Home

And all the people went to their homes.
2 SAMUEL 6:19

PSALM 134

Our family life largely determines our church life. Our worship of God at home during the week has a telling effect upon our worship of God in church on Sunday. That probably explains why the weekend is really the "weak-end" for so many people.

But the opposite is also true. Our worship of God in his house on Sunday has a powerful influence on everything we do during the week at home, at work, and at school. So it works both ways. The church and the home are mutually involved in each other's affairs.

It was a great moment when the ark of the covenant was returned to the tabernacle. David and his people observed it with a splendid service of worship. There were songs, sacrifices, and rededication to the service of God. Everyone was deeply impressed.

But then what? The record says simply, "And all the people went to their homes." That's really the end of the long story of the travels of the ark. It was now at home again, and "the people went to their homes." But would they carry the inspiration of that high moment with them and continue in their homes to live in the faith they had expressed so warmly in God's house? Would they remember the lessons they learned and repent of the sins they committed? They now had a God-filled church again. But what about their homes?

PRAYER

Gracious God, may the lessons we learn in church live on in our home today and every day, and may our home be a blessing to our church. In Jesus' name we pray. Amen.

Listen and Be Still

Reformation of the Home

*"He will turn the hearts of
the fathers to their children."*
MALACHI 4:6

MALACHI 4

It was never easy to keep the gospel promise alive in this world, but it became practically impossible near the end of the Old Testament era. Why? Because family life had degenerated among God's people. As a result, there had to be a reformation in the people's home life before Christ came to fulfill the promise of a Savior. Faith had to be restored in the hearts of parents and their children. The godly community needed to be reestablished. If it weren't, Christianity might not have flourished so well in the generation to whom it came.

That's what Malachi meant when he said that God would send a prophet who would "turn the hearts of the fathers to their children." God would send a prophet to reform the home and thus prepare the way for Christ. We know that prophet was John the Baptist, whose birth was foretold by an angel using the very words of the prophet Malachi (see Luke 1:17).

Twenty centuries have elapsed since that day, but again it is becoming more and more difficult to keep the gospel promise alive in the modern home. There's a great spiritual chasm between the generations in many families. The hearts of parents and children are not turned toward each other in mutual Christian faith.

We need another reformation. And the most important place for it to occur is right in our own homes!

PRAYER

Lord, we stand amazed by how you fulfilled your promise and
preserved your people throughout history. Bring the power of
your Word to bear on us. In Jesus' name, Amen.

Listen and Be Still

Fulfillment—at Home

Joseph [was] the husband of Mary,
of whom was born Jesus.
MATTHEW 1:16

MATTHEW 1:18-25

The day for which the years had been yearning had arrived at last! It was the crucial hour of human history, the sacred moment around which the centuries revolved. God was ready to redeem his covenant promise, sending his Son, the Savior of the world.

But the Son of God did not come to this earth as a full-grown man. Nor did he come by way of the temple, the marketplace, or the school. He came by way of the home. He was born! He had a mother!

She, of course, was a child of the covenant. God was thinking of her when he promised Adam and Eve that he would bring forth a Savior from their home—their seed—to crush the serpent's head. Mary became a mother to fulfill that promise. Her baby was the Son of God.

No, he didn't have a father on earth—only in heaven. And he didn't have a mother in heaven—only on earth. He exchanged his heavenly home for an earthly home so that he could save us from our sins. It took a tremendous miracle to fulfill the gospel promise, the miracle of the incarnation! And it cost God a high price, the blood of his Son, to provide someone who could earn salvation for us.

From the beginning, the home was God's point of contact with his world. Now he used it to send his Son as the Savior of the world.

PRAYER

Lord Jesus, thank you for entering this sinful world by way of a humble home. Sanctify our homes with your saving presence. In your name alone we pray. Amen.

Listen and Be Still

Truly Christian Homes

To those who believed in his name, he
gave the right to become children of God.
JOHN 1:12

JOHN 1:6-14

When you read about the blessings that came to the house of Obed-Edom during those ninety days while the ark of the covenant was there, you might be inclined to say, "Well, that was a very exceptional case; it couldn't happen again; we could never have homes like that today."

But we can! In fact, we can have homes that are even better, with even greater blessings. We can have the ark in our homes for a lifetime. You see, everything that was symbolized in that ark was fulfilled in Jesus Christ. And to those who receive him as their Savior he gives the spiritual power to become the children of God. By his Spirit, he lives with them in their homes day by day.

He is Immanuel, "God with us," the New Testament ark of the covenant. Thus we can have truly Christian homes. Millions of people have been born and raised in such homes, and then they go out to set up homes of their own like that. Indeed, these homes constitute the Most Holy Place of the kingdom of God! They are the heart of the church.

When people come to your home, do they see Christ in the center of things? Do your children feel that the Son of God really governs their home? What if Jesus entered your house, in the flesh—would he feel at home there? And would you be quite comfortable with him?

PRAYER

O God, help us to make our homes truly Christian, a place where your Word is the lamp, where your Son is Lord, and where your Spirit is our strength. In Jesus, Amen.

Listen and Be Still

At Home with Christ

A woman named Martha
opened her home to him.
LUKE 10:38

LUKE 10:38-42

If Jesus came to your house to spend a day or two…
If he came unexpectedly, I wonder what you'd do;
Oh, I know you'd give your nicest room to such an honored
  guest,
And all the food you'd serve to him would be the very best….
But when you saw him coming, would you meet him at the door
With arms outstretched in welcome to your heavenly visitor?
Or would you have to change some things before you let him in?
Could you let Jesus walk right in where he had never been?…
Would life for you continue as it does from day to day?
Would you keep right on saying the things you always say?
Would you be glad to have him stay forever, on and on,
Or would you sigh with great relief when he at last was gone?
It might be interesting to know the things that you would do
If Jesus Christ in person came to spend some time with you.

–Lois Blanchard

PRAYER

Our Father in heaven, we are ashamed that we often make our
Lord uncomfortable in our family circle. Help us to be more
faithful to the promise we have made to you. In Jesus' name,
Amen.

Listen and Be Still

Salvation in the Home

Jesus said to him, "Today salvation has come to this house."
LUKE 19:9

LUKE 19:1-10

The case of Zacchaeus gives us a very valuable insight into the ministry of Jesus. He found the sinner along the way, but he insisted on going home with him so that he could bring salvation to that house. In other words, it was a family matter. The Lord was concerned not only about Zacchaeus but also about everyone in his house.

Notice that Jesus called attention to the history of that home. He identified the head of the house as a son of Abraham, with whom God had established his covenant many years ago. Zacchaeus had forsaken that heritage. He was a lost son. But Jesus brought him back, and that's how he brought salvation to his house. The sinner found his Savior right in his own home, in the family circle. There, in the person of the Son of God, he saw the fulfillment of God's promise and evidences of God's faithfulness.

Jesus went out of his way to direct his ministry to the home. Many of his parables are set in family situations—the prodigal son, the marriage feast, the rich man and Lazarus, just to name a few. Many of his miracles also involved family problems. Each time he raised someone from the dead, it was in a family setting: a widow's son, a little daughter, a dear brother.

Like his Father in heaven, Jesus made the home his main point of contact, and he still does that today!

PRAYER

Lord Jesus, we confess that a Christian home is a privilege we often take for granted. Help us to make the most of this gift, to serve you better. In your name we pray. Amen.

Listen and Be Still

The Pentecost Promise

"The promise is for you and your children
and for all who are far off. . . ."
ACTS 2:39

ACTS 2:29-47

The New Testament church began in a house. That's where the disciples were assembled when the Holy Spirit descended upon them. And immediately they began to preach to the people who gathered in and around that house. And what was the text of that Pentecost sermon? It was a "family text"—the verse at the head of this page. It put the whole Christian gospel in the context of God's relationship to his people.

Thus the New Testament church began—with a family gospel—for the families present, and for all those who were yet "far off," who would be brought into God's family circle throughout the centuries.

That sermon set the pattern for the whole mission program of the early church. The Holy Spirit, whom Jesus had promised to send to his church, took the same covenant gospel and carried it forward into the New Testament world. Like the Father and the Son, the Third Person of the Trinity made his point of contact with human beings by way of the home.

Three thousand people were converted that day as a result of Peter's sermon. It was spectacular. But even more spectacular is the fact that many times that number have been converted since that day with the very same gospel! This is the gospel that builds the Christian church.

PRAYER

O Lord, help us to sense the tie that binds us to those who have gone before us in the long history of your church. We thank you for our place in it. In Jesus, Amen.

Listen and Be Still

From House to House

*"I . . . have taught you publicly
and from house to house."*
ACTS 20:20

ACTS 20:17-24

It's interesting to observe the method of the first missionaries of the Christian church. As a rule, they didn't set up big meetings to draw big crowds. To be sure, they did preach to crowds whenever they were given the opportunity. But their main approach was quite different. They spoke to little groups here and there, many of which were families. They went into the home.

When Paul reviewed his ministry in Ephesus, he summarized his method with this statement: "I...have taught you publicly and from house to house." This is a beautiful picture of mission work. The gospel was presented in the family circle. Parents and children were taught the meaning of the gospel promise. And that was a very important thing to do in the Gentile world, for most of those people were probably not familiar with the history of God's promises to Old Testament believers. They had to know what was behind the gospel of Christ, what had produced it. They had to see themselves included in a long line of God-filled homes that reached back to the beginning of time.

Missionaries are still settting up Christian homes in unchurched cultures today—"from house to house." And our churches are made up of such homes, where faith is passed along through the generations. Indeed, many of us have come into Christ's church that way.

PRAYER

Thank you, dear Lord, for the privilege of public worship and for the privilege of having the gospel right in our own home. In Jesus' name we pray. Amen.

Listen and Be Still

And Your Household

"Believe in the Lord Jesus, and you will be saved—you and your household."

ACTS 16:31

ACTS 16:23-31

Acts 16:31 is one of the most abused verses in the Bible. It is usually quoted this way, without the last four words: "Believe in the Lord Jesus, and you will be saved." But there is not a period there, for Paul added the words "you and your household."

Without those last four words, that sentence is not the gospel. Without them, the rest of the gospel is distorted.

There's a wrong theology behind the abuse of this verse. It implies that the salvation of a soul is strictly a personal matter between an individual and God. In other words, the gospel is supposed to find individuals here and there, one after another, bring them to salvation independently, and then string them all together as you might string beads. The church of Christ, according to this view, is gathered one by one.

But that's not the way Paul preached the gospel to the Philippian jailer, nor to anyone else, and that's not the way the church has been built in history. To be sure, salvation is a personal matter, but it is much more than that. And it can never be only that. It always involves other people. No one is saved as an island. Humans are social beings, with roots in homes.

That's why God has given us a family gospel, the one that Paul preached—the gospel with a promise to parents and children.

PRAYER

Our Father, may each member our family believe in the Lord Jesus Christ and be saved. May we have this one thing in common, by your grace. In Jesus' name, Amen.

Listen and Be Still

With All His House

He had come to believe in God—
he and his whole family.
ACTS 16:34

ACTS 16:29-40

Here is a beautiful picture of family evangelism from which we can learn a few lessons today.

Immediately after Paul told the Philippian jailer that the gospel was for him and his household, he found himself in the family group, teaching them the Word of God and explaining the gospel promise to them. We don't know how many were there, but we do know that everyone in the household "had come to believe in God." The word "house" implies that there were children present, so the children were included in this family conversion. No wonder the jailer "was filled with joy."

Many experts today are saying that modern society is coming apart because its basic unity, the family, is disintegrating. And they are right. There is plenty of evidence to support this claim. Some students of social problems have even suggested setting up special public boarding schools for preschool children, to take them away from the bad influences in their homes. This is a national concern in many countries.

But we have a gospel that is designed precisely to solve the number-one problem of our times—we have a family gospel with the promise of salvation for parents and children. How tragic if we preach it any other way than the way Paul preached it: "Believe in the Lord Jesus, and you will be saved—*you and your household.*"

PRAYER

O Lord, reach into today's homes with the family gospel. Bless those who take it from house to house. Bless the families who hear it, we pray. In Jesus' name, Amen.

Listen and Be Still

For Children Too

Then immediately he and all
his family were baptized.
ACTS 16:33

LUKE 18:15-17

Having traced the line of the covenant home in the Bible, it should be obvious that we cannot exclude children from the sacrament of holy baptism, if in fact they are the children of Christian parents. We call baptism "the sign and seal of the covenant." So, if the gospel promise is given to both parents and children, then both should wear its sign and seal.

No, baptism does not save the souls of children. But neither does it save the souls of their parents. The water itself does not wash away sin. But it does point to the washing away of sin through the blood of Jesus Christ. This is what Christian parents believe. They simply trust in the promises of God—and not only for themselves but also for their children. They are in this together.

Baptism, then, must be more than a mere formality, a christening service—or worse, a sort of religious status symbol. When the Philippian jailer was baptized with his whole family, they took the sacrament seriously. And it was the finest hour they had ever known in their home—a whole family receiving the sign and seal of God's promise because they really believed it! "One faith, one Lord, one baptism!" Another home was added to the church of Jesus Christ that day—a God-filled home.

PRAYER
"Our children, Lord, in faith and prayer, we now devote to Thee; let them Thy covenant mercies share and Thy salvation see." In Jesus' name alone we pray. Amen.

Listen and Be Still

Covenant-Breakers

*They went out from us, but they
did not really belong to us.*
1 John 2:19

Sometimes children go astray. There are those who never accept the gospel promise when they grow up, in spite of excellent training at home, church, and school. And there are those who do accept the promise but then forsake it later.

It happened already in the early church. The apostle John says that those who forsook the faith proved thereby that they never really had it. The sign and seal of God's promises meant nothing to them. Among them was one of the first missionaries, Demas (2 Timothy 4:10).

How do you explain a thing like that? You don't. But neither do you use it as a reason to doubt God's covenant promise. After all, the overwhelming majority of children raised by Christian parents grow up to maturity in the Christian faith. This is the rule in the history of the church; those who break the covenant are exceptions. Since we are all conceived and born in sin, the wonder is not that some children forsake the faith but that so many believe it and live by it.

Besides, don't forget that some of those who leave do come back! John Mark did. And so have many others. God brings some back through radio and television media; he brings others back through personal contact with a believer. Parents and families never stop praying for those who have left. God wants them to be saved!

Prayer

Lord, we pray for those who have left the faith. Please bring them back. We are asking for miracles, which you have done so often for the sake of Christ. In his name, Amen.

The Mind of Christ

*Bring them up in the training
and instruction of the Lord.*

EPHESIANS 6:1-4   EPHESIANS 6:4

The covenant with our God carries with it some very heavy duties. If we accept this gospel promise in true faith, for ourselves and our children, we obligate ourselves to train our children accordingly. Indeed, it will be the burning desire of our hearts to "bring them up in the training and instruction of the Lord."

One of the most powerful influences in the lives of our children is formal education. They spend more of their waking hours at school than at home or church—at least five hours a day, five days a week, for nine or ten months every school year. During that time they are exposed to all the mighty forces of learning. The world of knowledge opens before them—-act and fiction, philosophy and poetry, science and art, history and religion. They are subjected to truth and myth of all kinds.

Children raised by Christian parents have special privileges. God wants them to see his world the way he sees it—in the light of his Word, with the cross of his Son at the center of it. God doesn't want them to have an education that excludes him. Wherever our children are educated, we want them to know Christ.

That's why Christian parents in many communities provide Christian schools for their children. They want not only the highest academic standards and the best teachers but, above all, teaching in the Christian faith. Wherever our children are educated, we want them to know Christ.

PRAYER

Father, in this world of exploding knowledge, give us the mind of Christ, "in whom are hidden all the treasures of wisdom and knowledge." In his name we pray. Amen.

Listen and Be Still

Mixed Marriage

Do not be yoked together with unbelievers.
2 Corinthians 6:14

2 Corinthians 6:14-18

In the long history of the Christian church, nothing has done it more damage than mixed marriage. Young people who marry outside the Christian faith soon find themselves living in a home that is divided against itself. And it can become a bitter battleground, unless one of the spouses surrenders—but it usually turns out to be the wrong one. There simply is no way to harmonize belief and unbelief.

The children of such homes are often casualties; even if one parent permits the other to control their religious training, the children can feel the tension; they know what's going on behind the scenes. And often they resent it so much that they rebel against all religion.

As a rule, young people who enter mixed marriages often refuse advice from anyone. They think their "love" can overcome all obstacles. All who enter marriage, however, must consider seriously that their marriage is not strictly their own business. Marriage affects not only them, but it will also affect their children and the church of Jesus Christ. And with that we may not trifle!

The only solution for a mixed marriage is to "believe in the Lord Jesus, and you will be saved—you and your household" (Acts 16:31). Both parties must find their salvation in Christ and then reestablish their home on his promise. Thank God that this can and does happen!

PRAYER

Gracious God, we pray for those who have spiritual struggles in their homes. Help them to find each other at the cross of your Son, Jesus, and to live wholly for him. Amen.

Listen and Be Still

The Heart of Our Faith

If God is for us, who can be against us?
ROMANS 8:31

ROMANS 8:31-39

The doctrine of the covenant is the heart of the Christian faith. God is determined to keep his promise alive in this world. Even in times of great evil when the spread of the gospel was in grave peril, God broke through the opposition to revive his people and bring them back to him. And each time, people rediscovered the fundamental truth of Paul's triumphant question: "If God is for us, who can be against us?"

In today's world as families are torn apart and when biological families often do not function as God intends, God shows himself to be for us by adopting us as sons and daughters into his own family. God's family often incorporates our biological families, but it also transcends the biological family.

If we are part of a Christian family by birth or by adoption, we need to thank God for this wonderful blessing and do all we can to live faithfully for him.

If we are not part of a family in which our parents or siblings live by faith in Jesus, we need to recognize that God is creating a family for us, in the church. There we will find people who will be brothers, sisters, and even spiritual parents to us, giving us nurture and direction for Jesus' sake. Thank God for the family that transcends all boundaries!

PRAYER

Thank you, Lord, for homes that stand in the living tradition of your covenant promise. We rededicate ourselves and our families to your service. In Jesus' name we pray. Amen.

Listen and Be Still

LIVING THE LIFE OF FAITH

INSPIRING OUR FAITH

30 MEDITATIONS AND READINGS

BY REV. HENRY P. KRANENBURG

REV. HENRY P. KRANENBURG

Most people can identify a person or group of persons to whom they look up. That's why, as Christians, we try to model and teach what it means to believe in Jesus, and we hope others will catch on. But it's not just a matter of being models or good examples to others; we also need godly models.

In Hebrews 11 God gives us a list of several people in the Bible who serve as models or "heroes" of faith. Since God is the one who tells us about these people, it's a good idea for us to look at them and try to see what God wants us to see in them. In this way we can be encouraged and grow in our faith.

These reflections guide us in looking at heroes of faith in Hebrews 11 and in other passages as a way of "pumping up" our faith and inspiring us to live by faith each day in God's strength.

Rev. Kranenburg has served as a pastor in a number of Christian Reformed churches in Canada.

Faith Makes a Difference

"According to your faith
will it be done to you."
MATTHEW 9:29

MATTHEW 9:27-31

I don't know about you, but my faith experience through childhood, youth, and adulthood up to the present makes me a little anxious about passages like the one we're looking at today. It implies that the blind men were healed because they had enough faith to believe Jesus could do it.

Part of the reason for my anxiety is that I feel some guilt. I wonder, "If I had more faith, could I do more for other people, like moving 'mountains' of sickness or famine or relationship problems?" Another part of the reason is that I wonder if I really measure up to what God expects of me. Jesus said to some people that he was pretty impressed with their faith; I wonder what he thinks of mine.

My guess is that you might wonder about these things too. Over the years I've come to understand more deeply, though, that faith isn't really intended by God to be about "performance." Faith is about my relationship with God, a relationship that isn't just about "church" stuff but about life itself—every part of life.

What's exciting and encouraging is that Jesus says our faith is something we can work on. Faith can grow and develop. That means my faith is about where I am going—and growing. Whether you're young or old, I hope you will be encouraged to grow in faith.

PRAYER

Lord, we believe many things about you. Yet sometimes we struggle with faith and what it should mean for us. Please help us grow in faith as you want us to. In Jesus' name, Amen.

Listen and Be Still

Faith Helps Faith

*[May] you and I. . . be mutually
encouraged by each other's faith.*
ROMANS 1:12

ROMANS 1:7-12

When God gives suggestions to help our faith, that tells me God isn't just taking note of my weaknesses—God wants to help me. This tells me that faith is not just my own personal battle but that God involves himself in it too. A passage like Romans 1, which tells us how we can grow in faith, lets me know that I don't need to hide a weaker faith because God has already been working on ways to help me.

I have a cartoon in my files. Two people are standing looking at an almost flat tire on a car. The one says to the other: "My faith is like that tire. It has a slow leak, but if I pump it up once a week, it'll hold."

God provides ways for us to "pump up" our faith: Bible reading, prayer, study groups, times of reflection, church worship, and more. And in several of these ways God provides other believers to encourage us. Just as Paul notes in Romans 1, God wants us to be encouraged and strengthened—"pumped up"—by the faith of other believers. That's why it's good to take a look at people who are faithful witnesses, "heroes" of faith.

Maybe you know such faithful people in your life. Or perhaps God has used your faith to help someone else. Either way, people of faith are important to people of faith. Thank God for such people in your life, and ask him to remind you how their examples have helped you.

PRAYER

Thank you, Lord, that my faith is not just about me. Help me to find encouragement from other believers. Help me also to be an encouragement to others. In Jesus' name, Amen.

Listen and Be Still

Heroes Make a Difference

"Do not be misled: 'Bad company corrupts good character.'"
1 CORINTHIANS 15:33

2 TIMOTHY 1:3-7

Have your parents ever said they don't want you hanging around with a certain "crowd"? Maybe they said something like that, and it bugged you. Or maybe you appreciated that they had your best interests in mind. Either way, at the heart of that kind of concern is an important principle: the people that are part of our lives have an effect on us.

Paul recognized this truth, and he pointed out something similar in the life of Timothy, a young church leader who was raised in "good company."

For many of us, our parents and grandparents are the major shapers of our lives. Others of us can point to helpful guardians, teachers, and other role models. All of us are influenced also by the other people around us—classmates, co-workers, neighbors.

That's why God points out that when it comes to our faith, who we "hang out" with makes a difference. God invites us to shape our faith by "hanging out" with heroes or good models of faith, people whose faith is noticeable.

Looking at faith heroes and inspiring examples of faith is an interesting and helpful way to have our faith "pumped up." It's also a good reminder that God uses people of faith in our lives, just as he may use us in others' lives.

PRAYER

Lord, sometimes we feel alone in our faith, and at times we even feel lonely. Thank you for people who accompany us on the journey. Help us to learn from them. In Jesus, Amen.

Listen and Be Still

Faith

*Faith is being sure of what we hope for
and certain of what we do not see.*
HEBREWS 11:1

MATTHEW 8:5-13

Faith would be a lot easier if we had more proof. But then, of course, it wouldn't be faith.

God knows that we struggle with faith. He talks about it in the Bible and calls us to work on it. And what we have to work on is "being sure of what we hope for and certain of what we do not see."

You and I can hope for a lot of things; often we can feel pretty certain about a number of things; and there really are a lot of things that we just plain know for sure (unless we're terribly skeptical). But as we think about faith, we need to understand that faith is not the ability to "psych" ourselves up about unproved things. No, when our Lord speaks to us in his Word about faith, the focus is on God and all his promises.

One of the teachings I learned as a child puts it nicely. It's from the Heidelberg Catechism, and it says that faith is both a knowledge that everything God says in the Bible is true, and an assurance that all this is actually true for me. This means I trust in God and in what God says—even when I can't prove it—not because I am such a good "truster" but because God is such a trustworthy God and Savior.

The centurion of Matthew 8 had that kind of faith. He went to Jesus and believed what Jesus said. The centurion had faith, but Jesus did the healing.

PRAYER

Lord, please help us to keep in mind that faith is not an end product; you are the object of our faith. Help us to trust you and to see you working in our lives. In your name, Amen.

Listen and Be Still

God Created

By faith we understand that the universe
was formed at God's command. . . .
HEBREWS 11:3

GENESIS 1:1-3

There certainly has been a lot of debate about creation and evolution since Darwin, also among Christians. If the author of Hebrews had written this after Charles Darwin, I wonder if he might have written a little more.

But the fact is that God does not say more here. The matter of creation is also a matter of faith, and God expects us to accept that—even if we don't know and can't understand all the details.

If you take time to read the whole of Genesis 1, you'll notice a few repetitive "refrains." The one I'm referring to is "And God said. . . ." I may not understand precisely what took place on each day God created, but whatever and however it happened, it clearly happened "at God's command."

It's important that we understand this fact. God wants us to keep in mind first of all that he is the Creator and we are creatures; this is God's world. And I think God also wants us to know that this world and you and I are not here by accident: we are here "at God's command."

Faith won't tell me all the details of the creation event. It tells me to trust the Word of God given to us in the Bible. Faith understands that the issue isn't how—the issue is God. And if I trust God at all, I accept God's Word. That's why the Bible—and Jesus (the Word made flesh)—are crucial to faith.

PRAYER

Father, thank you for your Word by which you created this world—including me. Thank you that I am no accident. Help me to hear all your words for me, in Jesus. Amen.

Listen and Be Still

By Faith—Abel

By faith Abel offered God a better sacrifice. . .
[and] was commended as a righteous man.
HEBREWS 11:4

GENESIS 4:1-16

Abel is the first "hero" of faith mentioned in Hebrews 11. At first glance he doesn't seem particularly special. What's so significant about Abel's faith?

The story of Cain and Abel is really a story about two brothers at worship. Something about Abel's worship rings far more true with God than Cain's does. What's interesting is that on the surface Cain doesn't seem bad. At least he brings sacrifices to God, which is more than some do.

But the point is that that's not the point. Faith is not just about doing some proper religious actions, like showing up for worship and bringing your "sacrifice." There's something deeper. Faith is about what's on the inside when you do these religious actions. God isn't looking for performers, he's looking for people to trust him and love him. God wants our heart to be where our action is. And when it's about our heart, it's about all of life, not just a worship ritual or other religious action.

When Sunday comes, I hope you will go to church to worship God, because that's what God wants. But I hope you also remember that what God is interested in is your heart, not just your performance.

Abel's worship had integrity. God says that if we come with a sincere desire to love and serve him, he will accept our worship. And it will make a difference.

PRAYER

Lord, you don't look for award performances when it comes to faith. Help me in honesty to confess my sin and bring my heart to you in Jesus. Help my faith to grow. Amen.

Listen and Be Still

By Faith—Enoch

By faith Enoch was taken from this life. . .
commended as one who pleased God.
HEBREWS 11:5

GENESIS 5:18-27

We don't know much about Enoch. We know he had a son named Methuselah who lived 969 years. And we know that Enoch pleased God and walked with him. Enoch also lived a relatively short life—compared to his father and his son. Enoch lived 365 years. Actually, though, Enoch didn't die. He was "taken from this life, so that he did not experience death." And the reason, says Hebrews 11, is that he "pleased God."

So how does one please God? The answer Hebrews 11 gives is this: pleasing God means you come to him, you believe he exists, and you believe that he rewards those who earnestly seek him.

That's the kind of person Enoch was. He didn't just go after some earthly things that God could give him, like health, or money, or good grades, or fine children. He looked for and found God. That seeking and finding was part of his life, and the end came in finding what he had searched for.

We still may not know a lot about Enoch, but we know something that he didn't know. We know that the way to seek God is by seeking Jesus. No one can come to God except through Jesus (John 14:6).

God says that if you are looking for him in Jesus, you will find him. And he will be pleased because that's how he wants us to grow in faith.

PRAYER

Lord, sometimes we think that faith is a one-step deal—that once we have the facts, it's complete. Help us to keep seeking and to keep finding you through Jesus. Amen.

Listen and Be Still

Earnestly Seeking a Savior

Believe that he exists and that he
rewards those who earnestly seek him.
HEBREWS 11:6

JOHN 12:12-19

Palm Sunday is the day we remember that Jesus made his "triumphal entry" into Jerusalem, just six days before he was crucified. The people in Jerusalem were pretty excited about Jesus' coming into the city. Many of them figured this was the beginning of a national uprising to throw out the Roman government. That's the kind of leader they were earnestly seeking, and Jesus seemed to be the one sent by God to do it.

So these God-believing people, who had already been waiting for years for someone like Jesus to come to their political rescue, were pretty excited. Thus the palm branches and shouting and excitement.

Six days later that same crowd switched from shouting "Hosanna!" to shouting "Crucify him!" They were earnestly seeking someone all right, but Jesus wasn't coming through with what they had in mind. Figuring he was just a disappointing fraud, these people now wanted him out. They were seeking the kind of savior needed to fit their idea of salvation. So when the Savior actually came, they didn't recognize him.

Jesus' triumphal entry is a reminder that earnestly seeking God has to do with who God is, not who we want him to be. That's why God points us to Jesus; he's the only Savior, and we can't afford to miss him.

PRAYER

Lord, sometimes we get caught up in our ideas of who you ought to be and how you ought to help us. Please forgive us, and help us to seek you, not our idea of you. In Jesus, Amen.

Listen and Be Still

By Faith—Noah (1)

*By faith Noah. . . in holy fear
built an ark to save his family.*
HEBREWS 11:7

GENESIS 6:9-7:5

A look through my files and a search on the Internet tell me that there's no scientific certainty of a great flood that covered the earth. No proof to help my faith there. But then, this story is about Noah's faith—Noah, who with his family spent more than a year in an ark with animals of every kind.

Church school pictures or nice wall hangings of an ark full of smiling animals don't do justice to what happened: a terrible flood, people destroyed, and a long "cruise" that couldn't have been pleasant. But Noah did it. God had determined that even with the flood, the world must go on, and Noah was part of the plan.

Imagine being in Noah's shoes. You believe in God and have a solid relationship with him. Then one day God tells you to build this huge boat on dry land. You've never built a boat before, and you've never collected animals. Your neighbors think you're crazy, and the more "theological" ones tell you that a loving God of course wouldn't do this. But you know what God said.

So Noah "in holy fear built an ark." He trusted God more than he trusted his neighbors, even if he didn't fully understand how this "flood plan" would work. Faith in Jesus means following God's Word. It takes courage and trust that God means what he says, even if people laugh and we don't know the entire forecast.

PRAYER

Lord, sometimes we compromise your Word so that people won't think we're odd. Help us not only to obey but also to trust you, knowing that you hold the future. Amen.

Listen and Be Still

247

By Faith—Noah (2)

By his faith [Noah]
condemned the world. . . .
HEBREWS 11:7

JOHN 3:16-21

It took great faith on the part of Noah and his family to build an ark, gather the animals, and then actually get in the ark themselves. Noah couldn't check with any meteorologists for the long-range forecast to verify what God was planning. Noah just knew that God meant what he said. And at the same time Noah's faith "condemned the world." What does that mean?

If faith has to do with a living relationship with God, then Noah's faith made it clear to everyone who knew him that he believed in God. And his building of the ark showed that he took God seriously. In his "holy fear" Noah knew that God takes sin seriously, and if Noah believed and knew, no one else had any excuse (Romans 1:20).

The truth behind Noah's faith in the building of the ark is that God will not ignore sin. God knows we can't be perfect, but he expects us to pursue what is right and confess what is sinful in our lives. You can't claim faith in Jesus and at the same time simply go your own way.

Noah's faith is a painful illustration that also points to the seriousness of our sin and a God who will not tolerate it forever. The good news is that in this same Bible the Lord tells the story of Jesus, who came to earn forgiveness of sin for us. Ultimately God is not interested in condemning the world but in saving it.

PRAYER

Lord, Noah's faith was one of trust and one of holy fear. Give us wisdom to know the seriousness of your anger with sin and the depths of your love and forgiveness. Amen.

Listen and Be Still

Abraham—A Faith of Obedience

By faith Abraham. . . obeyed and went,
even though he did not know where he was going.
HEBREWS 11:8

GENESIS 12:1-8

What Abraham did was a lot tougher than we first might think. Abraham didn't have heroes of faith to encourage him, and he didn't have a Bible. He probably had a heathen father, and now he had the voice of God telling him to "go." "Just go," God had said. Abraham didn't even know where he was to go. He didn't have a map, although that wouldn't be much help anyway, if he didn't know where he was going. But Abraham trusted God, so he obeyed.

That's what God wants from us too. God gives us the Bible and tells us to trust him and follow his directions, and we will end up in the right place. "Just go," God says. "My Word and Spirit will guide you." And none of us knows in advance where the journey will take us.

That's not easy for me. I generally want to see where things are leading. I want to analyze everything carefully and make informed and thought-out decisions. I don't like to go places where I haven't been able to examine the path from at least one angle.

But Christian faith means following Jesus. And the only angle we have is one of trust. It doesn't seem to be a very secure business. But as long as it's Jesus we are following, we're guaranteed arrival at God's destination. Believing he's our shepherd means trusting that he knows where to go and wants to take us with him.

PRAYER

Lord, sometimes our faith is more comfortable just sitting. We can be afraid to follow you. Thank you for coming to be our shepherd. Help us to obey and follow you. Amen.

Listen and Be Still

Abraham—A Faith of Patience

By faith [Abraham] made his home. . .
like a stranger in a foreign country. . . .
HEBREWS 11:9

ACTS 7:2-8

Abraham's faith was a faith not only of obedience but also of patience. Abraham was traveling, but he didn't know where he was going. Not until he actually got to Canaan did God tell Abraham that this would be the land for him and his children.

Then we read that Abraham lived in this land "like a stranger in a foreign country," living in tents instead of permanent buildings. And Abraham never owned any of the land except for a burial plot he bought at a hefty price when Sarah died. No land—just a promise and a lifetime of wandering in the land that would one day belong to his family. But in faith, Abraham accepted all that, patiently trusting and obeying God.

Abraham's kind of patience is hard for us. Sure, we have faith in God, and we pray that God's will be done. But we also expect some action. We want results, and today we expect all kinds of results from fast food to e-mail responses to test outcomes to measurable improvements in behavior and learning. We don't have much time, and we expect God to act within our framework.

But faith that pleases God is patient with God's promises. It's the kind of faith that doesn't throw in the towel at the first hint that we're not getting results soon enough or the way we would like. Patient faith trusts that God will accomplish his plan for us in his time.

PRAYER

Lord, we often forget that faith is centered on you, not just on the things we would like to have. Help us entrust our plans and ourselves to your time. Give us patience. In Jesus, Amen.

Listen and Be Still

A Pitched Tent among Us

*The Word became flesh and
[pitched his tent] among us.*
JOHN 1:14

MARK 15:33-41

John 1:14 talks about Jesus "pitching his tent" among us by becoming a human being; Christ's death on the cross reflects on that "tent" coming down. The phrase "pitched his tent" is a translation of the Greek word used in John 1:14. As a previous meditation pointed out, tents are not permanent homes. If you live in a tent, it means you're just passing through. Saying that Jesus' incarnation was like pitching a tent, therefore, is like saying that the world and Jesus' earthly body were never intended to be Jesus' permanent home.

Jesus' followers, however, hadn't quite understood that. They wanted Jesus to stick around, not die. But Jesus did die, and his disciples felt as if everything Jesus had built and stood for had come down with his "tent."

But we know a little more. Jesus had a mission that included living for a while among us and then dying in our place. It was all part of God's plan.

God tells us that our lives are also like pitched tents. If we believe Jesus died for us, God promises that one day we will get new "tents" that will last forever. God doesn't intend for us to settle into this life; he is making us permanent citizens of heaven. This is possible because of what Jesus did for us on the cross at Calvary.

PRAYER

Lord, thank you for the time you spent among us and for the death you died for us. Thank you that through your death we have life and will live with you forever. Amen.

Listen and Be Still

251

Abraham—A Faith of the Big Picture

He was looking forward to the city with foundations,
whose architect and builder is God.
HEBREWS 11:10

REVELATION 21:1-8

Abraham's faith was about the "big picture." He could see beyond the events of a particular day or time. That kind of perspective would benefit each of us. Abraham kept in mind that moving to a promised land wasn't about some retirement plot for him and Sarah. It was about God and God's plans for the coming of Jesus and his kingdom. Without knowing all these details, Abraham knew he was part of something bigger than himself. Revelation 21 reminds us of that as well.

It's important to keep in mind that as followers of Jesus, we are part of that "something bigger" also. Sometimes we treat faith as being just for me—my peace of mind, my stability, my destiny. We can tend to look at church that way too—asking what a church can give me, or if its style of worship suits me. But faith has to do with a much bigger plan of God, even though I know I have an important place within that plan.

Abraham was just one player in the great work of God— wandering and without land. But that was okay with Abraham; he had the big picture in mind, and he knew his role was important to God.

Abraham's faith reminds us to keep in perspective what God is doing. That's why real faith gets involved in building the church, the body of Christ. I hope you are playing your role there too.

PRAYER

Lord, I'm thankful for all you have done for me. I'm also thankful that you are building your church. Please help me to play my part, following Jesus in living for you. Amen.

Listen and Be Still

Seeing and Believing

He saw and believed.
JOHN 20:8

JOHN 20:1-9

Too bad we couldn't have seen the empty tomb. John ("the other disciple") saw it, and it's interesting how he writes about it. He says that "he saw and believed." Even so, John writes, Jesus' disciples "still did not understand from Scripture that Jesus had to rise from the dead." Later John also records that Jesus says the ones who are really blessed are "those who have not seen and yet have believed" (20:29).

So what does all this mean for us? John knew that most people wouldn't get to see the empty tomb. But he also learned that real faith has to do with what we believe when we cannot see. The faith that is blessed is the faith that relies not on proof but on God.

This is an important observation. The disciples had seen it all and had spent time with Jesus, yet they didn't understand. We haven't seen it all, but if we understand why Jesus had to rise from the dead, then we are the more blessed. Christian faith is not about proving the resurrection but about confessing what God is doing through a living Savior and Lord.

John's words are encouraging. It's like he's saying, "Don't be jealous because of what we saw. If you understand what Scripture says about Jesus' resurrection, then you have already seen more than we did." That's the faith in Jesus we celebrate by his Spirit today.

PRAYER

Lord, thank you for those who saw the tomb and told your story. Thank you that we may believe without needing to see it too. Help us to see your lordship in all of life. Amen.

Listen and Be Still

Considering God Faithful

By faith Abraham. . .
was enabled to become a father. . . .
HEBREWS 11:11

GENESIS 15:1-6, 21:1-7

Can you imagine having a baby at ages 100 and 90? Most of us simply hope our pension plans will last that long; we certainly won't be thinking of starting a family! But that's what Abraham and Sarah did, and God points to these parents as heroes of faith.

God promised them a son, and to Abraham God's promise was more trustworthy than the general principle that you don't bear children in your old age. Abraham was sure, even though he had no evidence that Sarah could conceive, that his hope for a child would come true because God said so.

But this isn't about Abraham's positive outlook. Sometimes people think that if you really, really believe something will happen, and you're a Christian, then it will happen. Of course, if that were true, Christians could control government, rig the stock market, clean up our neighborhoods, and build the church of Jesus without opposition. But this isn't about having faith in faith, it's about having faith in God's faithfulness. Abraham had it right; he "considered [God] faithful."

God doesn't look at people and say, "Wow, they really think I will do what they ask. I guess I kind of owe it to them." Rather, God looks at us to see how we view him. Faith doesn't ask how strong faith itself is; it looks at how strong God is. Then it confesses God's faithfulness.

PRAYER

Lord, at times we pray and hope like people who want to guide your will our way. Help us to pray and hope, trusting that you already work for our good in Jesus. Amen.

Listen and Be Still

Faith Beyond Sin

*If we confess our sins, he is faithful and just
and will forgive us. . . and purify us. . . .*
1 JOHN 1:9

GENESIS 16:1-4A

Hebrews portrays Abraham as quite a hero of faith. But this passage in Genesis is a part of the story we don't want to miss.

The story of Abraham and Hagar is not a positive story about Abraham's faith. The fact is that in this episode Abraham was not so sure about God's faithfulness. He got to a point where he thought he at least ought to help God keep his promises. And so, contrary to God's plan, Abraham decided to have a baby through Hagar, Sarah's servant.

Abraham's faith is important for us to look at, but we also need to see that Abraham was an ordinary, sinful person who did not always trust in God with all his heart and strength. While that was not good for Abraham, the fact that God tells us about it reminds us that faith does not depend on how good we've been or if we've never committed any big sins. Abraham sinned with Hagar, but by God's grace Abraham recovered, and God forgave him and blessed him. Abraham learned that God's faithfulness is big enough to work even beyond our biggest sins.

I don't know what kind of a past you've had. But I do know the God who wants to be your Father in Jesus Christ. And because he is faithful, no matter what your sins are, God can strengthen you in faith and use you.

PRAYER

Lord, at times we wonder how you can care about and make use of sinful people and broken lives. Yet you do. Forgive us our sins, and show us how we can serve you. In Jesus, Amen.

Listen and Be Still

Faith Is Longing

They were longing for a
better country—a heavenly one.
HEBREWS 11:16

HEBREWS 11:13-16

The writer of Hebrews stops talking about specific heroes of faith for a moment to comment on a particular perspective of faith. Heroes of faith, we read, always seem to be looking for something better, "a better country—a heavenly one." That longing is part of a Spirit-led faith that pleases God.

Growing in faith means growing in the awareness that we are strangers here on this place called earth. The more we come to know God and understand what he has in mind for his people, the more our faith senses that the best is yet to come. Our present world is a bridge, as it were, to what is yet to come, and we don't build permanent homes on bridges. So when things in life don't feel right or well or fair, then faith reminds us we are longing for a heavenly home.

Sometimes we try too hard to "fit in" here on this earth. Sometimes we need to take a walk through a cemetery, or reflect on war, or think about abortions, the divorce rate, abuse, addictions, the sex-slave trade, cancer, depression—all parts of the sad reality of our world.

The reality of faith is that we long for a better home because we know what God has in store for us. Faith doesn't mean being satisfied with the way things are. Rather, it grows in longing for what will happen when our Lord Jesus returns.

PRAYER

Thank you, Lord, for good things in life. Help us to see the reality of a sinful world, and as we do, remind us that we long for a better place you are preparing for us. Amen.

Listen and Be Still

Faith Gets Tested

By faith Abraham, when God tested him,
offered Isaac as a sacrifice.
HEBREWS 11:17

GENESIS 22:1-14

God doesn't always make sense to us. One night God told Abraham he had to sacrifice his only son, Isaac. But God had also told Abraham earlier that Isaac was the son of promise, the one through whom Abraham would become a great nation. So when God told him to sacrifice his son, that wouldn't have made sense to Abraham.

Did Abraham lie there awhile figuring he must be imagining things? Or did he assess the situation logically, thinking that since Isaac could not be both dead and produce children, God must not really mean what he said? Or did Abraham perhaps think up some ways to help God out of this dilemma into which it appeared God was getting himself into?

We find no answers to these questions here. Instead, while it may not have made sense to him, Abraham knew what God had said. And because he trusted in God, Abraham did as God told him. God would handle being God, and Abraham would follow in trust.

God wants to know that our love for and faith in him are genuine, not self-serving. Faith is not just about saying we love God with all our heart, soul, and mind. It means being ready, in trust, to put our money where our mouth is. Christian faith is about following Jesus, not second-guessing him. The good news is that for us too God will make his plans work out.

PRAYER

We confess, Lord, that your ways are not our ways, and yet your ways don't always make sense to us. Help us to trust you to guide us at all times. We put our faith in you. Amen.

Listen and Be Still

By Faith—Isaac

By faith Isaac blessed Jacob and Esau
in regard to their future.
HEBREWS 11:20

GENESIS 27:19-40

So where is the faith in this story?

Jacob gets the blessing by way of deceiving his dad, and Isaac goes against what God said earlier about who should have the blessing—he tries to give it to Esau instead (see Genesis 25:23; 27:1-4).

We need to understand that the blessing was not simply a matter of dividing up some family furniture and property. It meant passing on to the next generation the blessing—namely, that through Abraham and his offspring all nations on earth would be blessed. This was a blessing that had to do with Jesus' coming. And now Isaac was just going to give it away to Esau because he favored his older son; whereas Esau, until now, hadn't even cared much about the blessing.

Suddenly, in a moment of horror, Isaac saw that his sons were playing the same kind of manipulative game he was playing. Isaac also saw that in spite of sinful maneuvering, things ended up the way God said they should. When Isaac realized that, he didn't take back the blessing as Esau wanted him too. In a moment of truth, he recognized he couldn't fight against God's will.

There are times in life when we come to realize how wrong we have been about some things. Faith enables us to see wrong for what it is. Faith recognizes that while there is life, there is time for change.

PRAYER

Lord, our own ideas and pride not only lead us to sin but can also keep us from seeing our sin. Help us to see where we are wrong, and give us faith to change. In Jesus, Amen.

Listen and Be Still

By Faith—Jacob

*By faith Jacob, when he was dying, blessed
each of Joseph's sons, and worshiped. . . .*
HEBREWS 11:21

GENESIS 47:29-31; 48:8-20

Jacob was now an old man, and now it was his turn to bless his children and grandchildren. It probably brought back some memories of what he went through to get a blessing from his own father.

It's interesting as well that Jacob deliberately gives the special blessing to the younger of Joseph's sons rather than to the elder. "Not fair," some of the others may have yelped. "The older son is supposed to get the blessing." But people of faith learn that for believers, life doesn't always go the way others expect it to.

That's an important lesson in faith. God's way of building his people—his church—doesn't always fit our traditions or expectations. Faith is not a matter of making sure God fits into our tradition. It's about following God in spite of what we have gotten used to or what we might expect.

Think about how God used a huge ark to save people and animals from a flood, a crying baby floating on the Nile, a youth killing a giant, a childless husband and wife to start a nation, a younger son blessed instead of the older one. When we live under God's blessing, things don't always happen the way we expect.

God's ways are not our ways, but God's ways are for our good. God wants us to trust him on that. Knowing what he has done in Jesus, we surely can trust God.

PRAYER

Lord, thank you for traditions and stable aspects of life. But help us not to hang on to them so tightly that we miss what you are doing. Keep us open to your surprises. Amen.

Listen and Be Still

259

Joseph—A Faith of Vision

By faith Joseph, when his end was near,
spoke about the exodus of the Israelites. . . .
HEBREWS 11:22

GENESIS 50:22-26

Joseph was sold into slavery by his brothers and wrongly imprisoned for attempted rape, and yet later God used him to save Egypt from famine and made him a powerful leader. It's a great life story. But to point out Joseph's faith, God reminds us what Joseph said about a future exodus to the land God had promised.

Although he was near the end of his life, Joseph's mind was on the future. At 110 years of age, Joseph knew his life wouldn't go on forever. But he was thinking far into the future about what would need to happen with God's people after he was gone. Joseph's faith was a faith of vision.

Life in Egypt had been great for Joseph and his extended family. But Joseph knew Egypt was not their home. Canaan was where they had to go; that's where God had said the promised land would be.

Joseph did not get distracted by all the power and people that were at his disposal. We know how easy it can be to get sidetracked by the blessings we enjoy in this life, and also by sufferings and hardships. There's another land, however, where God is leading us. It's a new heaven and a new earth, and one day we will make our exodus from here. People of faith keep that in mind. Having such a vision keeps us from either being too satisfied or too disheartened with this life.

PRAYER

Lord, keep us sensitive to the real value and main focus of the life you give us. Help us not to be distracted by riches or by struggles. "Teach us to number our days aright." In Jesus, Amen.

Joseph—A Faith of Belonging

By faith Joseph. . . spoke about the exodus. . .
and gave instructions about his bones.
HEBREWS 11:22

ROMANS 8:35-39

It may sound strange that while Joseph is talking to his family about a vision for the future, about the exodus that would have to happen someday, he also gives "instructions about his bones." What's going on here?

Some people despair when they sense that life on earth isn't going to get much better and that death is all that's left for them. We know Jesus will come back and God's kingdom will come, but it often seems so big and far away while death seems much closer.

That's not how Joseph felt. Joseph knew he would die before the people ever left Egypt. He knew that in spite of his power in Egypt, he wouldn't live to see the promised land. But Joseph also knew that his future wouldn't stop when he died.

Joseph knew, in faith, that if we are God's people in the present, we are also God's people in the future. That's why Joseph made sure his bones would go with his family, God's chosen people. God was his God, Israel was his people, the land of promise was his land, and he was not going to be separated from the work of God in the future.

That's the kind of faith we can have in Jesus, because God promises in Jesus that nothing will separate us from his love, not even our death (Romans 8:38-39). In Jesus, we're tied to the future, in life and in death.

PRAYER

Father, thank you for your promise that nothing will separate us from your love in Jesus. Thank you that not even death will keep us from a future land of promise. Amen.

Listen and Be Still

261

By Faith—Moses' Parents

By faith Moses' parents hid him. . .
and they were not afraid of the king's edict.
HEBREWS 11:23

EXODUS 1:22-2:10

It's hard to imagine that a Pharaoh could just order all male Jewish babies to be killed. But Pharaoh felt threatened by the growing Jewish nation, and babies are pretty vulnerable people. So Pharaoh gave the order. The amazing thing is that while Moses should have been killed when he was born, he not only stayed alive but wound up living in the very palace of the king who said kids like him should be dead.

But in our passage from Hebrews God is talking about the faith of Moses' parents. Those three months must have been a scary challenge for them. It might have been more convenient just to let Moses be killed. It probably would have been safer for the family and the rest of the community. After all, everyone else's baby boys were being killed. They could have just let it happen to their child too.

But they didn't. They feared God and defied the king. They stood up for God's values in spite of what others might have thought. Moses' parents had faith that God and his way would serve them better in the long run than simply doing what other people wanted or thought was convenient.

Faith means we choose God's values for our families and children, even if they don't always like it and it's not so comfortable.

PRAYER

Lord, sometimes it seems easier just to follow the decisions of others or to choose what is convenient. Help all of us, especially parents, to make good choices in life. In Jesus, Amen.

Listen and Be Still

By Faith—Moses Refused

By faith Moses. . . refused to be known
as the son of Pharaoh's daughter.
HEBREWS 11:24

ACTS 7:20-29

We assume Moses was taught the basics of belonging to God's people in the early years of his life in his parents' household. But most of Moses' youth was spent in the palace of the Pharaoh. From the Bible and history we know that Moses became a powerful leader and speaker. He was a man of influence. When Moses spoke, people listened.

But Moses didn't want to be connected to the palace and to people who did not acknowledge God. Moses refused to hide behind his high social status and the safety of belonging to the "in" group. So he made the gutsy move of openly claiming that he was a Hebrew. That would be like a general in the German army of the Third Reich standing up and claiming he didn't want to be known as a German, but as a Jew, like the rest of his people. It was a move that would destroy his standing in Egypt, but Moses knew he belonged to God. And that was far more significant than anything else, so he claimed his rightful heritage, even with its risks.

Do people at school or in your neighborhood or at work know about your faith? Sometimes we're too sensitive to what they think. Moses is a great example of what it means to affirm that we belong to the Lord. Today is a day in which you can clarify that fact with someone who may not know. It will strengthen your faith.

PRAYER

Lord, at times we care too much about how others may see us and think of us. Help us to care more about what you think, and to serve you openly as Savior and Lord. Amen.

Listen and Be Still

263

By Faith—Moses Chose

He chose to be mistreated
along with the people of God. . . .
HEBREWS 11:25

HEBREWS 11:25-28

I'm told that one reason for Wayne Gretzky's success in hockey is that he didn't go where the puck was; he went to where the puck was going to be. That's vision, and in hockey, not everyone has it.

Our general human tendency is to go to where the "action" currently is. We tend to pursue what's currently fashionable or faddish, wanting to be seen with the "right" people and identified with the "right" lifestyle.

Moses, however, played more like Gretzky than like most human beings. Moses knew what was expected of him. He knew the high life of palace living, where the money could be made, and how the riches could be accumulated and enjoyed—and it certainly wasn't in Goshen, where the Israelites lived. Moses also knew, however, where the action in God's plan was going to be, so he went where God was going.

We all make choices about what to do, where to go, what courses to take, which careers to pursue, how much to depend on God, and more. Someday we will stand before God, just like Moses, Gretzky, and everyone else. Then it will be clear whether the choices we've made will show that we know the "play" will end up at God's throne.

Moses knew, and he made his choice. God calls us to make the same choice for Jesus today.

PRAYER

Lord, the temptations of sounds, sights, and opportunities are all around us. Often they keep us from seeing where life is really going. Help us to choose wisely in Jesus. Amen.

By Faith—Moses Knew Value

*He regarded disgrace for the
sake of Christ as of greater value. . . .*
HEBREWS 11:26

PHILIPPIANS 3:4B-11

Moses didn't know Jesus, and he didn't know much about Jesus. But he knew "the Christ" was to come from the Israelite people.

Moses also knew that the coming of "the Christ" would have far more significance in the world than anything he himself could do as an Egyptian leader. Moses didn't give in to the "immediate gratification" attitude that wants whatever it can get right away. He planned a long-term investment strategy and stuck with it. He knew that investing in Jesus would yield more dividend than anything else. That's how Moses could put up with the mocking and whatever else happened to him when he made clear he belonged to the people of God.

Today each one of us has 24 hours until tomorrow at this time. We have a certain amount of energy, ability, resources, and opportunities. There are people we will see, and there's work we'll have to do. The only question is how we will invest these things over the next 24 hours. And that depends on what we value.

Moses knew value. He knew that the greatest reward is to belong to the Lord, who owns and will renew the earth. So Moses made choices accordingly. Whether your day includes school, home, office, barn, prison cell, hospital . . . you will be making choices. Faith pursues value in Jesus. He is the One we should value above all!

PRAYER

Lord, thank you for today, even if my circumstances may not be what I would like. Help me to consider you in all the choices I make, and to choose accordingly. In Jesus, Amen.

Listen and Be Still

265

By Faith—Many Others

These were all commended
for their faith. . . .
HEBREWS 11:39

HEBREWS 11:29-40

In Hebrews 11:32 the author writes, "And what more shall I say? I do not have time to tell about Gideon, Barak, Samson . . . ." That is still true today. There are many more heroes to look at, other people who, in spite of tough circumstances in their lives, simply followed the Lord.

I think that's how God intends to leave it. God doesn't name every faith hero there is. Nor does God say specifically what each one did. Maybe God simply wants to get us started so that we will continue to look up these people of faith on our own. That would be a good way to strengthen our faith. After all, the whole point of Hebrews 11 is that believers be encouraged by other people of faith because we all need encouragement.

It's a good idea to look at biblical heroes, but God also intends that we get together with modern-day believers. Going to church is not just about a good habit or about getting information from a sermon. It's God's way for believers to come together, with all their weaknesses and sins—and their faith—to support and encourage one another.

The heroes of Hebrews were pretty ordinary folks. Faith is not about spiritual giants; it's about people who trust in God's gigantic love. Meeting with these people, God says, is a way in which we "pump up" our faith.

PRAYER

Lord, thank you for your church and its people of faith. Remind us that faith and church are not about being sinless but about growing in faith and encouraging others to grow too. In Jesus, Amen.

Author and Perfecter of Our Faith

Let us fix our eyes on Jesus, the author
and perfecter of our faith. . . .
HEBREWS 12:2

HEBREWS 12:1-2

We have been looking at how faith works—how to increase it and build it and live in it. We have been looking at people who are witnesses of faith in God. And we have prayed and hoped that our faith will grow in the process.

In Hebrews 12 God gives us a message of real comfort and assurance. Sure, we have to take steps to grow and live in faith. And, yes, God calls us to do that with others. But it is Jesus who is the author of true faith. Jesus is the One who has started faith in our lives.

And now God tells us to keep our eyes fixed on Jesus because he is also the perfecter of our faith—Jesus will make our faith complete, perfect, the way God intends it to be.

While I am responsible to do the best I can to "pump up" my faith from day to day and from week to week, it's not up to me alone. I need Jesus to work on my faith as well.

That's where God has been taking us on this walk through stories about faith-filled believers. We are surrounded by witnesses who encourage us, but Jesus is the One whom all faithful believers look to, and he is the One we all follow.

Jesus has already run the race and finished it. He will bring me through where I need to go.

PRAYER

Lord, at times we think our faith is a work to be rewarded with salvation. Keep reminding us that even faith is something you start and complete in our lives. In your name, Amen.

Listen and Be Still

Encouragement from God

Consider [Jesus] who endured such opposition. . .
so that you will not. . . lose heart.
HEBREWS 12:3

LUKE 22:31-32

Almost everyone gets weary and loses heart sometime, especially when things aren't going well. We tend to get more tired when we are running against the wind, dealing with opposition, nursing wounds.

Sometimes it helps when someone we love and respect comes alongside us in those times and says, "Hey, I care about you. Don't give up or give in. I'll go through this with you." It helps if we know we are not alone.

And who is saying that in our Scripture reading for today? Our Lord Jesus is. He cares about our faith. He doesn't just "grade" our faith but also encourages and nourishes it.

In Luke 22:31-32 Jesus says he even prays about our faith, in spite of sin that may have led to troubles we are experiencing. That's because our faith is not just about us, it's about each one of us in relationship with God. And God wants that relationship to grow.

God also gives us Hebrews 12:3 to encourage us. He says, "Look at Jesus. I sent him because I want you to be my child. I know there are times in life when things are tough, when it's hard to keep going. But look at Jesus and remember that all of this is not just about your faith, it's about us. And I will strengthen you."

Keep your eyes on Jesus, and in God's strength through the power of the Holy Spirit, you can keep going.

PRAYER

Lord, thank you for walking with us—and ahead of us. Thank you for caring about each of us and for nurturing our faith. Please keep praying for us along the way. In your name, Amen.

JOURNEY TO DELIVERANCE

31 MEDITATIONS AND READINGS

BY DR. CALVIN L. BREMER

Coming to Faith in Christ

Dr. Calvin L. Bremer

Throughout history many oppressed and enslaved people have found strength and comfort in identifying with the people of "the exodus."

We include the following reflections based on the exodus of God's ancient people from Egypt in the hope that we will find strength and comfort as we move from sin's bondage toward God's promised land that is filled with freedom and joy.

Dr. Bremer served as the Executive Director of the Back to God Hour and as editor of the TODAY from 1996 until 2005. He also served Christian Reformed congregations in Michigan and Illinois from 1972 until 1996.

History for Today

These are the names of the sons of Israel
who went to Egypt with Jacob. . . .
EXODUS 1:1

EXODUS 1:1-4

"Epic"—"thrilling"—"bound to hold your attention!" Words like these are often used to describe books, plays, and screen productions of the events we are going to examine in this group of devotional readings.

There's something compelling about the story of the exodus from Egypt. The people of Israel had becomes slaves in a foreign land. Then they rallied around a leader who had been exiled, and finally they were freed. Throughout history many differing and distinct groups have felt the tug of identification with the children of Jacob who were delivered from oppression. African American people in the United States, Zionist Jews in Europe, Latin Americans struggling for justice—these are just some of the groups who have identified with the Israelites of the exodus.

But for all the similarities we can see, we must also be aware of some differences. History does not merely repeat itself, as some people say. The Ruler of history is moving it toward an end. We're looking at this segment of God's liberation plan not because it gets repeated in history but because it shows God's intentions for his people.

We'll see how God takes his chosen people out of slavery. And we'll focus on our relationship to our Deliverer, Jesus Christ—the Prophet like Moses whom God provided for us (Deuteronomy 18:15).

PRAYER

Almighty God, remind us how you have acted to free us through Jesus Christ so that we too can become your people. In his name we pray. Amen.

Listen and Be Still

271

Changes

Joseph and all his brothers. . . died,
but the Israelites . . . became exceedingly numerous.
EXODUS 1:6-7

EXODUS 1:5-8

Joseph had been the "prime minister" of Egypt during his lifetime (see Genesis 41). While he was alive and in power, and even for a while after his death, his relatives were well cared for. A sense of indebtedness for his leadership and the political savvy of the Egyptians insured that kind of treatment.

But time tends to dull memory, and change comes to every society. Eventually the day came when the memory of Joseph's power no longer protected his family.

About 400 years passed between the time of Joseph and the events we read about in Exodus 1. And in those years many things had happened. Isn't it striking how so many years and so much family history is condensed into just a few short verses of the Bible? Babies were born, old people died, young people died, heroic deeds were performed, cultural institutions were maintained, the Israelites contributed to the building of the society—but all of that seems to have been forgotten. How quickly we pass away. Two hundred years from now few people will have any memory of what we have done.

Change is the agent of history's movement. How quickly the kingdoms of this world pass away with only a few lines to record their effect on history. There is only One who remains the same yesterday, today, and forever—and that One is Jesus.

PRAYER

Father, as generations pass and memories of our work fade, help us to remember the work of our Lord Jesus and the work your people have done in his name. Amen.

Listen and Be Still

Slaves

"We must deal shrewdly with them or they will. . .
fight against us and leave the country."
EXODUS 1:10

EXODUS 1:8-14

Sin is motivated by many attitudes and by considerations that often look wise to the outside observer—and to the sinner. Notice how the king of Egypt speaks: "We must deal shrewdly with them." He thinks only of what he can gain for himself and his own interests. To people under the influence of the devil, that seems like wisdom.

Numbers are a big concern to this king, who says, "They will become more numerous." The king of Egypt is frightened by how many Israelites there are, fearing that they might become more numerous than the Egyptians, and thus more powerful. The king is concerned about power and control.

Another concern is economics. The king is afraid that if the Israelites leave his land, he will lose an important resource: workers. So he forces Israel into slavery to build store cities and do other work for him.

Notice, though, that there are no free people in this scene. The Israelites are the slaves of Pharaoh, and Pharaoh is a slave of fear and of its ally, hatred. Israel is treated as if they are less than human, and Pharaoh and his slave masters act less than human. Both need to be freed from tyranny.

The King of history is interested in complete liberation for the children of Israel and for the children of Pharaoh. The King of history will provide a liberator.

PRAYER

"Come, thou long-expected Jesus, born to set thy people free; from our fears and sins release us, let us find our rest in thee." In your name we pray, O Savior. Amen.

Listen and Be Still

Infanticide

"If it is a boy, kill him. . . ."
The midwives, however, feared God. . . .
EXODUS 1:16-17

EXODUS 1:15-22

In his oppression of the people of Israel, Pharaoh decided next to kill all their newborn boys. If he could destroy the next generation of Hebrew males, Egypt could completely absorb the Israelite nation into its culture as Egyptian men married Hebrew women. But that was not God's design.

Even in those hard times, God provided for his people. The midwives who delivered babies in Israel ignored Pharaoh's murderous instructions about how to handle "problem children." Instead the midwives chose to fear and honor God. And their obedience to God does not go unnoticed. In fact, we read this important note: "Because the midwives feared God, he gave them families of their own." But as for Pharaoh and "all his people" who threw children into the Nile, God's judgment would come, sadly, upon their own children.

The health of any culture can be gauged by the way it treats its weakest members. In Egypt's culture, and in many "civilized" countries of our world today, the choice was to kill infants for the "good" of the whole population.

God still provides for his people. The collective judgment we face for infanticide is paid for only through the gift of the firstborn Son of God, Jesus Christ. Let's fear and honor him in the tradition of the midwives.

PRAYER

Lord God, as we see sin abound in our culture, help us to be obedient to your will for life. Help us to seek life only in him who is the Life—your Son, our Lord. Amen.

Parental Faith

By faith Moses' parents hid him. . . .
Hebrews 11:23

Hebrews 11:23-27

Children often take on the characteristics of their parents. Whether the link is genetic or environmental, there's a link between parent and child. Moses was shaped by his parents' decision. His was a family that believed in God and acted on its belief. Pharaoh had issued a decree demanding death for every male child born to the Hebrews. But in this family the decision was made to hide the child from the authorities.

The first act of faith came in deciding to save the baby Moses. Can you imagine the effect this would have on a child growing up, knowing what his parents risked so that he could live?

The second act of faith was the hiding of the child within their home "for three months." Can you imagine the tension as Moses, like any other baby, would cry? As the bond between mother and son grew, so did the resolve to act in faith in the face of what seemed to be certain doom. When he could no longer be hidden, Moses was put in a basket and left along the riverbank (Exodus 2:3). For Moses' mother that little ark was a boat of faith.

The choices parents make influence the lives of their children in subtle and profound ways. The choices of Moses' parents live in the annals of faith. Do your choices show your complete dependence on God?

Prayer

Father, teach us the importance of obediently following your will. Teach us to love you more than we fear any other authority or the influence of others. In Jesus' name, Amen.

Listen and Be Still

275

Family Faith

His sister stood at a distance
to see what would happen to him.
EXODUS 2:4

EXODUS 2:1-10

Faith is often a family matter. The hiding of Moses in the family home was not something the parents could do by themselves. Given the presence of an older sister and brother, Moses' life depended on their being able to keep quiet about his presence in the home.

But let's think about the act of sending Moses' sister to watch the little ark in which Moses floated on the Nile. Think of all the potential dangers—floating away, the basket leaking, being discovered by animals, or being discovered by others who would obey Pharaoh's orders to drown Hebrew baby boys. Many of us would fear traumatizing a child by asking her to watch the baby from a distance.

We can understand Moses' mother's decision about this if we see it as an act of faith. Moses' mother believed that God would provide. A mother who lived by promise and obedience would wisely send her daughter to witness God's further protection of this special child. When Pharaoh's daughter found the baby, Moses' sister, with faith-shaped courage, offered to find a woman to nurse the baby. So in this way Moses' mother received him back to care for him till he "grew older"!

Are we placing ourselves and our children at the vantage points where we can watch God unfold his wonderful ongoing plan of redeeming the world?

PRAYER

Father in heaven, teach us the importance of modeling faith in our families. May we help each other see what you are doing in our lives to protect and save us. In Jesus, Amen.

Listen and Be Still

Food for the Hungry

Pharaoh's daughter said to her,
"Take this baby and nurse him for me. . . ."
EXODUS 2:9

EXODUS 2:7-10

The cry of a baby, the need for nourishment, the suggestion of a little slave girl, and the decision of a king's daughter—through all of these God brings a son back to be nursed by his own mother.

What divine irony! The son who has to be abandoned is brought back to his mother, who is then paid by the king's daughter to do what she is overjoyed to do. Imagine the joy in Moses' family that day! Imagine the laughter in the slaves' quarters as the news filters through that a slave mother is being paid to nurse her own son for the king's daughter!

God provides for the care of Moses in most unusual ways: at his own mother's breast and at the king's table. Both offer Moses the food and nurture he needs for solid growth.

Today again families of faith will draw sons and daughters together to be fed. Parents, obedient to God's calling and grateful for God's promise in their lives, will again coo words of love and affection to their children. But most of all they will see to it that their children are fed spiritually.

In family devotional times, in their education in school, and in their involvement in the life of the church, parents do all they can to make sure their children hear the Word of God and know the story of Jesus.

PRAYER

As you provided for Moses' growth, Lord, also provide for our growth through the community of faith. Use parents and others to stimulate our spiritual growth. In Jesus' name, Amen.

Listen and Be Still

Looking the Wrong Way

Glancing this way and that and seeing no one,
he killed the Egyptian and hid him in the sand.
EXODUS 2:12

EXODUS 2:11-15

I recently read of a person who was severely injured trying to cross the street. Bystanders said the person had been looking in one direction but had failed to see a truck coming from the other direction.

Moses made a similar mistake. In the New Testament we are told, "Moses thought that his own people would realize that God was using him to rescue them, but they did not" (Acts 7:25). Moses was looking to redeem his people, but he failed to look to God for his timing. While Moses was looking in every direction to make sure no others could see what he was doing, he forgot he was living before the face of God.

As we think about our own lives, let's admit to ourselves that too often we fail to remember we are living before the face of God. While we look around in every direction for opportunities and loopholes and advice from experts, we often fail to look up and seek God's direction before we act. Let's also admit that even when we are conscious of God's presence in the things we do, we often fail to sense God's timing. It's so easy for us to set our own agenda and adopt our own timetables for the events of our lives.

Let's be thankful for Jesus Christ, our Lord, who came in the fullness of time and said, "I seek not to please myself but him who sent me" (John 5:30).

PRAYER

Lord, we are often wrapped up in our work and other things.
Deliver us from slavery to ourselves. Teach us your ways and
timing so that our actions will not be in vain. Amen.

Listen and Be Still

Who Are You?

Moses. . . went out to where his own people
were and watched them at their hard labor.
Exodus 2:11

Exodus 2:15-22

Who am I? Who do other people think I am? Questions about identity and the problems of knowing oneself have been with us from the beginning of time.

Moses seemed, on the outside, like one of the Egyptians. He was a grandson of the king, so the culture of Egypt, with its language and customs, was his. That fact becomes apparent in our Bible reading for today. When Moses fled to the land of Midian and helped some young women with their flock, he was, in their eyes, an Egyptian. They looked at his clothes and listened to his speech and concluded that he was an Egyptian.

In his own eyes, however, Moses was clearly an Israelite, one of God's people. Back in Egypt he had to go out "to where his own people were." He lived in Pharaoh's court surrounded by people who were not his own, and he had to make a special effort to be with his own enslaved people.

This reminds us that the Israelites were the people of promise; they had a land promised to them other than the one they lived in. "By faith Moses, when he had grown up, refused to be known as the son of Pharaoh's daughter. He chose to be mistreated along with the people of God rather than to enjoy the pleasures of sin for a short time" (Hebrews 11:24-25).

With whom do you identify yourself? Whose are you?

Prayer

Dear Jesus, we're tempted to identify with the world, since its sights often look so pleasurable. Help us to identify with your people, the family of God. In your name, Amen.

Listen and Be Still

279

Heard and Remembered

God heard their groaning
and he remembered his covenant. . . .
EXODUS 2:24

EXODUS 2:23-25

When you cry alone, does anyone hear? Does anyone care that you are crying? The Bible makes clear that God watches over what happens in our world.

Early in Genesis we read of God's coming to Cain and telling him that his brother's blood cried out from the ground and that God had heard it (Genesis 4:10). And in our reading for today we see that God hears the groaning of his people and remembers his promises to Abraham, Isaac, and Jacob.

The whispered complaints of the oppressed Israelites, the muttering under the breath about unfair demands, the whimpers and cries of beaten slaves—all are heard by God. And today God still hears the cries of children forced to the streets by the policies of unrelenting governments. God still hears the mutterings of a mother left without support by a husband who chases the wind. God still hears the prayers whispered by weary prisoners in the gulags of our world. God still hears us crying ourselves to sleep at night.

Even more important, though, is that God also remembers his covenant with those who live in faith. God has promised to be our God and to make all things new. God hears our cries, and God remembers, and God promises that a better day is coming for all who follow the Son—a day without night, a day with no more tears.

PRAYER

Sometimes, Lord, we say through our tears, "Does Jesus care when my heart is hurting?" Remind us that you not only hear but also remember us for your Son's sake. Amen.

Listen and Be Still

Formal Education

Moses was educated in all the wisdom of the Egyptians and was powerful in speech and action.

ACTS 7:22

ACTS 7:17-22

Education is often the gateway to opportunity. But sometimes for those going through it the benefits are not obvious. Many students have asked, "What is all this for? Does all this knowledge lead anywhere? Does it have any purpose?"

Moses was educated in the best knowledge of Egypt. As a grandson of the Pharaoh, he had access to the wisdom of the court. And, according to these verses from Acts, he distinguished himself in the way he applied his knowledge: he "was powerful in speech and action."

It's interesting to note that after forty years in the land of Midian, Moses returned to Pharaoh's court not as a naive, unsophisticated person, awed and uncertain of how things are done in the highest arenas of power, but as one whose formal training had prepared him for his return to the court, with a firm knowledge of its language and customs.

Some of us fear that too much education drives away faith, but there is no ground for that fear. Just look at the stories of Moses, Daniel, Paul, Apollos, Augustine, John Calvin, and so many others in the history of God's people. God uses formal training to build his kingdom.

Are you faithful in your educational preparation? God will use it in his own time in the unique place he has planned for you. Take care to prepare yourself.

PRAYER

As we sit in classrooms and pore over books at home, instruct us in your wisdom, Lord, so that we may become wise unto salvation and useful in your kingdom. In Jesus, Amen.

Listen and Be Still

Informal Preparation

*Moses. . . fled to Midian, where he settled
as a foreigner. . . [for] forty years. . . .*
ACTS 7:29-30

ACTS 7:23-29

Could you wait forty years for something important to happen? Remember, Moses thought God was going to use him to deliver the Hebrews from Egypt. That was part of his thinking when he killed the Egyptian. And that event led to his flight to Midian, where he worked for his father-in-law for forty years.

During this time God was teaching Moses, preparing him for leadership. Moses needed to learn that the timetable for liberation belongs to the One who sets it. It's clear that later in life Moses still struggled with being patient (see Numbers 20:1-13). In Midian God taught Moses to wait for the time of God's choice.

During this same time Moses gained an additional benefit in his leadership preparation. Because the Hebrews were a slave people, they had become toughened to endure the oppression they suffered. Now God was preparing Moses, who'd led a pampered life in Pharaoh's playground, to grow strong and sturdy. God sent him up and down rocky mountains till he knew the ways of the wilderness and had the toughness to handle the rigors of travel. Now he was also physically ready to lead a slave people in the wilderness.

God uses ordinary, everyday things to prepare us for the work of his kingdom. Rejoice today that through the everyday things in your life God is preparing you.

PRAYER

Father, keep us from being impatient with your timetable or with our present area of service in your kingdom. Thank you for what you are doing in our lives right now. Amen.

Listen and Be Still

In the Right Place

When the Lord saw that he had gone over to look, God called to him. . . .
EXODUS 3:4

EXODUS 3:1-6

Where you are often determines what you see. Whether you're at the opera or at a soccer match, the place from which you watch has an effect on your enjoyment, knowledge, and involvement. If you claim to be an avid soccer fan but you always sit in the last row of the bleachers and look away from the game, people will wonder about your claim of being an enthusiast.

Moses made some conscious choices about being where God showed himself. He went to the mountain of God, making his way through the wilderness to get there. The writer of Exodus also shows that Moses made another decision after noticing the burning bush: "he thought, 'I will go over and see . . . why the bush does not burn up.'" It pleased God to reveal himself to someone who was choosing to look for him.

When God's people look for the Lord in his Word and when they gather to worship and hear God's Word proclaimed, the Spirit of God promises to use God's Word to show God to them. The decisions we make about reading the Bible and gathering with God's people, about being where God shows himself, may affect whether we have "mountaintop" experiences with God.

Whenever you can, join with the people of God in prayer, praise, and giving; gather around the Word of God with his people to hear God speaking to you.

PRAYER

We desire to hear your voice, Lord, but too often we run around in the wilderness rather than going to the place where you are speaking. Lead us to hear you. In Jesus' name, Amen.

Listen and Be Still

O God

"Take off your sandals, for the place
where you are standing is holy ground."
EXODUS 3:5

EXODUS 3:4-10

When we exclaim or cry out, "O God," it's clear from our tone of voice, or more accurately, our tone of heart, whether we're showing respect for the God who is holy.

The reaction of much of the world to the presence of God is seen in the way God is portrayed on television, in plays and movies, in books, and elsewhere. Usually God is shown as an ineffective or whimsical old man with idiosyncrasies we are all forced to endure. In cases like these, the creature acts superior to the Creator.

Moses' meeting with God strikes a wholly different note. God announces his holiness, and Moses' reaction is consistent with that holiness. As a sign of respect for God's holiness, showing awe mixed with fear, Moses hides his face from the Lord.

Nowadays the announcement of God's holiness and righteousness is made through God's Word, the Bible—and most poignantly through the proclaimed Word of God based on the Bible. In worship and in all of life, people are called to acknowledge the Lord as God, serve as God's most gifted creatures, and honor the earth as the Lord's footstool.

The day is coming when people will no longer be able to deny the presence of God; nor will they be able to simply ignore God's presence. God's holiness will not only be announced but will be revealed for all to see.

PRAYER

"Holy, holy, holy! Lord God Almighty! All thy works shall praise thy name, in earth and sky and sea." O God, allow us into your holy presence through Jesus Christ. Amen.

Listen and Be Still

Excuses, Excuses

*Moses said to the Lord, "O Lord,
I have never been eloquent."*
EXODUS 4:10

EXODUS 4:1-17

Moses was full of excuses, even though he had lots of reasons to do what God was calling him to do.

God had chosen Moses; God had spoken to him in a place where Moses had made himself available; God had shown Moses signs he could use in Egypt to prove he was sent by God. The signs would support the message of God's deliverance.

But despite all this help, Moses begged God to send someone else. So, to put Moses' excuses to rest, God provided for Aaron to go along with Moses and do the talking for him.

In Jesus Christ, God has taken away all our excuses. Jesus came with signs and wonders to support his message, his good news about God's coming kingdom. The signs and wonders of Jesus' life and of his death on the cross showed the powers of this world that God's kingdom is coming. And Jesus' resurrection to new life is God's sign that the Son, Jesus, is God's spokesman to this world.

As God gave Moses signs and wonders and even a spokesman, so God has given us signs and wonders as well as an eloquent spokesman—the Word who became flesh—all in the person of Jesus. "How shall we escape if we ignore such a great salvation?" (Hebrews 2:3). In Jesus, we have no excuses not to serve the true God.

PRAYER

Lord, give us eyes of faith to see the cross and the empty tomb, which point us to the risen Lord Jesus as the answer to all our excuses. We pray in his name. Amen.

Listen and Be Still

Blood Brothers

She said "bridegroom of blood,"
referring to circumcision.
EXODUS 4:26

EXODUS 4:24-26

Moses was on his way to Egypt, but at a lodging place he met the Lord, who was angry with him. The reason for the Lord's anger was Moses' neglect. While living in Midian, Moses had failed to have his son circumcised. He had failed to have the sign of God's covenant placed in his son's flesh.

Here we have a clear case of Moses' failing to keep the covenant even as God was working through him to make good on the old covenant promises to Abraham. And it was Moses' wife, a mother raised outside the people of promise, who placed the sign of promise and of judgment on her son's flesh. God's anger was aroused not simply because of the neglect of physical circumcision but also because of the neglect of the covenant it symbolized. Failure to be circumcised symbolized being cut off from the people of promise.

The sight of blood made Moses' wife call him "a bridegroom of blood," meaning that initiation into Moses' family involved shedding blood. Today it's not circumcision of the flesh that counts, but circumcision of the heart (Jeremiah 4:4; Colossians 2:11). For the real "bridegroom of blood," Jesus, was cut off for the sake of his people.

Are you a member of the family of Jesus? You can be—by faith. Or will you face an angry God because you neglected God's provision to become part of his family?

PRAYER

Lord Jesus, thank you for purchasing us through your shed blood. Take us into your family through the initiation of faith in you. Mark our hearts with your love, we pray. Amen.

He Said What?

*Aaron told them everything the Lord
had said to Moses. . . . And they believed.*
EXODUS 4:30-31

EXODUS 4:27-31

Do you remember what God said to you yesterday? More important, does it make any difference in your life?

God sent Aaron to meet Moses on his way to Egypt. And God used Moses as his mouthpiece to speak to Aaron. Then, when they arrived in Egypt, God used Aaron to speak the words of God.

Aaron spoke and displayed the signs that were given to him, and the people's response was belief and worship. Today God still sends people who point us back to the Scriptures and help us to see the Lord.

God speaks to his gathered people through preaching on the Lord's day. Sometimes God speaks to us through a discussion of a sermon. Sometimes God's Word comes to us through hearing what God is saying to someone else—through books or sharing of personal experiences. Sometimes this happens through radio or television. In each case we must listen carefully to make sure that what we hear or read is based on God's Word.

When the children of Israel heard God's words through Aaron, they knew God cared about them, so they believed and worshiped God.

When we hear God speak, we must believe and worship. What is God saying to you today? And what will you do in response?

PRAYER

Lord, you speak so eloquently—even through the faltering speech of human lips. Help us to hear as you speak through human voices. May we believe and worship. In Jesus, Amen.

Listen and Be Still

Smoke Screen

"Lazy, that's what you are. . . . That is why
you keep saying, 'Let us go and sacrifice. . . .'"
EXODUS 5:17

EXODUS 5:1-18

Smoke often hides what is really happening. The ability of firefighters to rescue people and to put out fires is often hampered by the amount of smoke they have to deal with.

This is often true in people's lives as well. Too often people put up smoke screens in order to hide what's really happening in their hearts and lives. They make accusations that only touch on what's really bothering them. They make excuses that have little to do with the reason for their actions. Sometimes the person involved does not even realize this is happening. It can only be observed from a distance.

Pharaoh put up a smoke screen when he accused the Israelites of wanting to worship their God simply because they were lazy. For a people so vigorous that they had become more numerous despite Pharaoh's working them to death and killing all their baby boys, the accusation of laziness couldn't stick.

The real reason for Pharaoh's displeasure was clear when he first spoke with Moses and Aaron, saying, "Who is the Lord, that I should obey him and let Israel go?" Pharaoh had rejected Israel's God.

Christians often have to face false accusations from people who don't know the Lord or what God does. Misunderstandings like that are as old as history.

PRAYER

O Lord, as we hear criticism from unbelievers, give us the wisdom
to hear what is true and to see through the smoke of falsehood.
Keep us from losing heart, we pray. In Jesus, Amen.

Listen and Be Still

Why, Lord?

Moses . . . said, "O Lord, why have you brought trouble upon this people?"
EXODUS 5:22

EXODUS 5:17-6:8

Living with our faith stretched to the limit is hard work. Our expectations of how and when God should act can make us vulnerable to discouragement. Even the faith-filled person sometimes asks, "Why, Lord?" or, "Why this?" or, "Why now?"

The people who so eagerly heard the announcement of the Lord from Aaron are the same people who now accuse Moses and Aaron of putting a sword in Pharaoh's hand to kill them. This accusation takes its toll on Moses, who turns to God and asks why.

Isn't it strange how vulnerable we can be to the pressures of others and to their opinions about our life and our faith? The Bible speaks openly of the difficulty we experience in the life of faith. It shows "heroes of faith" coming with their "why" questions—Moses, Elijah, David, and Peter are just a few examples.

But God's faithfulness to us and to his promises does not depend on the highs or lows of our spiritual experiences. God simply announces again what his intentions are for Israel.

As each of us comes with frustrations in our spiritual lives and honestly asks God, "Why is this happening to me?" let's also remain quiet long enough to hear God speak again of his intentions for us in Jesus Christ: "I have chosen you, you are mine." Then we can go on.

PRAYER

Thank you, Lord, for not making the varying degrees of our affection the barometer of your faithfulness. Your intentions for us remain the same, in Jesus. Amen.

Listen and Be Still

Unhearing

They did not listen to [Moses] because of
their discouragement and cruel bondage.
EXODUS 6:9

EXODUS 6:9-12; 7:1-4

There are times when we just can't hear. When all the energy we have is being used to do something else, we are oblivious to some sounds around us. We human beings learn to screen out certain sounds or signals that we think are unhelpful to the task or the activity we're focused on.

The Israelites were so broken that they didn't hear what God was saying to them. They were spending all their energy on coping with the cruelty of their slavery.

We need to recognize that effect in others when it seems as if they have "tuned us out." Christians are often frustrated because of persons who don't seem to hear what God is saying to them—their children, for example, or their neighbors.

God could see very well what had happened to his people. So again God charged Moses to speak to Pharaoh. But this time God changed the picture by saying that when Pharaoh refused to obey, God would demonstrate his power.

Some of us may be so broken that we haven't heard God speak. But God is saying right now that he cares for us. We need to listen carefully for God's voice.

We also need to follow God's example and speak again—with love—to those broken persons who have not yet listened to what God is saying in their lives.

PRAYER

Lord, keep us from becoming so immersed in our activities that we tune out what you are saying to us. Speak to us again, reassuring us, for Jesus' sake. Amen.

Listen and Be Still

God Gains Attention

"The Egyptians will know that I am the Lord when I stretch out my hand against Egypt."
EXODUS 7:5

EXODUS 7:1-13

The old farmer walked out to where his mule was standing, quietly lifted a baseball bat, and hit the mule on the forehead. When asked what he was doing, the old man replied, "First I have to get his attention; then we can start plowing."

Sometimes God has to get our attention. And to do that, God chooses to use events that are tools of judgment. God told Moses that the reason for his judgment on the Egyptians was to make them know that the Lord is God. Everything God does shows us something about who he is, but in this instance God expressed that his intent was to reveal himself clearly to the Egyptians. And God was successful in this, for later on we read of the magicians telling Pharaoh, "This is the finger of God" (Exodus 8:19).

There may be events in our lives or in our nations that are the actions of God's judgment, for the truth is that God is judging us already now. God's judgment gets our attention, all right—but do we see God clearly? While time remains, we need to acknowledge God, see his hand behind the events of history, and worship him.

I know that the Lord is almighty;
supreme in dominion is he,
performing his will and good pleasure
in heaven, on the earth, in the sea.

PRAYER

O Lord, help us to see how you use the events of our lives and in our world to show yourself as the Holy One who redeems his people. In Jesus' name we pray. Amen.

Listen and Be Still

Plagues

"This is what the Lord says: 'By this you will know that I am the Lord.'"
EXODUS 7:17

EXODUS 7:14-24

〜Many of us have become desensitized to the spectacular. Too many movies and too much television have dulled our sense of what is truly dramatic.

The Egyptian people were treated to a series of plagues that disrupted their patterns of living, weakened their society, and shook their faith in their own gods. All this demonstrated that the God of Israel was the Lord of all creation. From the swallowing of the snakes, to the changing of the Nile to blood, to the death of the Egyptians' firstborn sons (Exodus 12:29-30), the plagues were visible demonstrations of the superiority of the God of Israel.

We know enough from the history of Egypt, and we know enough about the gods the Egyptians worshiped in those days, to see that the plagues were not just some variety of punishments that God selected at random. The plagues were visible manifestations of the battle between the God of Israel and the worthless gods of the Egyptians. What the Egyptians trusted in and used for worship failed them now.

Could it be that the plagues of our society—the drug culture, the occult, pornography, pollution, terrorism—are God's way of reminding us that the gods of medicine, spiritual powers, sex, industrial development, and economic power are false gods?

PRAYER

"The dearest idol I have known, whate'er that idol be, help me to tear it from thy throne and worship only thee." Lord, help us to serve you only. In Jesus' name, Amen.

Listen and Be Still

Compromise One

"No! Have only the men go;
and worship the Lord. . . ."
EXODUS 10:11

EXODUS 10:7-11

"Politics is the art of the possible." This bit of common wisdom governs how we function in much of our lives. We willingly compromise certain things in order to achieve or gain our desires.

Pharaoh's advisors were astute politicians. After hearing their advice, Pharaoh was willing to let the Israelites go to worship the Lord—on the condition that only the men should go. The women and children would have to stay home.

In offering this compromise, Pharaoh showed his misunderstanding of God's claims on the families of Israel. If the fathers of Israel had accepted this compromise, they would have denied, in practice, the promise of God's covenant that extended to their families. For the Lord had said, "I will be their God" (Genesis 17:8).

How many of us have accepted the compromises of the "pharaohs" of our day? Have we accepted any compromise that allows the demands of God to hold for one group but not for others—a compromise, for example, that gives the benefits of the covenant to adults and not to children? How often do we talk of children in the church as the church of the future, rather than the church of the present and the leaders of the future?

God accepts no compromise, only unconditional surrender of entire families.

PRAYER

O covenant God, teach us what it means to worship with our entire families. Keep us from compromising in regard to anyone's worship or spiritual growth. In Jesus' name, Amen.

Listen and Be Still

Compromise Two

*"Go. . . . Even your women and children may
go with you; only leave your . . . herds behind."*
EXODUS 10:24

EXODUS 10:21-29

"If at first you don't succeed, try, try again." That motto must be hanging in the devil's office, for it's certainly the way he treats us humans. When the devil's agent, Pharaoh, found that his earlier terms were not acceptable to Israel, he came back with an alternative plan.

This time Pharaoh would let the people take their women and children with them, but their flocks and herds would have to stay behind. Again the Israelites refused, due to the all-encompassing demands the Lord made on them. There could be no worship unless it involved all the people and all their possessions.

God's redemption does not simply involve people; it involves the whole creation. In God's plan, people are not isolated from their possessions; all their goods are part of God's kingdom and have a purpose in it.

A compromise in regard to material wealth often sneaks up on us without our noticing it. For instance, do we factor inflation into our giving, as we expect our employers to do with our earnings?

Pharaoh demanded the compromise of worship without wholehearted material commitment. Israel didn't accept it; neither should we.

Total commitment of life and resources takes thought and reflection. God is not pleased with compromises; God wants our all. After all, he's given his all to us.

PRAYER

O Giver of every good and perfect gift, accept our heartfelt worship as we bring before you all you have given us. Hear us in the name of Jesus, your greatest gift to us. Amen.

Listen and Be Still

When I See Blood

"When I see the blood, I will pass over you."
EXODUS 12:13

EXODUS 12:1-13

The news passed through all the slaves' quarters—there was to be a special meal. Instructions called for a lamb to be killed and roasted, for the blood to be sprinkled on the doorpost, and for all who ate the meal to be dressed and ready to go. The blood on the doorpost was a sign that inside the home the lamb was being eaten and the family was participating in the deliverance the Lord would provide. The day of liberation had come.

But so had the night of judgment. The Lord was coming to judge Pharaoh and the Egyptians, and the judgment would come to anyone who did not have the sign of blood on the doorpost. As the angel of the Lord came bringing death, the blood on the doorpost was the only thing that would turn the angel away from bringing the sentence of death into that home.

The judgment of the Lord is coming to all nations; the angel who executed death for the Egyptians is coming again at the appointed time to bring death to the people of the world. The only thing that will turn the executioner away is the blood of another Lamb, the One whom John the Baptist announced: "Look, the Lamb of God, who takes away the sin of the world!" (John 1:29).

Are you feasting on the Lamb of God, with your preparations made for the journey? Will the angel see the blood of the Lamb protecting you?

PRAYER

The sentence is upon us, O Lord. When the time of judgment comes, may the angel see the blood of the Lamb, your Son, our only hope for salvation. In his name, Amen.

Listen and Be Still

295

Fond Farewell

*The Egyptians urged the people to hurry
and leave the country.*
EXODUS 12:33

EXODUS 12:29-36

How quickly life changes. One day the king is unyielding, opposed to having the people of Israel leave; the next day he urges them to be gone. We should recognize that what appears to be a fickle reaction of a spoiled monarch is actually a human response to the movement of God's hand.

Someone once said that it seems as if God's "judo principle" is operating here. In other words, those who struggle the hardest to be on top suddenly find God using their own momentum to place them on the bottom. Here God turns the momentum of the oppressor to eagerness to see the slave people leave. In fact, the Egyptians are now so eager to have the Hebrews leave that they also give up their silver and gold to hurry the slaves along. Suddenly the back wages of hundreds of years are eagerly paid by the oppressor. Egypt is despoiled by slave bands marching with troughs of dough on their shoulders. What divine irony!

By identifying with Jesus, who emptied himself and took the form of a slave for our sake, we can be sure that the riches of this world will have lasting value. Why? Because all the wealth of the kingdoms of this world will be given to the Son (Isaiah 60:5; Revelation 21:24-26).

Will you be part of the slave band that sees God's "judo principle" operating again?

PRAYER

Lord, we know we are bound by the limitations of our culture and time, but we look forward to the day the head of our slave band will set us fully free. In Jesus, Amen.

Listen and Be Still

Both Ways

Moses took the bones of Joseph with him. . . .
EXODUS 13:19

EXODUS 13:11-19

"Look both ways before you cross the street!" That advice for young children also applies to the Christian standing in the midst of history.

Moses had just stressed the importance of passing the memory of the exodus on to Israel's children. And then, as if to illustrate the importance of looking back, he took along the bones of Joseph to the new land the Lord had promised Israel. Almost four hundred years of history were tied up with those bones—years of memories of how the people had come to the land of Egypt.

After looking back, the people of God also had to look toward the future. Joseph, after looking back to the promise given to Abraham, had been able to look forward, convinced that Abraham's sons and daughters would someday leave Egypt. Joseph was a person who lived with his eyes to the future, to the fulfilling of God's promises. So he had asked that his bones be kept, saying, "God will surely come to your aid."

With Moses the people also looked to that future of God's fulfilled promises. The Passover celebration was a symbol of future hope, a celebration to continue until in Jesus that hope would be fulfilled.

All Christians must also look both ways: back to God's promises and great acts of salvation, and forward to Jesus' return and the full coming of God's kingdom.

PRAYER

Lord, give us a two-dimensional view: a hearty celebration for all you have done for us in Jesus Christ, and an eager anticipation of his return. In his name we pray. Amen.

Listen and Be Still

297

Led by God

By day the Lord went ahead of them in
a pillar of cloud to guide them on their way.
EXODUS 13:21

EXODUS 13:20-22

If you have to travel, it's nice to have someone with you who knows the road: where it turns, where the bridges are, what corners to be careful of.

The Israelites were on a journey through land unfamiliar to them. God gave them a visible sign to assure them that he knew the way. The divine Navigator would show them the route to the promised land.

We too are making a journey through life, and at times we might think to ourselves how nice it would be if only God had a pillar of cloud waiting for us each morning to give us directions for each day. Then we could simply follow the cloud and know that we're traveling within God's will.

In reality, God has given us the promise of something even better than a pillar of cloud for each day and a pillar of fire for each night. Jesus said: "I will ask the Father, and he will give you another Counselor to be with you forever—the Spirit of truth. The world cannot accept him, because it neither sees him nor knows him. But you know him, for he lives with you and will be in you" (John 14:16-17).

So there's no need for us to have a pillar of cloud like the Israelites had. Through Jesus our hearts can be filled with the Holy Spirit, who will live in us always and guide us to the promised land.

PRAYER

Lord, if we ask for wisdom, you will give it freely. We need wisdom for making choices each day, so please give us your wisdom through your Spirit, we pray. In Jesus, Amen.

Listen and Be Still

Fear Not

"Do not be afraid. Stand firm and you will see
the deliverance the Lord will bring you today."
EXODUS 14:13

EXODUS 14:10-18

Fear can do strange things to us. Sometimes it gives us great strength to perform feats that seem beyond our ability; other times it immobilizes us, leaving us unable to function. But most often it leaves us in an agitated state somewhere between those two extremes.

The Israelites' fear, like ours, was not necessarily brought on by circumstances. They had pillars of cloud and of fire; they had walked out of Egypt with the spoils in their knapsacks; they had seen the powerful plagues by which God showed himself to Egypt. But at the sight of "Pharaoh and all his army" following them, they caved in to fear.

In that agitated state the Israelites began accusing Moses of getting them into this fix, and they began justifying their own actions of the past. As we listen to their conversation, it may sound to us like the whining of little children. But is that all it is? When we are frightened, don't we often sound the same? If we fear for financial stability, isn't it easy to blame our spouses or our bosses for our insecurity? Or if we fear for our children, don't we quickly blame outside influences?

It's good to know that our salvation doesn't depend on our own efforts. When we are scared because of what we can't do, the prophet like Moses will say, "Stand firm, and . . . see the deliverance [of] the Lord"!

PRAYER

"Your power alone, O Son of God, can all my sin erase. No other work but yours . . . no strength but that which is divine can bear me safely through." In your name, Amen.

Listen and Be Still

They Saw

When the Israelites saw the great power
the Lord displayed. . . the people feared the Lord.
EXODUS 14:31

EXODUS 14:26-31

〰️Stand firm and watch. This teaching technique is as old as the Red Sea and as modern as today's high school laboratory.

Moses had told the people of Israel that all they had to do was stand still, and the Lord would fight the battle against the Egyptians for them. With knees still quivering, the Israelites did exactly that.

Afterward they stood on the seashore to survey what the Lord had done. As the bodies of Egyptians floated ashore and caught in the reeds, what they had witnessed made its impact on them. They had just seen the vindication of the Lord before their eyes; truly the Lord was God. Now, as they looked out over the sea, they saw where the Lord had made a path for them through the middle of it; they saw the way of escape.

Among the ordinary events of our lives, we catch glimpses of God's salvation as we stand next to friends healed from a life of sin who profess their new life in Jesus. We see in Jesus God's way for our escape.

Though we now see only dimly and catch only glimpses, someday we will stand by another sea and see how all the enemies of the Lord are defeated. And we will see clearly how the face of our Deliverer, who has led us through this life and whom we already worship, shines with glory (see Revelation 15).

PRAYER

Lord, thank you for glimpses of your saving power, but give us also a longing to see the salvation of our God complete. Give us faith, Lord, to await that Day. For Jesus' sake, Amen.

Listen and Be Still

Song of Triumph

Moses and the Israelites sang. . . "I will sing to the Lord, for he is highly exalted."

EXODUS 15:1

EXODUS 15:1-18

In the previous reading we left the saints standing by the sea, looking at what God had done. But the people of Israel do not remain there quietly. Soon the whole people are straining in song, lifting one united voice in praise to God for their deliverance. Throughout this song are the themes of God's love for his people and God's judgment for those who stand in the way of his plans for them.

Throughout history Christians have joined in singing about the mighty acts of God. From the chants of psalms to the Latin liturgy, from pipe organs to amplified guitars, Christians have found many ways to celebrate the victory of the Lord over his enemies. When, along with Pharaoh's voice, the voices of a thousand petty dictators have been stilled under the waves of God's judgment, the stillness will be broken by believers who sing of the love and power of God.

Lift your voice today to sing of the triumph of God; praise God for his love and strength. Remember the vision of John in which he saw those who had been victorious with God standing beside the glassy sea and singing "the song of Moses the servant of God and the song of the Lamb" (Revelation 15:3).

After slavery and the Red Sea, and because of the love of Christ and his deliverance from judgment, God's people keep right on singing—into eternity.

PRAYER

"Who will not fear you, O Lord, and bring glory to your name? For you alone are holy. All nations will come and worship before you." We praise you forever, O Lord. Amen.

Listen and Be Still

MISSION MAGNIFICENT

30 MEDITATIONS AND READINGS

BY DR. ROGER S. GREENWAY

DR. ROGER S. GREENWAY

The Christian faith is not built on imagination or a collection of wise sayings; it is built on actual historical events. Among them are Jesus' crucifixion, his resurrection from the dead, his ascension into heaven, and the breath-taking expansion of the church since the day the Holy Spirit came and set God's mission in motion.

In these reflections, we learn of God's ages-long mission that was set in motion at Pentecost, when the Holy Spirit was poured out on the church. The Holy Spirit is the Spirit of Christ and the Spirit of mission. The Holy Spirit's coming began the spread of Jesus' gospel to the world. Nothing is more important than this mission.

Dr. Greenway, a retired minister of the Christian Reformed Church, served for many years as a missionary to Ceylon (Sri Lanka) and to Mexico. He has also served on the board of Christian Reformed World Ministries and has taught at Westminster and Calvin Theological Seminaries.

The Source of Life and Power

"You will receive power when the Holy Spirit comes on you; and you will be my witnesses."
Acts 1:8

Acts 1:1-8

The source and power of the church's mission are found in the Holy Spirit. He is the Spirit of life and of witness.

Christians around the world celebrate Pentecost. In these next meditations we will remember and reflect on that great, historic event. On that day, spiritual power was unleashed—the likes of which the world has never seen. And, since Pentecost, the world has never been the same.

This set of meditations will focus on events in the early days of the church. They are recorded in the book of Acts. Acts tells us about the faith and actions of Christians who became filled with the Holy Spirit. Therefore, Acts has a lot to teach us about living and serving God today.

Jesus promised his followers that they would be "baptized with the Holy Spirit." And Jesus asked them to wait for this experience with the Spirit, because he did not want his followers to begin their mission without it. He knew that if they tried to accomplish God's mission in their own strength, they would surely fail.

As we read about what happens when believers in Christ are gripped by the Spirit and turned loose upon the world, we are struck by the importance of Pentecost for Christian missions. Do we see ourselves as part of God's mission?

Prayer

O God, thank you for the power of the Holy Spirit. We want to learn more about him and to experience his power in our daily life and witness. Open our hearts to your teachings. Amen.

Listen and Be Still

305

Spiritual Health in a Hostile World

They. . . joined. . . constantly in prayer, along with the women and Mary the mother of Jesus, and his brothers.
ACTS 1:14

ACTS 1:12-14

Jerusalem was not a safe or happy place for the followers of Jesus. But Jesus had commanded them not to leave Jerusalem until they had received the gift of the Holy Spirit (Acts 1:4).

Though dangerous, Jerusalem was also the place of greatest possible influence. Very soon the ancient Jewish feast of Pentecost would be celebrated, and people from all over the Roman Empire would be pouring into the city for the religious celebration. Whatever might happen of spiritual significance in Jerusalem at that time would make an impact far and wide.

We should note that the early followers of Jesus did two things: they found a place where they could be together in the midst of the city but apart from the hostile crowd, and they were constantly in prayer. Each of us can do these things. We must cling to the circle of believers, however small or isolated, and pray as much as we can.

Serving God in tough places may not be our choice. But if God wants us there, he will provide the strength we need not only to survive spiritually but to bear witness for him. Very often it is the presence of adversaries that provides the opportunity for fruitful service. It was, after all, in hostile Jerusalem that the outpouring of the Spirit occurred.

PRAYER

Lord, sustain us by your Spirit and grace. May our spiritual life not waver, nor our steps wander. Help us to be a light for Jesus where we work and live. For his sake, Amen.

Listen and Be Still

Judas and the Holy Spirit

"The Scripture had to be fulfilled which the Holy Spirit spoke long ago. . . concerning Judas."

ACTS 1:16

ACTS 1:15-22

The story of Judas is one of the saddest in the Bible. Chosen by Jesus to be one of his closest followers, Judas might have become a leader in the church and a great missionary of the gospel. Instead, he struck a deal with Jesus' enemies and betrayed the Lord for money. Overcome by the results of his treachery, Judas soon died by his own hand (Matthew 27:5).

Acts tells us that the Holy Spirit had predicted Judas's treachery many years earlier. The apostle Peter recognized these predictions in Psalms 69 and 109, and he drew implications from them about finding a replacement for Judas. Judas had occupied a position of leadership, and since that place was now empty, it should be filled by a qualified person.

Judas had heard the gospel again and again. He had witnessed the wonders Jesus had performed. Along with the other disciples, Judas had been groomed for leadership in the mission of the church. But his heart was evil. He felt no love toward the Lord Jesus. Even the miracles he saw did not bring life to his soul.

The gospel message does not act by itself; the regenerating power of the Holy Spirit is necessary if a heart is going to be changed. The gospel is simple, and the Word is clear, but the human heart is entirely set against them until the Holy Spirit instills life and faith.

PRAYER

Lord, forgive us our sin and keep us close to yourself. By your grace and Spirit, prevent us from falling and make us useful. In the name of Jesus, our Lord, we pray. Amen.

Listen and Be Still

The Missionary Drive

All of them were filled with the Holy Spirit and began to speak in other tongues as the Spirit enabled them.
ACTS 2:4

ACTS 2:1-4

Gathered at Jerusalem for the Pentecost festival were Jews from all over the world. Their languages were as diverse as the nations they came from. Often they had difficulty communicating with each other, but when they came to where the Spirit-filled Christians were assembled, they all suddenly heard the gospel being announced in their very own language.

Behind this explosion of universal witness to Jesus lay the inner compulsion of the Holy Spirit. Once believers had been filled with the Spirit, nothing could keep them quiet. The Holy Spirit is the Spirit of Christ's mission, and his chief interest is to proclaim God's saving work, accomplished through Jesus.

Pentecost stamps the word "missions" on everything the church does. The Spirit, who gives life, health, and vitality to the church, is the missionary Spirit of the Lord. He refuses to be silenced. All who know his presence become his mouthpieces. And his message is always about the saving goodness and greatness of God.

Churches and individuals who are filled with the Spirit are always lovers of missions and evangelism. For them, witnessing is natural. In word and deed they give evidence that an inner compulsion will not let them rest. This is the missionary drive of the Spirit, who bears witness to the saving goodness of God.

PRAYER

Spirit of God, breathe into us the same missionary love and zeal that were so evident at Pentecost. Move your church to witness boldly, and bring everyone to learn of your salvation. Amen.

Listen and Be Still

God-Fearing Jews in Missions

There were staying in Jerusalem God-fearing Jews
from every nation under heaven.
ACTS 2:5

ACTS 2:5-13

The dispersion of the Jews at the time of Christ provided a marvelous opportunity for the spread of the gospel. Jewish communities could be found in most parts of the ancient world. Jewish religious activities were a well-known part of city life. Jewish scholars had translated the Old Testament into the Greek language, and religious teachers were busy propagating the Jewish faith among Gentiles.

Acts 2:11 says that "Jews and converts to Judaism" were present at Pentecost. Foreign-born Jews could be distinguished from locals by their language, customs, clothing, and skin color. But they were all united in their fear of God and respect for the Scriptures.

God used the Jews to prepare the world for the gospel. God chose this people to be the channel for his revelation and for the incarnation of his Son. On his human side, Jesus was a Jew. The apostles were Jews, and the early church was heavily Jewish. The Holy Spirit was poured out on a Jewish feast day.

Jews and Gentiles heard the gospel together on Pentecost, and they came into the church arm and arm. The way the gospel unites different people is glorious. As we prepare for Pentecost this year, let us pray that through faith in the Spirit of Christ many peoples, now separated, will be united.

PRAYER

Spirit of the living God, open the eyes of Jews and Gentiles to the truth about Christ and the gospel. Convict us of our sin, bring us to repentance, and unite us in love at Jesus' feet. Amen.

Listen and Be Still

The Cross and the Resurrection

"You, with the help of wicked men, put [Christ] to death. . . . But God raised him from the dead."
ACTS 2:23,24

ACTS 2:14-24

When Peter addressed the crowd, he took out the Scriptures and got right to the point: God has fulfilled his word. Salvation is only through Christ. People who should have received him crucified him instead. But God raised Jesus from the dead. Jesus is now at God's "right hand"—the place of power and authority over the universe. The only safe thing for anyone to do is to repent, receive Christ by faith, and be baptized. Christ's Holy Spirit came upon all who believe.

The gospel spoken by Peter at Pentecost is the same message that Christ's followers must bring to the world today. Likewise, Peter's faith in God's plan and purpose is the missionary's confidence. People may do their worst, but God's power outdoes the opposition.

Samuel M. Zwemer, the great missionary to the Muslims, stated the matter this way: "Apart from God in Christ there can be no missionary enterprise. In Jesus Christ the work of missions finds its basis, its aim, its method, its message, its motive and its goal. The evangelization of the nations is not a human but a divine project....The message of the New Testament to the world was redemption from sin. The word of the Cross was the message of the apostles; the power of the Cross was their motive; and the glory of the resurrection was their hope."

PRAYER

O God, enable all who preach the gospel to set forth Christ and the gospel clearly and according to your Word, so that none may escape the eternal issues of Christ. For his sake, Amen.

Listen and Be Still

The Pentecostal Church

They devoted themselves to the apostles' teaching and to the
fellowship, to the breaking of bread and to prayer.
ACTS 2:42

ACTS 2:40-47

On Pentecost Sunday, Christians who are able attend church. Some Christians have very little choice about which church to attend. Others have many congregations to choose from. If given the opportunity to describe the kind of church they'd like to be a part of, most Christians, I imagine, would describe a church like the one that began at Pentecost.

What was so marvelous about the church formed at Pentecost? The first thing that strikes us is its size—three thousand were converted and baptized. There was excitement—the apostles performed signs and wonders. A kind of electrifying enthusiasm over their new faith brought Christians together—not just on Sunday, but every day—and the church kept growing.

But there was more. There was a quality, a depth of commitment, in the Christians that went deeper than excitement over signs and wonders. These people were devoted to solid, biblical teaching. And they loved each other so much that they didn't let anyone remain poor. They opened their homes to one another and celebrated the Lord's saving work in holy communion.

The Spirit of the Lord made the church a living witness to God's reign in human lives. What prevents us from having the same fellowship is our reluctance to be like the early Christians in every detail.

PRAYER

Dear Father, we long to see our churches strong and growing, praising you and loving all your children. Let the faith, love, and power of Pentecost multiply in churches today. In Jesus, Amen.

Listen and Be Still

A Beggar at the Gate

A man crippled from birth was being carried to the temple gate. . . where he was put every day to beg. . . .
ACTS 3:2

ACTS 3:1-10

The story of the beggar's dramatic healing has thrilled Bible readers for centuries. The beggar hoped for a coin, but he received something much greater. "Silver or gold I do not have," said Peter, "but what I have I give you. In the name of Jesus Christ of Nazareth, walk." Then Peter took the beggar by the hand, helped him up, and the man could walk!

Let's reflect on the disciples' concern for this cripple. Why did they bother with him at all? With all the exciting things happening in the growing church, the apostles could have rushed on by.

Peter himself provided the explanation later, when he defended himself before the temple authorities. He described what had happened as "an act of kindness shown to a cripple." It began with an act of love for an individual who lived on the fringe of society. Others rushed by, but Peter and John heard the man's pleas and stopped to give him attention. They were moved by the impulse of the Spirit and acted boldly, in faith. God did the rest.

The basis for our attention to the poor is God's love for us and ours for him. The Spirit of God living in us forbids us to ignore their desperate need. He tunes our ears to their cries and moves our hands to lift them. And when we lift them, we tell them about Jesus.

PRAYER

Spirit of God, deepen our love for God and our neighbors. Turn our attention to the poor, and make us instruments of your healing. By our acts of kindness, bring honor to Jesus. Amen.

Listen and Be Still

The Spirit's Theme Is Jesus

"The God of Abraham, Isaac and Jacob, the God of our fathers, has glorified his servant Jesus."

ACTS 3:13

ACTS 3:11-21

Spirit-filled people talk mostly about Jesus. Jesus himself predicted that this would be so. The Spirit, Jesus said, would explain his work and teachings so that future generations would know him, believe, and witness about him (John 15:26,27; 16:12-15).

This is illustrated by the sermon Peter preached after the lame man was healed. Don't look at me, said Peter. I'm not the source of this miracle. Look to Jesus, the holy and righteous one and the author of life. You had him killed. But God raised him from the dead. By faith in the name of Jesus, this lame man was healed. You must repent! Believe in him! He is coming again!

The ministry of the Spirit is always Christ-ward. He prompts witnesses to tell about Christ. He moves preachers to exalt the name of Jesus. The Spirit does not call attention to himself but always to Jesus and to salvation through Jesus. The theme of true pentecostal preaching is Jesus, followed by a call to repentance and to faith in him.

The Spirit inspires the same kind of proclamation today. Shame on those Christians who by their religious words and actions draw attention to themselves, make themselves famous, and even become rich. Such conduct is not truly Christian, for the Spirit does not operate this way. He gives all the honor to Jesus.

PRAYER

Spirit of God, show us where we have strayed from pure faith and practice. Teach us to measure all that is called "religious" by your Word. May we praise the name of Jesus alone. Amen.

Listen and Be Still

Bold Witnesses

They were all filled with the Holy Spirit
and spoke the word of God boldly.
ACTS 4:31

ACTS 4:23-31

Christians in China have experienced persecution much like that of the early days of the Christian church. And they have grown strong and bold. So highly do they value the things they learn through suffering that they pity Christians who live in lands where no high price must be paid for one's faith.

The Holy Spirit moved the early Christians to witness with amazing boldness in the face of vicious opposition. The powerful people who had crucified the Lord were determined to stamp out the budding Christian church. They imprisoned, intimidated, and in some cases stoned to death the followers of Jesus. But they could not destroy the faith or the courage of the believers. The believers used the opportunities provided by persecution to witness publicly for their Lord.

The Spirit-filled Christians in ancient Jerusalem gathered for prayer after a frightening time in prison. They recognized in Scripture that what they were suffering was related to the great spiritual war of the universe, between the powers of darkness and the Lord of light. But they did not ask that God spare them from persecution. They asked that he enable them to speak his word with boldness and that he confirm their testimony in supernatural ways.

How such faith and bold witness are needed today!

PRAYER

Father, we pray for those members of your family who suffer persecution. Keep them close and guard their faith. And may we who are free work hard to spread your saving word. In Jesus, Amen.

Listen and Be Still

Who Is the Holy Spirit?

"How is it that…you have lied to the Holy Spirit? You have. . . lied. . . to God."

ACTS 5:3,4

ACTS 5:1-11

Two young women were discussing religion before a church service in Philadelphia. "I can agree with most of what they teach here," said one, "but not with the Trinity. I think theologians made that up." The other said that she considered herself a "Trinitarian" but that she wasn't sure about the Holy Spirit as God.

No Christian should be hazy about something so important as the divinity of God's Spirit. We owe too much to the Spirit's word to doubt him. In passages like the one we read today, the Bible's teaching about the Spirit leaps from the page and grips us. He is not an impersonal power that we may acknowledge or ignore. He is God, and we must honor him for who he is.

Ananias and Sapphira failed to reckon with the Holy Spirit, and that caused their downfall. They pretended to make a gift to the church of all their proceeds from a land sale. But they kept back part of the money, still hoping to enjoy the church's praise for their generosity. The trick probably would have worked if the Spirit, who knows everything, had not exposed them. If you try to deceive him, you are in serious trouble.

Besides clear evidence of the divinity of the Holy Spirit, this episode teaches that God wants the witness of his church to be pure. God hates all sham and dishonesty, especially when his church is concerned.

PRAYER

Holy Spirit, rid our minds of any doubts about you, and make us reflect your purity in every thought, word, and deed. May we always serve you with fear. In Jesus' name, Amen.

Listen and Be Still

A Division of Labor

*"Choose seven men. . . who are known to
be full of the Spirit and wisdom."*
ACTS 6:3–4

ACTS 6:1-7

It takes a lot of wisdom to help the poor, and to do it in the special way that advances God's kingdom requires wisdom and wholehearted commitment to God. This is what the Bible calls the "fullness of the Spirit." It is an essential requirement among those who minister to the poor in the name of Christ and his church.

In the body of Christ there are various gifts and callings. All of them come from the Holy Spirit, but they are not all the same. The early apostles recognized this, so they divided the areas of labor. Deacons would minister to the poor, while the apostles would concentrate on the ministries of prayer and preaching.

It is significant that this story of the division of labor is followed by a verse that tells of the rapid growth of the church (v. 7). Today too, when ministries of word and deed are properly linked in the service of Christ, the Spirit blesses the church's mission.

By their services to the poor, Christians obey the Lord and bear witness to him. The Lord commands his children to be generous, to remember the poor, and to do good to all, especially to fellow believers in need.

Ministry to the poor is also a public statement of Christlike love and concern for our neighbors. Such ministry shows even critical and hostile people that the Christian faith is genuine.

PRAYER

Heavenly Father, make us Christ-like in our concern for those in need. Anoint many with the gifts and calling to serve the poor. And take away hunger from all your children. In Jesus, Amen.

Listen and Be Still

The Gospel Makes Some People Angry

*They could not stand up against [Stephen's]
wisdom or the Spirit by which he spoke.*
ACTS 6:9–10

ACTS 6:8-15

Stephen was among the first deacons chosen by the church to minister to the poor. He is described as "a man full of God's grace and power." God performed miraculous signs through Stephen, and Stephen's ministry had a tremendous impact.

It is not surprising, then, that severe opposition to Stephen soon arose. Stephen was arrested, and false witnesses were lined up against him. They argued and accused him, but the Bible says they "could not stand up against his wisdom or the Spirit by which he spoke."

Christians should never be surprised by the world's rage against the gospel and its spokespersons. The proclamation of the gospel arouses the anger of securalists in the West and of adherents to non-Christian religions in the East. Like Stephen, some Christians are struck by physical blows and die as martyrs, while others suffer more subtle abuse for days and years.

The twentieth century has seen many martyrs for Christ, and many believers are suffering severely even today. There are pastors in prison in Africa and in the Middle East because they were found preaching. Lay persons are in jail for distributing Bibles. Many are tortured and subjected to the lowest forms of humiliation.

All, like Stephen, are objects of the world's wrath because they represent Jesus.

PRAYER

Father, hear the cries of all who suffer for the gospel. Fill them with your Spirit and support them in their need. Bring lasting fruit from their suffering and release them soon. In Jesus, Amen.

Listen and Be Still

A Dangerous Religion

On that day a great persecution
broke out against the church.
ACTS 8:1

ACTS 7:54-8:3

On my desk are reports of persecution being waged right now against Christians in four different countries. Do Christians in the so-called "free world" realize the price some believers are paying for their faith?

Report number one: A pastor and a deacon in Africa have spent six months in jail for distributing Bibles. They have been beaten, and there is no promise of their early release.

Report number two: In an important Mideast country, ten Christians have been arrested this year. The charges? They forsook their old faith and became followers of Jesus Christ. Pending legislation in that country would make conversion to Christianity punishable by life imprisonment.

Report number three: The death penalty has been decreed in a certain country for anyone who wrongfully uses the name of the country's hallowed religious teacher. The law is considered extremely dangerous for the Christians in that land.

Report number four: In another country a young woman, a recent convert to Christianity, mysteriously disappeared. There are reports that say she was tortured and killed because she changed her religion.

Would we hold on to such a dangerous faith if persecution came to us?

PRAYER

Lord, give those who suffer for their faith the grace to persevere. And make all who follow Christ aware of just how dangerous their faith is. Make us all strong, now and always. Amen.

Listen and Be Still

A Wise and Spirit-Filled Person

*Philip began with that very passage of Scripture
and told him the good news about Jesus.*
ACTS 8:35

ACTS 8:26-35

The first description the Bible gives of Philip says he was full of the Spirit and wisdom. Philip was one of the first seven deacons of the church (Acts 6). He demonstrated Christ's compassion in his ministry to the poor.

The next time we hear of Philip, he is deeply involved in evangelism (Acts 8:4-17). When persecution broke out in Jerusalem, Philip went to Samaria, where very few people had heard the gospel. He proclaimed Christ there, and many wonderful things happened. Converts were great in number, and the whole city felt the joy that Christ brings. Soon afterward, Peter and John, the two leading apostles from Jerusalem, joined Philip, and a "second Pentecost" occurred when the Holy Spirit came upon the Samaritan believers.

In today's reading we see Philip on a lonely desert road. There he met an important Ethiopian on his way home from Jerusalem. The Ethiopian was reading from the Scriptures and was hungry for true religion. But he did not yet know about Christ. Philip explained the Scriptures to him and told him the good news about Jesus. The Ethiopian believed and was saved.

The last we hear of Philip is that he is in Caesarea, married, the head of a godly household, and working as an evangelist (Acts 21). What a beautiful, fruitful life he lived! The world needs more people like him.

PRAYER
Holy Spirit, we want to be used as Philip was. Please take over our lives and fill us with your truth and wisdom so that we can be useful in the church for the glory of Christ. Amen.

Listen and Be Still

The Vision of Christ

"Who are you, Lord?" Saul asked. "I am Jesus, whom you are persecuting," he replied.
ACTS 9:5

ACTS 9:1-6

Anyone who has ever been charged by a bull will never forget the eyes full of fury and the loud and heavy breathing of the animal lunging forward, intent on piercing its victim.

Like an angry bull, Saul made charge after charge against Jesus' followers. He was "breathing out murderous threats" against them, says the Bible. He seized men and women and threw them in prison. He was determined to stamp out Christ's followers.

But, suddenly, as he journeyed to Damascus, where he expected to extend his persecution, Saul was stopped in his tracks. A brilliant light shone down from heaven, and he fell to the ground and heard a voice: "Saul, Saul, why do you persecute me?"

People today hear Jesus' voice in many different ways. The Word comes to people by radio, through literature, and often simply by the quiet witness of a friend or neighbor. Missionaries travel thousands of miles to convey Christ's message in places where other gods and other faiths are embraced by millions.

When he heard Jesus speaking, Saul fell to the ground and surrendered. Suddenly he saw the truth as never before. All the things he had trusted and the goals he had pursued turned to dust.

PRAYER

Lord, you confront us as we read your startling message in the Bible. May we surrender to you, as Saul did. Take our lives and make them yours completely. In Jesus' name we pray. Amen.

Listen and Be Still

A Persecutor Turned Preacher

*At once he began to preach in the synagogues
that Jesus is the Son of God.*
Acts 9:20

Acts 9:17-22

The believers in Jesus living in Damascus were braced for the worst. Paul the persecutor was coming their way, and they knew his murderous intentions. They expected bitter confrontations and imprisonment.

But none of that happened. Instead, the man whom they had feared came as a preacher of Jesus Christ. Just a few days before, Saul had despised Jesus' name and hurled accusations against all those who believed in him. But now he was arguing fervently for Christ.

Nobody was more shocked by this change of events than the humble man Ananias. Ananias had gone looking for Saul after God had revealed that Saul had met Jesus and was waiting for Ananias to come. Their encounter was dramatic. "Brother Saul," said Ananias, "the Lord—Jesus, who appeared to you on the road as you were coming here—has sent me so that you may see again and be filled with the Holy Spirit." Saul had been blinded in his encounter with Jesus, but when Ananias spoke to him, he could see again, and he arose and was baptized.

Let nobody underestimate the power of God's Spirit to turn a sinner around. What God did for Saul he can do for anyone. Through faith and baptism, Saul entered the great company of those who by God's grace and Spirit have been turned from death to life.

Prayer

O God, do in the lives of many today what you did in the life of Saul. Show your power, turn sinners around, and glorify your name through people who once scorned your Son. Amen.

Listen and Be Still

A Woman Well Remembered

All the widows stood around him, crying and showing him the. . . clothing that Dorcas had made. . . .
ACTS 9:39

ACTS 9:36-43

In Joppa a woman died whom nobody could forget. Her life had been marked by good deeds and loving concern for the poor. Dorcas used her gifts and energies to meet the needs of other women and to relieve some of their suffering in poverty. When she died, a host of people were cast into mourning. Here had been a woman who demonstrated the Spirit of Jesus.

How many will mourn when we die, and why? Will we leave behind us tangible evidence of our faith and concern for the poor and suffering? Will we be remembered as great and generous men and women of God?

For most middle-class people it is terribly hard to realize how much suffering there is in the world. Where many of us live, we don't see it. Our refrigerators are full, and our children never go to bed hungry. Poverty is not something many of us daily touch or feel. Yet one-fourth of the world goes hungry and many a mother grieves over her malnourished child—including some readers of this devotional.

Peter got down on his knees and prayed over Dorcas's body. "Get up," he said, and she opened her eyes and sat up. Her life was prolonged, and her ministry continued. The poor had their Dorcas back; God showed his mercy to them by restoring her back to life. And to us he demonstrated dramatically how much the world needs the ministry of people like Dorcas.

PRAYER

Dear God, help us to live as Dorcas did. Help us to show our faith by our deeds and to uproot the world's misery with our love and mercy. May we do all in the name of Jesus. Amen.

Listen and Be Still

God Has No Favorites

*[They] were astonished that the gift of the Holy Spirit
had been poured out even on the Gentiles.*
ACTS 10:45

ACTS 11:15-18

The news burst like a bombshell on the church. The Holy Spirit had come upon Gentiles, just as he had come upon Jews. A new day had dawned. God had no favorites. His saving grace and Holy Spirit were extended to people of all races and nations.

Direct action of the Holy Spirit was required for this breakthrough. There was much to be changed: old barriers and prejudices had to be burned away by divine fire. A new set of people would soon become members, and many of the old believers found this unsettling. It forced them to rethink their understanding of God, his ways, and their mission.

But the Holy Spirit brought about the change. He is the great teacher of divine truth, and he keeps expanding the church's horizons. It was shocking at first for the church to realize the breadth of God's love and missionary intentions, and some members continued to resist the widening scope of the gospel. But, on the whole, the Spirit's direction was accepted, and old barriers came down.

Intellectual questions may linger, but divine love's fire cannot be quenched. Arguments drop aside when the Spirit leaps forward, pulling the church to broader frontiers. All peoples of the earth need Christ, and the Spirit signals God's people to move onward!

PRAYER

O God, around us are people and nations that do not know Christ. We who know him want nothing more than to tell them about our Savior. Lead us on in our mission, for Jesus' sake.

Listen and Be Still

Through Ordinary People

Some of them. . . began to speak to Greeks also, telling them the good news about the Lord Jesus.
ACTS 11:20

ACTS 11:19-24

One of the most remarkable churches in history, the church in Antioch, was founded by people whose names we don't know. All we know is that they came originally from the Mediterranean island of Cyprus and the North African country of Cyrene. They had spent some time in Jerusalem, but persecution had forced them to flee. They traveled to Syria, and in Antioch they began telling Gentiles as well as Jews about Jesus, the Lord. A great number of converts were won.

The founders of the church at Antioch were not the original apostles whom Jesus had commissioned to evangelize the world. These were so-called lay-people, ordinary Christians in whose hearts the Holy Spirit lived, giving them the good news to tell others.

The fact is that most of the work in Christ's kingdom is done by people whose names and labors go largely unnoticed by others. Yet what marvelous things the Spirit accomplishes through them, and how great will be their eternal award in heaven!

Every believer has at least one gift for kingdom service, because the Holy Spirit passes no believer by. And most believers have many gifts. We cannot imagine the amount of witness, service, and church growth that would occur if all believers recognized and used all the gifts and callings of the Spirit.

PRAYER

Give us the grace, Lord, to genuinely assess ourselves. Forgive us for minimizing our talents and leaving kingdom work to others. Stir us by your Spirit to some new service today. Amen.

Christians

The disciples were first called
Christians at Antioch.
ACTS 11:26

ACTS 11:25-30

Jesus' disciples have been known as Christians for so many centuries that most people have forgotten where the name was first used. It was first coined to degrade Christ's followers in Antioch, Syria.

In those days millions of people were slaves, and they usually did not have their own personal names but were known by the names of their owners. Neither did slaves have the privilege of doing as they pleased. Their wills were not their own. They lived, worked, dressed, and behaved according to the wills of their owners and masters.

Against this background we can understand the implication of the name Christian.

The disciples of Jesus spoke of him as their Lord and Master. They said their chief goal in life was to do Christ's will and to advance his interests. They spoke of being owned by Christ and "bought with a price," namely, Christ's blood. "They talk like slaves," smirked their enemies. "So we'll call them Christians, 'slaves of Christ.'"

When the critics of Christianity look at us today, can they detect the attitudes and behavior that so distinguished the disciples at Antioch? They were people who rightly could be described as "full of the Holy Spirit." Are we prepared to be like them, slave-like in devotion to Christ?

PRAYER

Lord, lead us to the spiritual level of the Antioch disciples. Take our goals, hopes, and dreams and make us Christians in every sense of the name. What more can we ask? In Jesus' name, Amen.

Listen and Be Still

Through the Night, to the Light

Peter was kept in prison, but the church
was earnestly praying to God for him.
ACTS 12:5

ACTS 12:1-10

Christians are sometimes exposed to the world's worst evils. Anger, hostility, and moral pollution surround them every day. They find it difficult to keep their spiritual and moral lives intact. Perplexed, they struggle to pray and do not know what to ask. What are the solutions? Where is the escape? Often their lives are something like Peter's experience in prison.

God's Holy Spirit can provide the power and grace to overcome such conditions. He who is called the Comforter knows all about our situation. He who sustained Jesus can also sustain us.

In Scripture, the Spirit describes and interprets many of life's ugliest realities. He tells us of escape routes we never would imagine. His options far exceed our imagination, and his answers bewilder us until later we look back.

Peter's miraculous escape from prison illustrates God's power in answering prayer. The Bible says the disciples were "earnestly praying to God," which is the way all prayer should be. We should note, though, that their expectations were disappointingly meager. When Peter knocked at the door, they couldn't believe that God was actually answering their prayer. They had to learn, just as we do, that God delights in advancing his cause by answering his people's prayers.

PRAYER

Lord, we often travel through the cruel night of temptation and fear. We pray for strength and perseverance. By your Spirit, lead us to victory. Through Jesus Christ we pray. Amen.

Listen and Be Still

Sent by the Spirit

The Holy Spirit said, "Set apart for me Barnabas
and Saul for the work to which I have called them."
ACTS 13:2

ACTS 13:1-5

There are many Christian missionaries throughout the world, and their number is increasing. If asked, most of them would say they became missionaries because of a call from God. They felt moved by the Holy Spirit to leave homes, friends, and occupations to become Christ's messengers.

In most cases, churches play a large role in commissioning and supporting missionaries. This is as it should be, because the Bible clearly shows that the Spirit moves the church to be involved in missions.

Barnabas and Paul were active workers in the church in Antioch. The Spirit moved the church to see that God had special work in distant places for these two people. So the church commissioned Barnabas and Paul to go forth with the gospel. They were sent by the church and by the Spirit.

People who have little or no acquaintance with the Bible cannot understand the spiritual dynamics of missionary calling. They often attribute strange and unworthy motives to missionaries and portray them negatively. Yet such people are intrigued that missionaries keep going forth century after century, with churches sending and supporting them.

To those who understand the Spirit, missionary work is the most exciting in the world.

PRAYER

Lord, thank you for those who brought us the gospel in years past. We thank you that this work continues. Holy Spirit, anoint all who proclaim the gospel today. In Jesus' name, Amen.

Listen and Be Still

The Great Divider

When the Gentiles heard this, they were
glad and honored the word of the Lord.
ACTS 13:48

ACTS 13:44-52

The message of the gospel is the great divider. It brings joy to some people, but it makes others angry and sometimes mean.

This is illustrated by the story we read today, which took place in Antioch in Pisidia—a different city from the one we've been discussing for the past few days.

After Paul and Barnabas had spoken, one group became abusive and did everything possible to prevent people from hearing more. But others loved what they heard. They believed it, rejoiced over it, and immediately got busy spreading the message.

Everywhere on earth, the sure test of spiritual life is a person's reaction to the Word of God. Where there is life, there is joy over the gospel. On the other hand, wherever spiritual ignorance and death reign, God's truth is sneered at, and its messengers are opposed.

The Bible says that in Pisidian Antioch the people who accepted the gospel were filled with joy and with the Holy Spirit. The uproar of the crowd and the hostility of their enemies did not discourage them. Salvation had come to their hearts through the Word spoken to them, and that was worth everything.

Today, too, we must expect that our belief in the gospel will separate us from others. But let the world mock and rage. We have joy and the Holy Spirit.

PRAYER

Lord, give us courage to speak about your truth and give us joy over all it reveals. Send your light to cities and towns throughout the earth for the salvation of sinners today. In Jesus, Amen.

Listen and Be Still

Strategies of the Spirit

[They spoke] boldly for the Lord, who. . . [enabled]
them to do miraculous signs and wonders.
Acts 14:3

Acts 14:1-7

The strategies found in the book of Acts provide important lessons for missions everywhere. The early messengers of the gospel consistently targeted the larger cities and important population centers. From the urban centers the gospel spread outward and eventually covered entire regions.

Moreover, the apostles searched for those who were most receptive to their message—that is, they moved along the line of least resistance. Invariably they went first to the synagogues, which were found in almost all the key towns of the empire. And when the Jews rejected them, they turned to the Gentiles.

Behind these strategies was the fact that the apostles leaned heavily on the guidance and power of the Holy Spirit. They knew that the Spirit went ahead of them, preparing the hearts of those who would later receive the message. The apostles submitted their human strategies to the Spirit's divine strategy. Wherever he opened doors, they were prepared to follow.

"Miraculous signs and wonders" were part of the Spirit's strategy in places where the apostles' message was vigorously resisted. Today, too, missionaries often experience that where difficulties are greatest, God's power and grace are poured out in special, even miraculous ways.

Prayer

Sovereign God, guide your servants today. Tear down before their eyes the towers of sin and unbelief. Honor your name and the Son, whom you gave. In his name we pray. Amen.

Listen and Be Still

Serious about the Church

Paul and Barnabas appointed elders. . . in each church and. . . committed them to the Lord. . . .
ACTS 14:23

ACTS 14:21-28

The Bible makes it clear that mission work is serious business, and the planting and development of churches is an essential part of it.

The trip that Paul and Barnabas took together cost them a lot of pain and trouble. But their mission was to preach the gospel in places where it had not been heard before, and they accomplished that. In each place where converts were won, the apostles also organized a church and, trusting in the grace of God to sustain them, appointed elders to represent Christ's authority and to give leadership to the believers.

The missionaries were not superficial workers. Nor were they overly hasty in heralding the gospel. Their goal was to establish lasting communities of believers that would carry on the work. The apostles later returned to each place to teach and strengthen the young churches. The New Testament books that we call the "epistles" were one of the means by which the apostles continued nurturing the churches.

It remains God's will that churches be established, supported, and attended. Churches are to be centers of fellowship, instruction, intercession, and service. To neglect the church is to disobey God, in missions as much as in personal discipleship. Churches remain God's special instruments for advancing his kingdom.

PRAYER

Lord, bless and multiply your church. Cleanse it from sin and imperfection, and instruct it by your Word in truth and righteousness. Make its fellowship increasingly precious to us.

Amen.

Listen and Be Still

Who's in Charge?

When they came to the border. . . they tried to enter. . .
but the Spirit of Jesus would not allow them to.
ACTS 16:7

ACTS 16:6-10

The missionary enterprise of the church of Christ has never been larger than it is today. There are missionaries from North America, Europe, Asia, Latin America, and Africa. They cross the borders of other nations, learn new languages, adapt to new cultures, and proclaim the gospel by every means imaginable. They follow in the footsteps of Paul and his companions. They labor under Christ's commission and aim to tell the world about the gospel.

Who is the chief administrator of this worldwide missionary enterprise? There are mission agencies and boards, mission councils and administrations. But do human beings really control Christian missions, or is there a divine hand governing the entire operation?

Paul and his fellow missionaries knew the answer. They had their plans and strategies, but they realized that their vision and abilities were limited. The Holy Spirit was really in control. When the Spirit opened doors, the work advanced. When the Spirit closed doors, there was nothing they could do. Missions was, and is, primarily a spiritual enterprise. In it, men and women labor and serve, but they do not control.

The secret of success in missions lies in accepting the direction of the Holy Spirit and following it boldly in the hope of his kingdom.

PRAYER

Lord, make all your servants attentive listeners to your voice and humbly obedient to your direction. Don't let your people try to do your work without depending on your direction. Amen.

Listen and Be Still

Did You Receive the Holy Spirit?

*"We have not even heard that
there is a Holy Spirit."*
ACTS 19:2

ACTS 19:1-7

There are Christians who like to talk about God's creation, Christ's incarnation, the cross, the church, and Scripture's prophecies about the future. But they avoid speaking about the person and work of the Holy Spirit. The result is spiritual malnutrition: preaching and teaching lose vitality, theology becomes cold and academic, and church life wanes.

The Bible clearly teaches that Jesus Christ accomplished his great work in the world to earn the right to send the Holy Spirit into the churches. It also teaches that the Father sent his Spirit to bear witness to his Son and that without the Spirit's witness the church has nothing to say. Conviction of sin, faith in Christ, new birth, and Christian growth are all the Spirit's work, and none of these can be done without him.

A church without the Spirit is a contradiction in terms. It has no power and no real message. Whatever else it may claim to be or do, it is quenching the Spirit.

Thousands of churches around the world are sadly in need of renewal. They need truth, wisdom, faith, holiness, love, zeal, and power. They also need our prayers. Hardly anything that we pray for is more important than the spiritual renewal of churches. Only congregations that have been cleansed and made alive can effectively tell the world about Christ's salvation.

PRAYER

Forgive us, Lord, for our ignorance concerning the Spirit and for ignoring our dependence on his work. Teach us to depend entirely on the Spirit's power and direciton. In Jesus' name, Amen.

Listen and Be Still

The Vision of Service

*"King Agrippa, I was not disobedient
to the vision from heaven."*
ACTS 26:19

ACTS 26:19-23

There are still times today when the Holy Spirit reveals God's will to an individual in an extraordinary way. When such a thing happens, people usually describe the experience as a "vision" from heaven of what God wanted them to know or do. Ordinarily, however, the Spirit speaks quietly, using the Bible as his chief instrument. He reveals God's will for our lives through the preaching and reading of his Word. When we hear it, the important thing is to believe it and obey.

On the hot, dry road to Damascus, the man known as Saul received a vision. This was a vision of salvation. He saw for the first time the Lord Jesus, and he realized that the person whom he had despised and whose followers he had persecuted was at the right hand of God. Saul surrendered completely. From that moment on, Jesus was his Savior and Lord.

Paul's vision also had to do with service. He had to be saved before he could properly serve, but, once saved, he moved immediately into a life of service to his God and Savior. And his service was not to gain merit or to earn his way to heaven; it was the service of a surrendered and grateful heart.

Pity the person without a vision of Christ for salvation and for service. We are saved to serve, and the challenges are all around us. Do you see Christ?

PRAYER

Jesus, reveal yourself to us, that we may embrace you by faith and serve you obediently. We realize that only in service to you, our Savior, can we find meaning in life. In your name, Amen.

Seeing God's Hand in Everything

*"Keep up your courage, men, for I have faith
in God that it will happen just as he told me."*
Acts 27:25

Acts 27:21-26

A disciple of Jesus should think about three things each day: God is all, God claims all, and God works all. These are the basic, guiding principles of Christian discipleship. They will hold you up in every situation.

Jesus, during his life and ministry on earth, lived and proved these three truths. The presence of the Father was for Jesus a continual reality. God's sovereign claim over every detail of life was for Jesus a fundamental principle. As Jesus lived by the power and Spirit of God, he exalted God in every area of his life.

Like his Master, Paul the apostle saw the Father's hand in everything and submitted to it. Acts 27 tells us about a terrifying storm and that Paul did not struggle against what was happening; he accepted his circumstances and saw what God would do through them. He had faith in God even when everyone around him was numb with fear.

The world seldom appreciates such people. The three basic truths of discipleship leave them cold. They mock and poke fun and say that Christians are fools. Sometimes they make life very miserable for Christ's followers. But the world cannot overcome the simple believer who holds on to what he believes. God has spoken, and that is enough. We trust God and await his solutions.

Prayer

Holy Spirit, help us to realize how everything depends on God's strength and blessing. Make us unshakable in our confidence that God is all, claims all, and works all. In Jesus, Amen.

GREAT SEASONS OF FAITH

THE ROAD TO BETHLEHEM
REV. GEORGE G. VINK

THE CROSS AND THE RISEN LORD
VARIOUS AUTHORS

GREAT SEASONS OF FAITH

THE ROAD TO BETHLEHEM

31 MEDITATIONS AND READINGS

BY REV. GEORGE G. VINK

THE ROAD TO BETHLEHEM

REV. GEORGE G. VINK

Year after year, Advent after Advent, Christians have focused their attention on the birth of Jesus in a little town called Bethlehem. These reflections take us on a journey that leads through Bethlehem.

But our journey does not stop at Bethelem. We pass through it on our way to the cross and the empty tomb.

As you journey through Bethlehem, we pray that you will come to see either for the first time or in some new light the Lord Jesus, the baby born to be the Savior, the Prince of Peace, the King of kings. And when you see him, please worship him and tell others about him.

Rev. Vink has served as a pastor to Christian Reformed congregations in British Columbia, Montana, Michigan and California.

Our Advent Journey Begins

*"Let's go to Bethlehem and see
this thing that has happened. . . ."*
LUKE 2:15

LUKE 2:8-15

Luke's account of Jesus' birth tells of shepherds, society's outcasts, who were terrified—and their terror was understandable. After all, when was the last time you had angels waking you, or God's blinding glory shining on you?

After assuring the fearful few that there was no reason to be afraid, the angel announced the good news. It was (and is) good news for all people, including fringe people like the shepherds. And, just in case they wondered if this was someone pulling the wool over their eyes, God provided a heavenly host as a back-up choir. God had done what he had promised, even if his people didn't really remember his promises.

After the heavenly messengers left, the night's silence hung heavy over the surprised shepherds. Finally one of them spoke: "Let's go to Bethlehem and see this thing."

Did they understand what had really happened? Sleepy shepherds and angelic announcements weren't a common combination, after all. They still aren't.

The surprised shepherds scurried off to Bethlehem in order to see with their eyes what their ears had heard. Let's journey with them. Our journey, however, will begin way back in the garden of promise so that we can see and understand a little more about "this thing that has happened, which the Lord has told us about."

PRAYER

Lord, sometimes we feel like those surprised shepherds. Lead us in our journey so that we may be ready for Christmas. In the name of Jesus, our Savior, we pray. Amen.

Listen and Be Still

The Long Road of Redemption

God. . . will soon crush Satan under your feet.
The grace of our Lord Jesus be with you.
ROMANS 16:20

GENESIS 3:14-21

God enjoyed making his world. Genesis 1:31 says that he saw it as "very good." A garden of delights and a perfectly matched couple crowned his creation. What could possibly go wrong? But something did go dreadfully wrong. And we have felt the effects ever since. A contemporary testimony puts it this way: "Early in human history our first parents listened to the intruder's voice. Rather than living by the Creator's word of life, they fell for Satan's lie and sinned!"

God sets out on a long road to reclaim the fallen as his people and the world as his kingdom. In the garden of guilt and fear God spoke his message of grace. The road has valleys and mountaintops, deserts and deluges. Again and again our forefathers thought they had arrived at the fulfillment of God's promises, only to be dismally disappointed. The peace promised through the crushing of the enemy's head didn't come right away.

The journey to Bethlehem turns out to be a journey requiring patience and persistence. When the apostle Paul wrote to the church at Rome that Satan's defeat would be "soon," the believers' hopes revived. The waiting, though, seems longer than the night before Christmas presents are opened. "Soon" is not soon enough, and we grow impatient, forgetting it's worth the wait.

In our journeying and waiting, we need the good word that says, "The grace of the Lord Jesus be with you."

PRAYER

Lord, your patience with us is amazing. We expect instant answers for long-term problems. Help us to wait, Lord, and to trust that you will keep your promises. In Jesus, Amen.

Listen and Be Still

Graves Along the Way

Rachel. . .was buried on the way to Ephrath
(that is, Bethlehem). . . . Jacob set up a pillar.
GENESIS 35:19-20

GENESIS 35:16-35

As a young family, we often traveled across many states and provinces to visit our parents. The most memorable trips were the ones that included a stop in a cemetery along the way. While one parent would make sandwiches, the other would walk the children among the graves, weaving a story of the lives as engraved on the markers. A young child's grave spoke of sorrow and dashed hopes. An aged grandmother's stone formed images of hot chocolate and peanut butter cookies. A young mother's marker brought tears and reminded me to be more appreciative of my spouse.

The long road of redemption is lined with graves, filled with sorrow, and stained with tears needing the comfort of God's grace. The pain of parting and moving on can cripple us if we stop only at cemeteries and stay there. The journey of life includes death; it's the only way out.

Rachel's tomb testified that Jacob loved his wife. In his sorrow he set up a pillar to mark her grave. She had died there giving birth to her second son.

As we journey onward to Bethlehem, we go to celebrate the birth of an only Son—whose death was not permanent and whose grave was only borrowed. There is no marker by a tomb somewhere saying, "Jesus Christ—Loved of the Father."

No wonder the angel said, "I have good news!"

PRAYER

Heavenly Father, help us to see even grave markers as signs of your faithfulness as we continue our journey to the place where your promises are fulfilled. In Christ, Amen.

Listen and Be Still

The Temptation to Quarrel

As they were leaving [Joseph] said to
them, "Don't quarrel on the way!"
GENESIS 45:24

GENESIS 45:21-28

As we journey to Bethlehem, we stop for a story that has moved listeners to tears since the day it happened. Parental favoritism and subsequent sibling rivalry brought about a divided family as well as unnecessary grief. Jacob's favorite son, Joseph, had been sold into slavery, and Jacob was led to believe he was dead. God intervened, however, by way of a royal-guard captain, a neglected wife, a cupbearer, and a baker. And Joseph rose to power and prominence in a foreign land. Then Joseph revealed himself to his frightened brothers and sent them home to tell Jacob that he who was dead was alive—and not only alive but ruling in Egypt.

The brothers told Jacob, "Joseph is still alive! In fact, he is ruler of all Egypt." Jacob's reaction was one of shock and disbelief. The news was just too good to be true. But son after son testified, "Yes, Father, he is alive, and this is what happened." Their repeated telling and Joseph's gifts eventually convinced the aging father to go to Egypt, where his own son ruled.

The good news of Jesus must overcome our tendency to quarrel along the way over differences that seem too much like sinful sibling rivalry. (In fact, that's often all it is.) Isn't the good news a good reason to reconcile with an estranged family member? Doing so will make the remainder of your journey more joyful. I know.

PRAYER

Teach us to journey with joy, O Lord. Help us, O Holy Spirit, to heal what has been broken. "Joy to the world! The Lord is come: let earth receive her King." In Jesus, Amen.

Listen and Be Still

An Aged Father Rallies to See His Son

*Israel rallied his strength
and sat up on the bed.*
GENESIS 48:2

GENESIS 48:1-7

It's an awesome thing to be in the presence of death. Pastors and nursing staff share the privilege with gratitude. To hold a hand, share a song, lift hearts in prayer, and hear God's Word while gathered around a bed where time and eternity meet is a privilege.

Joseph heard that his father, Jacob, was ill and dying. The mighty ruler of Egypt rushed to his father's house. The Bible then records what pastors and nurses have been seeing for years. Dying, weakened parents rally their strength because a son or a daughter has come to visit one more time. A few final words are spoken, some gestures of love are expressed, and soon there's quiet as the gasping for breath stops.

It's good to stop at Jacob's bedside for a few moments. Jacob, the deceiver, reminds his powerful son about the more powerful God. He says, "El Shaddai (God Almighty) has shown me the way. He appeared to me at Bethel (Luz). He has been faithful to his promises." Jacob continues in detail to remind his son about God's promises. Then he does something that prefigures God's adoption of children for his Son's sake. Jacob includes Joseph's sons among his own. "They are mine," he says.

Advent is a good time to remember that there's a Father who adopts people from all backgrounds as his children and heirs for the sake of his only Son.

PRAYER

Lord Jesus, we know that death may come, but we know you've gone that way before us and that you will walk with us. Lead us and guide us, we pray. In your name, Amen.

Listen and Be Still

Doing Your Own Thing

In those days Israel had no king;
everyone did as he saw fit.
JUDGES 17:6

JUDGES 17

As a young boy, I knew Saturday meant shining all the shoes in our family, especially the ones to be worn to church the next day. If I had done as I saw fit, everyone would have gotten the black polish all over their own hands. But our family had a king of sorts, and she ruled with authority.

Years and years before my Saturday shoe-shining, another mother and son worked out an arrangement after a confession of guilt. Micah had stolen some of his mother's silver, and she had responded by uttering a curse that caused remorse and repentance in her son. Mothers have an effective way of making sons feel guilty. But mothers also have forgiving hearts. When Micah told her he had the silver, his mom reversed her curse and said, "The Lord bless you." And, without much thought, mother and son had some of the silver made into idols. What a mess!

The writer of Judges makes clear that having no king meant anarchy. Everyone did as he or she saw fit. It sounds so contemporary, doesn't it? Children steal from parents. Parents curse whomever. God's blessing gets pronounced on whatever suits whomever. People appoint their own priests, and priests service the highest bidder. Today's road, as in Judges, is rough and rutted.

We all need a King. On to Bethlehem to find him!

PRAYER

"King of kings and Lord of lords" is a refrain of Christian submission. By your Spirit, help us submit to you, Lord, and to do as you see fit, for Jesus' sake. Amen.

Listen and Be Still

Welcome Home

*When [Naomi and Ruth] arrived in Bethlehem. . .
the women exclaimed, "Can this be Naomi?"*
RUTH 1:19

RUTH 1:16-22

Naomi didn't like her reception at Bethlehem. She wasn't coming home with a sense of triumph or accomplishment. She felt very bitter. The excitement of the women in town didn't please her at all.

And Naomi said so: "Don't call me Naomi. . . . Call me Mara, because the Almighty has made my life very bitter." She made sure everyone knew how unfairly God had dealt with her. She had left with a husband and two sons, and now they were buried. Bitterness became her booze, and she enjoyed its effects.

We've arrived at Bethlehem, but there is no manger here with a baby in it. It's still a sleepy little town with normal people like you and me, a town with people who come out to welcome one of their own who hasn't quite made it in the world beyond familiar fields.

During this Advent season, you might meet some people like those who welcomed Naomi and Ruth. Or your eyes may be blinded to any hope because you are overwhelmed with life. You may even be a little bitter. If so, may God's presence and comfort help you to focus on the psalmist's words, "It is good to be near God" (Psalm 73:28). It depends on your attitude.

Psalm 73:17 gives the remedy: "I entered the sanctuary of God; then I understood. . . ." It's no all-encompassing answer, but it's a good start.

PRAYER

O heavenly Father, we need your welcome embrace today. Thank you for people who welcome us in your name. Be near us today, we pray. Amen.

Listen and Be Still

What Happened since Yesterday?

The women said...."Praise be to the Lord,
who this day has not left you...."
RUTH 4:14

RUTH 2:1-7, 17-20; 4:13-17

The women didn't simply call Naomi "Mara," as she had told them to in her bitterness (1:20). God used the barley harvest and its traditional celebrations to fill the emptiness in Naomi's life. It seems so simple, and yet it is so profound. God's ways are not our ways, and he repeatedly surprises us.

Upon hearing about Boaz and his generosity, Naomi exclaimed to Ruth, "Blessed be the man who took notice of you!" (2:19). Then she praised God by acknowledging, "He has not stopped showing his kindness to the living and the dead" (2:20). This is a different tune from the lament Naomi had sounded upon her arrival home.

God's providing often comes by way of our doing what we are capable of doing. We have not been promised a comfortable beach chair, shaded just right with refreshments being served while waiting for "our ship to come in." We have to use our talents, our abilities.

Ruth married Boaz, and Naomi again had a "son." And the kinsman-redeemer's name became famous beyond Israel. Boaz, David's great-grandfather, would be an ancestor of David's "Son," our Redeemer. And he, too, would be born in Bethlehem, years later, with angels rejoicing at his birth.

The journey of redemption is long, with detours and apparent dead-ends. But everything is not as it seems.

PRAYER

Our Creator-Redeemer, thank you for showing Naomi the way of hope. When we're bitter, bring us to Bethlehem, for we all need to see Jesus. In his name, Amen.

Listen and Be Still

David's Son, Our Shepherd

The Lord is my shepherd,
I shall not be in want.
PSALM 23:1

1 SAMUEL 17:12-15

It seems that we're getting closer. We're reading about David, Jesse, Judah, and Bethlehem. These are familiar names associated with Jesus' birth.

Some of us may also often be reading Psalm 23 for comfort during this season. While many of us may be shopping and enjoying parties, others will be experiencing loneliness.

For some of us, this may be the first season without a lifelong partner. Death may have come suddenly, or a marriage may have died unexpectedly, without visible warnings of a terminal illness.

Somehow during this time of year we sense a bit more our need for shepherding. We may know the saying, "We all, like sheep, have gone astray" (Isaiah 53:6). In this Advent season we may also be having trouble getting into the mood of Christmas. All those cheerful Christmas carols may not be of help either.

When we feel this way, we need to hear David's Son. We need to hear and tell about Jesus, who grew up and said, "I am the good shepherd. The good shepherd lays down his life for the sheep" (John 10:11). These words have power to pick us up and point us in the direction of hope and healing. A relationship with Jesus provides what we need, whether it be forgiveness or fellowship. Usually, it's both.

PRAYER

Dear Jesus, our good shepherd, thank you for laying down your life for us. Help us to share your good news of comfort and joy with those in need. In your name, Amen.

Listen and Be Still

David's Triumph

David triumphed over the Philistine
with a sling and a stone. . . .
1 SAMUEL 17:50

1 SAMUEL 17:45-50

Reading about David and Goliath in just these few verses does not do justice to what may be the best-known story of the Old Testament. There's something about winning against overwhelming odds that encourages us. We identify with the Davids of this world.

God's people were paralyzed with fear as the giant Goliath taunted them day after day. Promises of wealth and a royal marriage hadn't enticed even one soldier to risk his life (17:25). When David offered, Saul warned him, "You are only a boy, and [Goliath] has been a fighting man from his youth" (17:33). But David told of his success with lions and bears that attacked his father's sheep. He credited the Lord for his deliverance and said God would protect him from Goliath too (17:34-37).

Saul saw that there was no stopping David, so he said, "Go, and the Lord be with you" (17:37). Parents still use this blessing when sending their children to college, a mission field, or some other new challenge.

The rest is history. David faced the enemy, declared that he came in the name of the Lord, and triumphed.

David's Son won a bigger battle years later. He faced the last and greatest enemy, death. The women spread the news as they raced from the empty tomb: "He's alive! He has risen!" Jesus had royally defeated the enemy. That's the real reason for this joyous season.

PRAYER

Dear, victorious Jesus, thank you for facing the enemy we couldn't defeat. Help us, by the power of your Spirit, to endure and keep spreading the news for your sake. Amen.

Listen and Be Still

Good Friends and Precious Water

"Should I drink the blood of these men
who went at the risk of their lives?"
1 CHRONICLES 11:19

1 CHRONICLES 11:10, 15-19

This next stop on our journey to the manger is an event in King David's life that takes place near Bethlehem, now host to a Philistine garrison.

The chronicler tells us that "David became more and more powerful, because the Lord Almighty was with him" (11:9). David had surrounded himself with mighty men, and his kingship was expanding. Resting in a cave with some of his chiefs, he expressed a desire for a special drink of water. Some of his mighty men risked their lives to secure it. Their devotion to David motivated them to risk their lives for their king. The way David received their offering gives us an indication why he had such a loyal following. He didn't consider himself superior and worthy of their sacrifice.

The gospel of John describes the coming of Jesus this way: "The Word became flesh and made his dwelling among us" (John 1:14). He became one of us. He took on our flesh and blood and experienced what it was like to be human.

In this case the King sacrificed himself for his subjects. And by his death he provided the water of life for all who believe. This sacrifice inspires not only our loyalty but also our worship. And in response we offer ourselves as living sacrifices (Romans 12:1). Will you offer yourself to Jesus today?

PRAYER

Lord God of David, help us to celebrate Jesus' birth. In this season our lives are so busy. May our preparations include a reflection on the greatness of your sacrifice. Amen.

Listen and Be Still

A Prayer of Confidence

I will lie down and sleep in peace, for you alone,
O Lord, make me dwell in safety.
PSALM 4:8

PSALM 4

Today once again there will be millions of children who'll go to bed tired. But before they snuggle under their covers or pull the mosquito netting over themselves, there may be a parent who will remind them to pray. Or, better yet, there may be a parent who teaches them to pray and prays with them. Many parents have taught their children a prayer similar to this age-old childhood prayer: "Now I lay me down to sleep. I pray the Lord my soul to keep. If I should die before I wake, I pray the Lord my soul to take."

As we journey toward Bethlehem, we've stopped at a familiar psalm. It's a psalm of simple prayer.

The psalmist begins with a simple request: "Answer me when I call to you." Any believer, new or experienced, knows the feeling that comes when God seems so far away. This can happen during a time of distress similar to what the psalmist experienced or during the demanding routine of daily work and commitments.

After telling God what has been happening, the psalmist concludes with confidence. Not all of the day's struggles may be gone. But he shows that he is able to sleep peacefully. He can rest, knowing that God does not slumber or slip away on tiptoe as Mom or Dad do when a child finally falls asleep. The psalmist is confident that God provides safety, whether he wakes or sleeps. Sleep well tonight.

PRAYER

O righteous God, we, too, need relief and mercy. We come in confidence. Fill us with your joy, that we may live in peace and die in peace. Through the Prince of Peace, Amen.

Listen and Be Still

Our Eternal Dwelling Place

Surely. . . I will dwell in the
house of the Lord forever.
PSALM 23:6

PSALM 23

Jesus made clear that he fulfilled the prophetic words of the Old Testament, including those in the Psalms. He is the King who ascends the throne (Psalm 21). He is the One who groans, "My God, my God, why have you forsaken me?" (Psalm 22). And it is Jesus who says, "I am the good shepherd. The good shepherd lays down his life for the sheep" (John 10:11).

Our long journey toward Bethlehem began with shepherds to whom angels came and announced good news. Along the way we've seen a little of David's life, the shepherd boy, hero, and king. And now we hear the conclusion of the shepherd's psalm: "Surely...I will dwell in the house of the Lord forever." It's a wonderful conclusion to a song of confidence. No matter what comes his way—evil or enemies—the psalmist will not fear. God provides for him. It may be the wonderful quiet waters of condo living or the green of a golf course. It may also be the valley of cancer or catastrophe. Yet the good shepherd comforts and strengthens.

The psalmist is assured of a place to live. No longer a nomadic, wandering shepherd. No longer being hounded by those who don't want him around. Our present dwellings, even if they're magnificent, cannot compare with the accommodations being prepared for us by our Lord in heaven (John 14:2).

PRAYER

Dear Shepherd God, thank you for leading us along our journeys in life. We are grateful for your constant care. Go with us to the very end, we pray. In Jesus' name, Amen.

Listen and Be Still

Did You Go for a Drink?

My soul thirsts for God, for the living God.
When can I go and meet with God?
PSALM 42:2

PSALM 42:1-5

The church at which I worship is very gracious to its preaching pastors. At every service, hidden from the view of thirsty worshipers, is a tall, ice-cold glass of water available to alleviate the preacher's thirst. There must be times when the listeners are tempted to ask for a sip or ask him to take no more sips and say amen.

Hunted, the deer runs for its life. It bounds into the woods, waits for the sounds of pursuit, and heads for the gurgling stream. Front legs spread, the deer drinks deeply and satisfyingly. The water restores life as it refreshes. The panting stops, and the deer begins to look around. Calm returns. The chase has ended. Relief.

People have plagued and taunted the psalmist, wondering where his God has been hiding. He painfully pours out his soul in prayer. He thirsts for the presence of the living God. He needs to worship and be comforted. He needs hope. He needs to praise God. He does not want to stay downcast forever.

The psalmist tastes his salty tears and cries out to God. He needs to drink in God's presence.

Jesus is the living water, the life-giving drink we need. He quenches our thirst in wonderful ways. He comes to us faithfully wherever we are. Will you meet him? "The festive throng" welcomes you, and the Lord Jesus invites you to join them.

PRAYER

Dear Lord, thank you for inviting us into your presence. We need you to refresh and restore us. Quench our thirst for you in Jesus' name. Amen.

352

Listen and Be Still

God Wakes Up

The Lord awoke as from sleep, as a man
wakes from the stupor of wine.
PSALM 78:65

PSALM 78:1-4, 65-72

Psalm 78 is a powerful, poetic account of God's dealing with Israel. Israel needed to be reminded of where they had been and how God had been at work in their lives. They had experienced God's leading in ways that we wish would happen to us. The parting of waters, water rushing out of a rock, or manna raining down would certainly make us sit up and take notice, wouldn't it? Did it work for Israel? Listen to the psalmist: "Their hearts were not loyal to him, they were not faithful to his covenant" (78:37). Israel's story is our story.

Sometimes when the journey gets long, we lose sight of our purpose and destination. Waiting is seldom fun. We're well into this journey to Bethlehem, and we're still not opening presents.

Despite the title at the top of this page, God does not sleep while we journey. It may appear that he is dozing or off doing something somewhere else. Not so. The picture our poet presents is an exaggerated way of teaching God's activity in behalf of his people. God responds and provides the shepherd that a wandering people need. Looking back, we can always see God's guiding hand and leading Spirit. It's a wise thing to stop, pray, and ask ourselves, "Where do we see God's leading?" or "Where is God leading us?" Take time today to list the ways in which God has acted in your life.

PRAYER

Almighty God, as you guide our journey, we see your grace revealed again and again. Help us to see it and to celebrate your covenant faithfulness. In Jesus, Amen.

Listen and Be Still

We're Over Half-Way—Praise God!

"Give thanks to the Lord. . . make known
among the nations what he has done. . . ."
ISAIAH 12:4

ISAIAH 12

Baby Jesus didn't come to give us a reason for a season of celebrations. He didn't come as God's great gift to provide an excuse for us to exchange presents. He didn't even come to occasion the singing of wonderful cantatas and Christmas carols. Baby Jesus came to bring deliverance to an enslaved people, caught in their own entanglements of deception and destruction.

The wells of salvation provide the water of life to a people doomed to die. It is with joy that we draw life-giving water. It is with joy that we celebrate Christ's birth and sing "Joy to the World."

The prophet preaches, "In that day you will say…" and from there he proceeds to suggest some things for us to proclaim. He makes clear that we have reasons to thank God for his mercies and to tell others the great things God has done for us. Now the question is "How can we best do that?"

Hopefully we've listened to the prophet's message that God brings salvation and comforts his people. Late one night, speaking to Nicodemus, Jesus put it this way: "God so loved the world that he gave his one and only Son…" (John 3:16). Certainly such good news is something to make us "shout aloud and sing for joy," isn't it? Have you done so? How? Whom have you told? What are you doing to tell the nations what God has done?

PRAYER

Lord God, thank you for turning away your anger and comforting us with the gift of salvation. Help us to tell others about your love and grace. In Jesus, our Savior. Amen.

Listen and Be Still

Walking Through Trials

"I see four men walking around in the fire. . .
and the fourth looks like a son of the gods."

DANIEL 3:25

DANIEL 3:13-27

The flames had been fanned furiously. The furnace had been heated seven times hotter than usual. The smell of scorched flesh hung in the air as soldiers removed the lifeless bodies of their friends who dutifully had gone too close. King Nebuchadnezzar was furious that Shadrach, Meshach, and Abednego had refused to serve his gods or bow down to his golden image. So they had been thrown into the furnace as a sacrifice to the king's pride and vanity. And God delivered them.

God's servants have never been promised a comfortable journey. Jesus' followers today have not been promised smooth sailing either. Even the Savior's own family didn't understand his mission. And his own people killed him for refusing to submit to their agendas.

Shadrach, Meshach, and Abednego were not killed, but, like them, many of Jesus' followers have refused to deny their Lord—and many have become martyrs. In our Christmas pilgrimage, it's good to remember those who have their hands tied and their tongues silenced by regimes that bow to different gods. It's good for us to pray that God will walk with our brothers and sisters through their trials and give them strength to say, "We will not serve your gods or worship [your] image."

Look with me at the manger. Is that a cross you see shadowing the baby's smile?

PRAYER

Father, sometimes we're scared of the heat that comes our way for not compromising our loyalty to you. Empower us with your Spirit to be faithful, we pray. In Jesus, Amen.

Listen and Be Still

Who Is Wise?

Who is wise? He will realize these things.
Who is discerning? He will understand them.
HOSEA 14:9

HOSEA 14

Many meetings of the church elders went much longer because of one elder's question. The decision would seem final after much discussion, and then he would ask, "I know it's right, but is it wise?" The chairman would sigh deeply, and the meeting would go a little longer into the evening.

If we read Hosea's question "Who is wise?" as it's stated here, we know it does not mean the same thing as the question "Who is right?" To know something or to have facts does not always lead to wisdom with regard to something. And discerning and understanding involve more than knowing.

The book of Hosea is the story of God's pain as well as his love. It's the story of his relentless pursuit of his people as a marriage partner, his repeated forgiveness, and his willingness to try again. When Hosea closes his prophetic words and asks the question about being wise, he indicates that the wise will realize things about life that people with knowledge—facts and figures—may not. Discernment leads to understanding God's ways, the right ways, the wise ways. Those who are righteous walk in God's ways. The righteous may not have all the answers, but they are wise enough to accept God's teachings and to obey them. On the other hand, the rebellious stumble and fall, with eternal consequences.

PRAYER

O wise and gracious God, show us where in our lives we need to act more wisely. Help us to discern your teaching so that we may understand your will for our lives. Amen.

Listen and Be Still

Calling on God's Name

"Everyone who calls on the name of
the Lord will be saved. . . ."
JOEL 2:32

JOEL 2:28-32

Our journey is rapidly drawing us closer to Bethlehem. We're almost tired of hearing the same carols played at the shopping malls while the crowds buy from merchants who are hoping the last-minute splurging will balance their books. We may find it more and more difficult to be excited about Jesus' birth. His humiliating descent gets hidden under tossed-aside gift wrappings waiting to be recycled.

Joel's prophecy speaks of a pouring out of power that we do not see displayed in Bethlehem.

Sometimes newly born Christians, having called on the name of Jesus Christ to save them, wonder about all the pouring out of power that is promised in Joel's prophecy. It just doesn't seem to happen. The routine of regularity dominates, and the rejoicing diminishes. Life's journey, whatever length, needs a certain amount of routine. But sometimes we need the challenge to "color outside the lines." Sometimes we need to climb a mountain to look back and see how far we've already come and to peer into the distance to see where we're going. We need to sing, "We've come this far by faith, leaning on the Lord." Even the routine requires God's help.

New Christians and experienced Christians need to smile at the manger and be amazed. The promised Deliverer smiles back at the celebrating survivors.

PRAYER

Dear Keeper of Promises, help us to understand that our journey is a matter of faithful obedience. In the midst of our hustling, help us to gaze on your grace in Jesus. Amen.

Listen and Be Still

Jonah, the Recalcitrant Prophet

*"Should I not be concerned
about that great city?"*
JONAH 4:11

JONAH 1:1-2; 4:5-11

Jonah, probably the best known of the minor prophets, is rather unruly. Told to go east, he heads west. Imagine an evangelist today getting a direct word from God to proclaim his message to Edmonton, and then heading off on a Caribbean cruise!

Jonah's deep-sea exploits caused by his disobedience (1:3-17) teach us about God's persistence to bring the gospel to those who are not on our list of favorite listeners. At least Jonah doesn't need to be told twice. Reeking from stomach acids and seaweed after being vomited onto dry land, Jonah heads for Nineveh. God gives him the message to bring, and Jonah obeys (3:3).

What happens next could be summarized by the following "three Rs": Ninevah repents, God relents, and Jonah resents it all.

God rebukes Jonah for his anger and teaches him a graphic lesson with a vine that's there one day and gone the next. Jonah responds with further anger and a pity party. He wants to die, but God isn't done with his surly servant. He rebukes Jonah and reminds him that he is a God of grace and compassion.

God leaves Jonah with a question that we need to ask ourselves. "Should we not be concerned about the neighbor who has Christmas lights on his house but doesn't know the real reason why they're there?"

PRAYER

Lord, sometimes like Jonah, we get stubborn or too comfortable.
Remove our cataracts of clannish vision so that we may see your
desire to save all people. In Jesus, Amen.

Listen and Be Still

He Will Be Their Shalom

He will. . . shepherd his flock in the strength of
the Lord. . . . And he will be their peace.
MICAH 5:4-5A

MICAH 5:1-5A

The Hebrew word for peace, *shalom*, is rich with meaning and application. But it can also be misunderstood. I have enjoyed the privilege of pronouncing God's blessing upon his people at the end of a worship service. And I always conclude with "Shalom." But I learned of a child who asked, "Mom, why does pastor always tell us to 'Shut up' when he blesses us?" Oops!

As we continue to prepare for Christmas, today is a good time to think about how the "Prince of Peace" has brought shalom to your life, to your world.

The shalom we seek is not simply an absence of hostility between people or among nations. The shalom we need describes a relationship between God and us that leads to wholeness in our relationships with others, beginning at home. Jesus spoke to his troubled disciples, saying, "Peace I leave with you; my peace I give you" (John 14:27). He was speaking about the result of his saving work, a work begun in Bethlehem. And when we know that peace, our hearts change and fears lose their power over us. But Jesus' peace doesn't come without bending the knee at the cross and believing he arose.

Will you celebrate that peace today? Doing so will make your Christmas the best you've had yet. Then God's words of blessing will have a wonderful new meaning for you and yours.

PRAYER

Lord Jesus, help us to make peace as those who know you. Guide us by your Spirit to honor you and serve you as our Prince of Peace, in whose name we pray. Amen.

Listen and Be Still

Free at Last! Free at Last!

The sun of righteousness will rise. . . .
And you will go out and leap like calves. . . .
MALACHI 4:2

MALACHI 4

How has your day been going so far? Perhaps you woke to sunshine and the aroma of freshly brewed coffee, and the words of "Joy to the World" ringing in your mind. But you were soon reminded that there is much more to do today than you will possibly be able to accomplish. As we continue to prepare for Christmas, the often-jaded expectations of the world tend to collide with the "good news of great joy" that is the true Christmas message.

"For you who revere my name," says the Lord, it will be different. And Malachi gives us a picture of salvation that elicits smiles and sunshine even on a dreary and hectic winter day. The sun of righteousness will bring changes in the lives of those who bask in the light of the Son, who says, "I am the light of the world." The Christmas lights on our trees and our houses remind us of his promise of healing as well as the elimination of the works of darkness.

Here Malachi pictures a scene of spring. Calves released from a winter of being cooped up in small pens leap for joy. No more restrictions. No straining for light anymore. What an accurate picture of those who have known the bondage of sin and have been released. They're free from the limitations they had while trying to do and be what God always intended for them.

PRAYER

Lord God, help us to see the promised Son and to show in our daily living the joy of being released sinners, saved by your grace. In Jesus' name we pray. Amen.

Are You Ready for Christmas?

"He will. . . make ready a people prepared for the Lord."
LUKE 1:17

LUKE 1:8-17

Do you, like me, find that every year Christmas seems to come a little quicker than the year before? There are so many preparations to make. We want the house decorated. We want the food ready for the family members and friends we have invited. Are you ready for Christmas?

Being ready for Christmas is more than having the presents properly packaged and placed under a newly decorated tree. Being ready for Christmas means turning hearts in the direction of loving relationships between parents and children. It means picking up the phone and calling home to say, "I'm so sorry. Can we work it out?" Being ready means a father calling the daughter whom he introduced to sexual experiences ever so wrongfully and confessing, "My dear daughter, will you ever find it in your heart to forgive a repentant father?" Being ready means....

Being ready for Christmas requires a housecleaning that cannot be hired out or done by anyone else. It means hearing the word of invitation to "come home" and leave our disobedience behind, whatever may be involved, however painful it may be. We cannot sing, "O little town of Bethlehem, how still we see thee lie," when there is really no stillness in our hearts because they're out of tune with God. But we can prepare by looking at our lives and getting rid of "stuff" that doesn't belong.

PRAYER

Dear Father, help us to heal any relationships that may need your healing grace. Help us to examine our hearts and prepare for your coming to live there. In Jesus' name, Amen.

Listen and Be Still

Leaping for Joy Again

"As the sound of your greeting reached my ears,
the baby in my womb leaped for joy."
LUKE 1:44

LUKE 1:39-45

When Dad drove the old Plymouth home faster than Mom considered safe, she would touch his knee or say something to show her displeasure. Although he had never driven a horse and buggy, he'd say, "The horse smells its stall," meaning that it's eager to get home.

We're getting very close to Bethlehem. The stall where Jesus was born seems close enough to smell. Yet we pause one more time before our arrival. Today we're at the home of Elizabeth. Mary has hurried there after the angel's announcement concerning both of them.

Excitement fills the air as Mary rushes into Elizabeth's house. And the Spirit causes Elizabeth to exclaim, "Blessed are you among women...! But why am I so favored, that the mother of my Lord should come to me?" Only the Holy Spirit could reveal such wonderful and yet unknown news.

Elizabeth's reaction includes her own baby's leaping within her womb. Only mothers know that feeling. As much as a father may listen for sounds and have his loving wife guide his hands to the movements of an eagerly expected baby, he cannot know the feeling of a baby leaping within the womb.

Do you know the blessing of believing that Bethlehem's baby was born for you? Has it ever made you leap or at least jump for joy?

PRAYER

Lord Jesus, thank you for being willing to submit to the humiliation of being one of us. Help us to experience the excitement of that good news. In your name we pray. Amen.

Listen and Be Still

We're There at Last

While they were [in Bethlehem]. . .
she gave birth to her firstborn, a son.
LUKE 2:6-7

LUKE 2:1-7

Christmas is another day to celebrate God's faithfulness. We celebrate the birth of Jesus in Bethlehem to a bewildered couple, far away from home. We've journeyed through many important stops and events since leaving the garden where we heard God promise that redemption would come by way of Eve's seed.

God has fulfilled his promise. He has waited until, as Scripture puts it, "the fullness of time." Now God has intervened in Bethlehem.

Coming to Bethlehem, we don't see any bright blue "It's a boy!" sign in the driveway. We see no reception at the "Bethlehem Bed and Breakfast" with Joseph and Mary as honored parents. It's still a quiet moment in Judea. "No room for them in the inn" meant using what was available—a shelter for animals. The King's throne was made of lumber, and the throne room smelled of animals, as a young mother tended to the needs of her newborn. Can we expect anything more humbling than what we see in Bethlehem?

The answer comes years later when we see his form on a rough, wooden cross, crying the pain of a dying, desperate man: "My God, my God, why have you forsaken me?" (Matthew 27:46). Celebrate his becoming one of us, accepting our punishment. And keep in mind that he came to die and to conquer death for our sake.

PRAYER

Dear Jesus, we rejoice in your willingness to humble yourself for our sake. Thank you for seeing past our sins to redeem us. May our celebrations today bring you glory. Amen.

Listen and Be Still

Worshiping as a Response

"God is spirit, and his worshipers
must worship in spirit and in truth."
JOHN 4:24

MATTHEW 2:1-8

We have a human need to worship something or someone. Something inside each of us says, "There's more to life, including my life, than meets the eye." We all look for a messiah. The woman at the well, as we find in John 4, expected a Messiah who would explain more about worship. But Jesus had already explained that worship must be done "in spirit and in truth."

Jesus' coming brings differing reactions. Christ's birth brought the Magi to Bethlehem. They understood him to be "king of the Jews," and, having seen his star, they came to worship him. Herod had a different reaction. Like all small minds in large places, he was threatened and frightened. Even a baby seen as king made him lie about worshiping.

In our world, Christ's birth appears to bring little reaction. Is that because we worship a baby, and not a king? Could it be that our celebrations are safe because we hide the Messiah? He seems such a good baby—certainly different from a noisemaker who upsets temple traditions as he sends tables flying and cries, "My house will be a house of prayer" (Luke 19:46). How well do we know this baby boy born to Mary? Have we stood at the cross with her and heard his last words?

What is your reaction to Jesus? Is it Herod's opposition or the Magi's worship?

PRAYER

Father, help us to worship you as you want to be worshiped. Tune our hearts to hear your words so that we may know the Savior we need. In Jesus' name we pray. Amen.

Listen and Be Still

Proclaiming as a Response

*"The Spirit. . . has anointed me to preach
good news. . . to proclaim freedom. . . ."*

LUKE 4:18

LUKE 4:14-21

Today's Scripture reading tells of Jesus' visit to the synagogue in Nazareth after he had successfully resisted Satan's temptations. It says, "He went into the synagogue, as it was his custom." Is there a lesson here for us?

Jesus was awarded the customary honor of reading the scroll and commenting on it. Now an adult, he found a passage in Isaiah and applied it to himself, saying, "Today this scripture is fulfilled in your hearing." Here again we learn that Scripture has a pattern of promise and fulfillment. God makes promises and keeps them.

Baby Jesus had become a man. The people recalled that he was Joseph's son, and they were amazed at the words he spoke. There is good news to be proclaimed. There is freedom from fear to be shared. There is recovery from addictions to be proclaimed. There is release from oppression to be made known.

But the good news of grace may not always be welcome. After all, the people in the synagogue of Nazareth responded by trying to throw this self-proclaimed Messiah over a cliff.

Even so, we respond best to Christ's coming when we proclaim the good news to those in prisons, whether prisons of steel bars or of a person's own making. We respond best when we take time to visit the lonely or encourage the hurting, as Jesus himself did.

PRAYER

Jesus, you risked your life by beginning your ministry at home. Help us to risk our comfort by sharing the good news and proclaiming freedom at home and everywhere. Amen.

Listen and Be Still

Muttering as a Response

All the people. . . began to mutter, "He has gone to be the guest of a 'sinner.'"
Luke 19:7

Luke 19:1-10

People's responses to Christ's birth are varied. Some ignore it or even reject it. Some pretend to hear but their actions betray their words. Some respond with a sense of worship and wonder in their hearts, and embrace it with determination to show in their lives that Jesus is Lord.

Journeying through Jericho, Jesus made a significant stop. He looked up and commanded Zacchaeus to get down from his sycamore perch. What a wonderful picture! The Savior sees the heart of a sinner and stops to save him. And where else do we find Jesus stating his purpose and passion so clearly? He finds the children of Abraham up a tree, in suburbia, on farms, in ghettos. Wherever they have gone, he looks them up, "for the Son of Man came to seek and to save what was lost."

But, all too often, some people's response to God's grace lacks compassion. They act as if they've earned their salvation and their brand of sinning is less despicable than that of the Zacchaeuses of this world. They forget that Zacchaeus obeyed Jesus and welcomed him.

Remember that to Jesus it doesn't matter if you're short or tall, black or white, rich or poor. "If you belong to Christ, then you are Abraham's seed" (Galatians 3:29). That's nothing to mutter about. God keeps his promises.

Prayer

Father, forgive us for muttering about people who are a little different from us. View us with compassion, Lord, and help us to view others that way. For Jesus' sake, Amen.

Listen and Be Still

Watching as a Response

All those who knew him. . . stood at a distance,
watching these things.
LUKE 23:49

LUKE 23:44-56

~This series of devotions is nearly finished. Our journeying has led us to Bethlehem, where we lingered long enough to wonder how much more humiliation Jesus would experience. In today's reading, we see a small crowd of followers at Jesus' cross, watching and wondering what went wrong.

Imagine the people's feelings. Imagine mother Mary's heart breaking. She and the other women watch and wait. So do some of Jesus' other followers. What did all this darkness over the land mean? Were the deeds of darkness winning while their hope for change breathed his last breath, committing his spirit to his Father?

In our lives, too, sometimes all we can do is watch and wait. God is at work, but we're left wondering about his snail-like pace. Looking back over the past weeks and months, we haven't always seen God's hand clearly at work, for often his ways are hard to figure out. Some things that happen made no sense to us. Some people who died should have lived longer, and others who had hoped to "be with the Lord" linger on. Someday it will make sense, but it's difficult to be patient until then.

The women watched as Jesus' body was laid in the tomb. They waited through a sullen Sabbath. God rewarded their patience. They saw first what we celebrate. They saw an empty tomb and first heard the news: "He has risen!" Darkness and death did not prevail. But God always does!

PRAYER

Dear Lord, sometimes we feel like helpless bystanders in our own lives. Help us to understand when we need to watch and wait and when we need to get working. Amen.

Listen and Be Still

It's Me! Look for Yourself

"Look at my hands and my feet. It is
I myself! Touch me and see. . . ."
LUKE 24:39

LUKE 24:36-44

Some things are so strange, so bizarre, that even seeing them does not convince us. After all, the scene in our reading for today is a long way from Bethlehem.

We've seen some strange sights on our journey. A prophet sulking over a city that repented. Three men—no, four—walking unharmed in a blazing furnace. A shepherd boy toppling a giant. A mother and son making gods as they saw fit. A slave becoming a powerful ruler.

We've seen the angels and shepherds outside Bethlehem. And we have watched as Jesus died. What are we to believe? The same women who saw him crucified came running and said, "He has risen!" Some men at the tomb even challenged them, "Why do you look for the living among the dead?" (Luke 24:5).

What do you make of today's encounter? Jesus stepped into the room without using the door. Suddenly he stood among the disciples and graciously greeted them: "Peace be with you." They were startled and frightened. This time there was no angel appearance to announce what had happened. It was Jesus himself! And they thought, "It's a ghost!"

What sort of experience will convince you? Jesus told Thomas, "Because you have seen me, you have believed; blessed are those who have not seen and yet have believed" (John 20:29). Whom will you believe?

PRAYER

Lord Jesus, help us to see you and touch you in your Word by the power of your Spirit. Our doubts come quickly. Convince us, we pray, and bring your peace among us. Amen.

Listen and Be Still

Spreading the Word

They spread the word. . . and all who heard it were
amazed at what the shepherds said.
LUKE 2:17-18

LUKE 2:15-20

The stores aren't playing Christmas songs anymore. The season is over. Clerks are busy helping customers exchange gifts they don't want or can't use. Many customers and clerks have heard and sung about God's greatest gift, but their lives haven't changed. They've heard the question "What child is this?" but they haven't answered it.

The shepherds knew what they had seen in the fields. They hurried to see Mary, Joseph, and the baby. And finding things exactly as the angel had said, they told others what "had been told them about this child." The excited shepherds witnessed without ever having attended a pastor's class or "Six Easy Lessons on How to Share Your Faith." They returned to their work, homes, families, and friends, "glorifying and praising God."

The long road of redemption led through a little town called Bethlehem. The trip to Bethlehem and the sight of Jesus changed the shepherds' lives. Everyone who sees Jesus is called to praise him. Like the shepherds, we have been at the manger. We've also seen the cross and the empty tomb. Where will we go from here? The road ahead looks hazy, and there's no road map or software program to show us. It's simply a matter of walking with Jesus, trusting him as he leads. It's an amazing journey with a wonderful destination and delightful discoveries along the way. Will you, too, share your amazement and tell others?

PRAYER

"O Master, let me walk with thee in lowly paths of service free. . . . Teach me the wayward feet to stay, and guide them in the homeward way." In your name, dear Lord, Amen.

Listen and Be Still

GREAT SEASONS OF FAITH

THE CROSS AND THE RISEN LORD

30 MEDITATIONS AND READINGS

BY VARIOUS WRITERS

The Cross and the Risen Lord

Various Authors

The Steadfast Face of God

As the time approached for him to be taken up to heaven, Jesus resolutely set out for Jerusalem.
LUKE 9:51

LUKE 9:51-62

Our faces reveal much about us—often more than we wish.

Outer things are told: Is the face young and still unjaded? Is its owner Oriental? African? European? Is the person healthy? Look into his or her face! Is he or she sick? Look at that peaked face!

Inner things are told too: There are kind faces, puzzled faces, angry faces, twisted faces. There are even lifted faces. Are you nervous or afraid? Your face may show it. Are you half-ashamed and half-amused? Your sheepish face tells all. The twitch of a lip, the narrowing of an eye or the raising of an eyebrow, the flaring of nostrils—all these things suggest what may be inside.

Now look at the steadfast face of our Lord. Here begins his steady, relentless movement toward the cross. On he goes, with that face set like flint against all the leers and grins of evil. At the end of his journey will be resurrection and ascension to heaven, but the road leads through Jerusalem, the city that rejected and killed the prophets. Ahead lies a terror that will test the courage of even the Son of God. Deliberately he turns to face it.

Look at the steadfast face of God, soon to be slapped red, running with the spit of wicked men, hot with the Judas-kiss. Resolutely this face is set for our redemption—until it is finished.

PRAYER

Truly, O Lord, you are a God who saves. We see it now in a glass or mirror, dimly, but one day we shall see face to face, through Jesus Christ, our Savior. Amen.

Listen and Be Still

Jesus, Friend of Sinners

"Neither do I condemn you," Jesus declared.
JOHN 8:11

JOHN 8:2-11

Some of the people around Jesus had hawk's eyes when it came to spotting sin. And what they couldn't see they could sniff out like spiritual bloodhounds. They were always at it—their eyes darted everywhere, and they snooped and sniffed to find sinners.

These people couldn't begin to understand the attitude of Jesus. Not only was he gentle with sinners, but he also became their friend. He associated with people of unsavory reputation and hateful occupation. He would sometimes seem to let people off the hook even when they were caught sinning. To them, Jesus just didn't make any sense, and they muttered and complained about his incomprehensible behavior.

But let there be no mistake: Jesus hated sin more than anyone. And he knew something about sin that the hawkeyes and bloodhounds didn't seem to understand: sinners can be forgiven and made whole again!

Now, Jesus also knew that sin would have to be punished and that this would have to be accomplished in a way that no human mind could fathom. Someday he would give his own life for the sins of the world!

Jesus will never let you take your sin lightly. But he won't let you take his grace lightly either. His grace and love are greater than your sins can ever become. That's why he is called the Friend of sinners!

PRAYER

Jesus, we're grateful to know that you are our perfect, loving Friend. May we never do anything to destroy your friendship or take advantage of it. Help us to be true. Amen.

Listen and Be Still

Nobody Wants a Crucified Savior

"Never, Lord!" he said. "This
shall never happen to you!"
MATTHEW 16:22

MATTHEW 16:21-23

Some of us have looked at the cross so long that we have lost our focus. Peter lets us know how Jesus' death looked to a person who saw it for the first time.

According to Matthew's record, Peter's world was beginning to come together. Peter was becoming more and more sure that Jesus was the Christ, the Son of the living God, and he felt fortunate to be on the inside track so far as Jesus' kingdom was concerned. Then Jesus told Peter about death at the hands of the religious leaders. The idea was threatening for Peter himself, but even worse, it was a massive contradiction. Thinking about the Son of God suffering and dying was like thinking about a square circle—an impossible idea.

On the face of it, nobody wants a crucified Savior. But that's the kind of Savior we have. And being a Christian involves understanding that such a Savior is necessary. Our God is a glorious God, but we are not saved in his glory; we are saved in his humiliation. Jesus, God in the flesh, had to become a common criminal. This was the only way to pay for sin.

Peter can teach us if his insight into the horror of Christ's death jars us into an understanding of how unspeakably horrifying it is that the divine Son of God had to die for us. That this was necessary speaks clearly of our wretchedness.

PRAYER

Forgive us for becoming accustomed to the cross, O God. May we, like Peter, see its ugliness. Thank you, Jesus, for becoming our crucified Savior. In your name, Amen.

Listen and Be Still

375

Jesus Only

*When they looked up, they saw
no one except Jesus.*
MATTHEW 17:8

MATTHEW 17:1-8

Jesus alone, striding toward Calvary—that's the basic message of the gospels. Physically that's the way it was. And many think that is all there was to Jesus' history—that he was just a lone man walking tragically toward his death.

But no. Jesus walked in company with God the Father and God the Holy Spirit. He was surrounded and supported by heavenly servants—"angels attended him" (Mark 1:13). And on the glory-filled mountain the brilliance of the Almighty broke out around him. For the disciples there could be no mistake; they heard the Father's voice: "This is my Son, whom I love; with him I am well pleased. Listen to him!"

Yes, Jesus is indeed the Son of God. When he was born, the glory of the Lord transformed the countryside and the angels sang (Luke 2:13-14). As a young man, he went to his Father's house (Luke 2:49). When he began his ministry, the Holy Spirit came upon him (Luke 3:22).

On the mount of transfiguration it happened again. The Father came near his Son as he began to walk the treacherous steps down into the inferno of divine wrath. It was the last moment of encouragement, when Jesus' consciousness of his own divinity was fortified by one last taste of his Father's majesty. So the Father readied his Son for death—and for the crown beyond the cross.

PRAYER

Help us, Father in heaven, to remember how close you were to Jesus every step of the way. Thank you for strengthening him so that he could die for us. In his name, Amen.

Listen and Be Still

Palm Sunday Weeping

Your enemies will. . . encircle you. . .
because you did not recognize. . . God's coming.
LUKE 19:43-44

LUKE 19:28-44

Right in the middle of all the Palm Sunday excitement Jesus does something unexpected. The air is heavy with messianic expectation, celebration, and coronation cries. Here was at least the man who would get Rome off the people's backs and Caesar out of their hair. In the middle of all the excitement, at high noon on Palm Sunday, what does Jesus do? He weeps over Jerusalem.

This is the city toward which Jesus has "set his face" (Luke 9:51, RSV). The Lord whose kingdom is not of this world has made his move toward the city. And when he is in sight of it, he weeps. What a dramatic contrast to the cheers of the fickle crowd! What a dramatic glimpse of the mind of Christ! On Palm Sunday the people are cheering and throwing down their coats and tossing up their hats. But the king has his head in his hands, and his body is shivering with grief. The face set like flint against sin is now stained with tears.

Jesus has tried to bring the people good news. God knows he has tried to gather them together (Luke 13:34)—but they would not. Now, toward the end, Jesus predicts judgment for the city that will reject him.

So many times God wanted to gather us. But we always grew soft toward sin and hard toward God. The heartbroken indictment of us all is that we did not know when redemption was at our door.

PRAYER

Temper your judgment with mercy, O God, so that we may yet see, and believe, and turn, and be saved through Jesus Christ, our Lord. We pray in his name. Amen.

Listen and Be Still

A Stone's Throw

He withdrew about a stone's throw. . . .
LUKE 22:41

LUKE 22:39-46

How far is a stone's throw? It depends on who throws the stone. A toddler picks up a pebble, hurls it mightily, and it falls at his feet. A hardy young person on the beach throws a stone out over the water, and it splashes two hundred feet offshore.

When Jesus withdrew a stone's throw from the disciples, they could probably still see him and hear him out there alone. Today, when we measure distances in light years, a stone's throw seems a fairly short distance.

Except here—for the distance represented by this stone's throw was so great that it defied human measurement. The gulf between Jesus and the disciples was infinite. If you doubt it, hear his cry: "Father, if you are willing, take this cup from me...." That cup held the bitter dregs of God's wrath against sin. Christ was beginning his descent into hell. That is why exact measurements—50 or 500 feet—are not important here. Christ was before the face of God, confronting eternal judgment. The issues of the struggle were eternally significant.

It was a stone's throw—but you couldn't walk over there. From him the anguish wrung sweat like drops of blood—but to endure what he endured there would destroy you. All you could do was watch and worship, praying that he'd endure and hoping that he'd come back to you. And that's what he did.

PRAYER

Blessed Lord, ours was the transgression, yours the deadly pain. Your forsakenness won our acceptance. Send us forth today in the joy of salvation. In your name, Amen.

Listen and Be Still

The Prayer in the Garden

*"My Father, if it is possible, may
this cup be taken from me."*
MATTHEW 26:39

MATTHEW 26:36-46

Jesus always seemed in perfect control of situations, whether subduing a stormy sea, encountering the funeral procession of a widow's son, or escaping hometown enemies intent upon stoning him to death. But in the garden we see him prostrate on the ground, writhing in spiritual agony. We see him facing death, with blood-like sweat pouring down his face. It is all because he holds in his hand a cup—not of blessing but of judgment, a cup of divine wrath and death. Let no one say, "How weak he has become. How courageous the death of Stephen was compared to this" (see Acts 7). For none faced such a death as his. No one else has ever gone to death with the sins of the world resting on him.

Listen! "Father, this cup is bitter; my lips burn; there is no grace in these dregs. I pass through the valley of the shadow of death, and you turn your face from me. If it be possible, let this cup pass from me."

Do not misunderstand this cry. Even in his agony Jesus was not asking to be freed from his redemptive mission. Rather, he was asking the Father if there were some other way—any other way—to redeem his people. But he rested in his Father's will.

The answer came back: "There is no other way. Take the cup and drink it." And he did.

What can we say but "What a wonderful Savior!"

PRAYER

Dear Savior, because you took the cup of suffering, we now take the cup of salvation and call on your name. Receive our praise and bless us today. For your sake, Amen.

Listen and Be Still

The Sword in the Garden

*"Put your sword away! Shall I not drink
the cup the Father has given me?"*
JOHN 18:11

MATTHEW 26:47-54

What a contradiction—Peter wielding a sword in defense of the Prince of Peace! But leave it to Peter—he was the one who blustered when he should have been silent, slept when he should have watched, cursed when he should have prayed.

Peter, in his defense of Jesus, placed a subtle temptation before the Lord. If his action displayed courage, it also showed ignorance. Though Jesus had spoken of the necessity of his death a few hours earlier, Peter had missed the point. Seeing soldiers surround his Master, he leaped forward, sword in hand.

Jesus recognized the temptation implied in Peter's action. It suggested that Jesus did not need to suffer and die. But Jesus dismissed the idea of the sword as an instrument to deliver him. By no means would he permit that sword to shatter the cup of suffering and death he held, given him by the Father.

Jesus points out here that he was not a victim. If it were a matter of needing to be rescued as a victim, the angelic hosts of heaven were available. The songwriter is correct: "He could have called ten thousand angels to destroy the world and set him free. But he died alone for you and me."

Jesus resisted the temptation to escape death. The Good Shepherd was ready to lay down his life for his sheep.

PRAYER

Good Shepherd, we praise you for laying down your life for us. Lead us today in paths of righteousness and restore our souls. We ask this in your name. Amen.

Listen and Be Still

Pleased to Meet You, Jesus

*When Herod saw Jesus, he was greatly pleased,
because. . . he had been wanting to see him.*
LUKE 23:8

GENESIS 4:1-12

On the road of humiliation that our Savior traveled there were many stopping places. One of them involved facing a flippant and superficial Herod.

Herod refused to take Jesus seriously. For him, this meeting turned out to be a trivial affair. Because he had heard strange things about the prophet of Galilee, he had wanted to meet Jesus. But beyond satisfying himself that Jesus was not John the Baptist returned to judge him for having John killed, Herod wasn't interested in Christ's claims. He paid no attention to the serious charges that the priests leveled against our Lord. Herod kept chattering away and plying Christ with questions. Appropriately John Masefield in his play The Trial of Jesus portrays Herod as a superficial, empty-headed, and hard-hearted ruler whose only interest in is Jerusalem's latest sensation. What a weight this careless attitude added to the heavy load of Christ.

There are many people like Herod today, interested only in a casual, superficial acquaintance with our Lord. They are pleased to meet Jesus only if the claims of the gospel are not pressed upon them. Such a meeting increases their condemnation. Have you met the Lord? Is your pleasure in meeting him rooted in curiosity or in your need for him? Has it led to a confession of your sins, a belief in his Word, and a surrender to his will?

PRAYER

Father of all mercies, deliver us from all cheap and casual interest in the Savior. Make us aware of our desperate need of your gracious forgiveness. For Jesus' sake, Amen.

This Is the Day

In him we have redemption through
his blood, the forgiveness of sins. . . .
EPHESIANS 1:7

LUKE 23:44-49

What a marvelous day that first Good Friday was! But none of the people who were there knew that.

The people who killed Jesus didn't know. The Pharisees didn't know. Pilate didn't know. The women didn't know. Even the disciples didn't know.

To most people Good Friday seemed like a total failure for Jesus. It looked like the end of the road. Jesus had done his best, but he just hadn't gotten anywhere. His followers were few, and most of them were nervous and afraid. There was nothing left for which to hope. The supernatural darkness that blanketed the scene typified the despair that shrouded the world that day.

But that was not how Almighty God saw Good Friday. It was the day he had been pointing to for thousands of years. It was the day Jesus had been talking about for months. It was the day on which Jesus, the Son of God, gave his precious life for the sins of the world! On this day Jesus made the one perfect sacrifice that made all other sacrifices unnecessary. This day gave meaning and sense to all the sacrifices and offerings and prayers of the past. Without this day, there would be no forgiveness, no salvation, no peace.

Because of Good Friday, there is victory for us! For everyone who repents and believes, sins are wiped away, buried, forgiven, and forgotten. Jesus paid it all!

PRAYER

We praise you, Lord Jesus, for that first Good Friday'! How wonderful is your love! Help us to repent of our sins and to trust you for our salvation. In your name, Amen.

Listen and Be Still

Taking a Stand

*Joseph. . . went boldly to Pilate
and asked for Jesus' body.*
MARK 15:43

MARK 15:42-47

Each of the gospel writers tells us about Joseph of Arimathea. Matthew tells us he was rich. Mark tells us he was an important member of the Jewish Council. Luke adds that he was a good and upright man, and John tells us he was a secret disciple of Jesus. Joseph was apparently a very special person. He had a lot to lose, therefore, and seemingly nothing to gain when he went to Pilate and asked for the body of Jesus.

Jesus, remember, was no hero on the day he died. When he was on trial, no public defender was appointed to represent him. No one came to his rescue or pleaded that his life be spared. Not even his disciples dared to help him. Jesus died as a common criminal under the worst of circumstances. Who, then, would want to claim the body of a person like that?

Joseph of Arimathea would!

Joseph decided to show his love for Jesus, no matter what happened. He would identify himself with his Lord, no matter what the cost. No longer did he care what others said or thought. He was ready to let the world know where he stood. So with love and compassion and boldness he asked for Jesus' body.

Many secret believers in Jesus are afraid to identify themselves publicly with him. But how impressive it is when Jesus' followers are not ashamed!

PRAYER

Father, help us never to be ashamed of your precious Son. Give us the courage to be faithful to him in every situation and to proudly bear the name Christian. In his name, Amen.

Listen and Be Still

Because He Lives

*If Christ had not been raised our preaching
is useless and so is your faith.*
1 CORINTHIANS 15:14

MARK 16:1-8

The well-known story of Jesus' resurrection is as thrilling today as when it was first told. The drama and surprise were so great that many who heard about it could hardly believe it had happened. But gradually the truth of it all began to sink into people's minds. And as the full meaning of the resurrection began to take possession of their lives, they knew it would become the central truth of the Christian faith.

Without Jesus' resurrection, nothing else that he did would matter. Jesus would have been just another teacher. We would have no assurance that our sins could be forgiven and no hope of peace with God. We would have no promise of life to come and no victory over death. All that Jesus taught and claimed would be meaningless and empty.

But now Jesus lives! And because he lives, we can face each day with calm assurance. We can even face death without fear. We can look forward to the day of our own resurrection and the eternal life to come.

Easter is a great day for those of us who believe. Small wonder, then, that we sing Easter songs with enthusiasm and joy: "Christ the Lord is risen today! Alleluia! All creation, join to say: Alleluia! Raise your joys and triumphs high; Alleluia! Sing, O heavens, and earth, reply: Alleluia!"

PRAYER

Father, we praise you for the joy of new life in you. Give us, we pray, the courage to face each new day and to live always in the power of Jesus' resurrection. In his name, Amen.

Listen and Be Still

Mistaken Identity

Thinking he was the gardener, she said. . .
JOHN 20:15

JOHN 20:10-18

We should not be surprised that many people do not believe Jesus rose from the grave. Mary's reaction to Jesus after his resurrection shows why. Mary thought he was the gardener.

The reason for this is simple. Recognition of people we know depends largely on whether we really expect that person to be present. I remember attending a worship service once on the island of Okinawa; a young man with whom I had been to college sat in the same row with me. I noticed him and thought he looked like my college friend, but I did not really recognize him because the last thing I expected was to meet him in that place. After the service we greeted one another, but with hesitation because neither expected the other to be there.

Seeing Jesus alive was the last thing Mary expected, for she had witnessed the devastating reality of his death. She never expected to see Jesus alive again. She didn't believe her eyes.

So it is that in her testimony—"I have seen the Lord!"—we have proof that Jesus was really dead and that he really rose again. That a dead person could live again is also the last thing we'd expect. In their closed universe, many people today cannot allow a dead person to rise. But it happened with Jesus, and someday the unexpected will happen as well with those who believe in him.

PRAYER

Lord, we are so thankful that because of the resurrection we may anticipate that one day the unexpected will happen to us. Thank you for Mary's testimony. In your name, Amen.

Listen and Be Still

The Glorious Impossibility

"It was impossible for death
to keep its hold on him."
ACTS 2:24

ACTS 2:22-28

The statement is so simple that we are apt to overlook it. But it sums up everything about the life, death, and resurrection of Jesus Christ of Nazareth: It was not possible for death to hold him.

Why wasn't it possible? First he was God, and God is life itself; when it comes down to it, death cannot hold life a prisoner. Second, Jesus Christ was the perfect man, and death has no claim on such a man. Third, Jesus had paid the price of human sin, so Satan, the prince of death, no longer had any claim on him.

So the Bible furnishes us with the glorious picture of God reaching down from the realm of heaven and releasing the Son of God from death's bondage. It had to happen. Death was powerless before the almighty power of God, and it had to surrender its victim.

In Peter's simple statement on Pentecost, the good news of the Christian faith is expressed fully: Death has met its match. For the first time since our forebears gave in to Satan's temptations, death touched Someone who would not lie still and slide into corruption.

In Jesus, God accomplished his great victory over sin—Jesus is victory itself, and when the victory of God met the best Satan could bring against it, death was "swallowed up" (1 Corinthians 15:54). If you are "in Christ," death won't be able to hold you either.

PRAYER

Lord, we thank you for the glorious impossibility that death cannot hold you. We have hope, knowing that you are all-powerful and death is not. We trust in your power. Amen.

Listen and Be Still

The Scandalous Jesus

*"Blessed is the man who does
not fall away on account of me."*
LUKE 7:23

LUKE 7:18-23

Jesus' contemporaries didn't understand his choice of friends.

He seemed to have an uncomfortable bias in favor of "the least of these" (Matthew 25:40). In Luke 7 today Jesus explains that, yes, he is the Messiah because, among other things, "the good news is preached to the poor." But this was surprising. People expected the Messiah to be more familiar with the corridors of power than with the corners of poverty.

Early in the history of the church, Jesus' followers began to take offense at his true humanity. They made up legends of boyhood miracles. They tried to explain away his limited knowledge about when the end of the world would come (see Mark 13:32). They pretended that he did not really die. How, after all, could God do any of these things? Jesus' humanity was a scandal.

In the modern church, as well as in the modern world, it is Jesus' true divinity that seems to be the stumbling block. Biblical witnesses are portrayed as primitive yokels who would believe anything. Jesus' miracles are explained away. Jesus' astonishing claims to authority and oneness with God are softened and qualified. Jesus' divinity is a scandal. Each age finds its own reasons to be scandalized by Jesus.

Yet, "blessed is the [person] who does not fall away."

PRAYER
Forgive us, O Lord, for taking offense where none has been given. Instead, let us rejoice in the deeds of the Messiah who has come. In his name we pray. Amen.

Listen and Be Still

Responding to the Resurrection

Since. . . you have been raised with Christ,
set your hearts on things above, where Christ is. . . .
COLOSSIANS 3:1

COLOSSIANS 3:1-12

Colossians 3 speaks of the new nature that believers receive, and the impression we get is that this nature is utterly different from what a person is outside of Christ.

But a Christian should not be described only in terms of what Christ through his resurrection has done for him. The Christian must do something too. Colossians 3:1 says, in effect, "If you are the blessed recipient of God's grace, don't just stand there; do something. You must seek the things that are above."

With this we face the great mystery that runs through the Bible—the mystery of how God's work and humanity's work are related. When God first created people, he gave them free will, and he allowed the destiny of creation to depend in some real way on the decision people would make. And when God re-creates people through the power of the resurrection, he re-creates them to serve him freely and with love.

Think what this means for you today, if you are a believer in Jesus Christ. Every moment is a moment of decision, every event is sacred. God is waiting to see whether you will order your life in terms of heaven's priorities or if you will disregard the gifts he gives. Turn your eyes upon Jesus, who has been raised and is at God's right hand.

PRAYER

Lord, help us love out of the power of the resurrection today.
Thank you for including us in your mysterious plan. Make us alive
and alert to your will. Amen.

Listen and Be Still

Practical Religion

Whatever you do, whether in word or deed,
do it all in the name of the Lord Jesus. . . .
COLOSSIANS 3:17

COLOSSIANS 3:12-17

The past few meditations have pointed out how the resurrection of Jesus affects the lives of those who believe in him; they are to seek the things that are above, where Christ is. Now the question is, What kind of people does the resurrection produce—are they, for example, so heavenly–minded they are of no earthly good?

Colossians 3 shows us the relationship between the heavenward interest of Christians and their daily life. In this chapter, we see that to seek the things that are above does not mean to abandon the things in this world. Not at all. Of all religions Christianity is the most practical. Heavenly–minded people know how interested God is in the creation he has made.

If people truly are followers of the resurrected Jesus and have the Lord's Spirit in their hearts, they will be better students, better carpenters, better teachers, better homemakers, better anything. And if a person claims to be a follower of Jesus and does not care about the quality of work he or she does or about his or her performance as a parent, spouse, sibling, or friend, we have reason to question the sincerity of that person's commitment. Heavenly–minded people do a superior job on earth.

That's because by faith they understand that what they do, they do "in Jesus' name." Anything that has Jesus' name on it has to be good!

PRAYER

Lord, thank you for enabling us to see that our ordinary activities can be important. May we approach them with enthusiasm in this day, in Jesus' name. Amen.

Listen and Be Still

The Unbeliever Convicted

*"Unless I see. . . and put my hand
[there]. . . I will not believe it."*
JOHN 20:25

JOHN 20:24-31

Thomas made his position clear. He was in a state of unbelief, and was not about to change unless he could see proof with his own eyes and judge for himself.

Nothing the disciples said to persuade him of the resurrection could change his mind. This man declared that Jesus alone could provide the evidence. For eight days the Lord let Thomas walk about in his self-imposed despair. (Sometimes God deals with us that way too.)

When Jesus came to minister to this unbelieving disciple, he spoke with a tone of rebuke, quoting Thomas almost word for word. "Here is the evidence. Put your finger here. And your hand here. Now do you believe?"

How far the Lord stooped in his grace to rescue his doubting disciple! He was willing to give what Thomas demanded, though he had every right to ask Thomas to meet his demands.

With reluctance and even pain, I am sure, Thomas touched the Master. Jesus uttered no word of praise. He simply said, "Because you have seen me, you have believed." And as John tells us, these events were recorded so that we might believe. For Thomas, it was "see and believe," for us it is "read and believe."

The last beatitude uttered by Jesus is not for Thomases: "Blessed are those who have not seen and yet have believed."

PRAYER

Gracious Lord, take the dimness of our unbelief away, and give us eyes of faith so that we who have not seen you may believe in you and serve you. For your sake, Amen.

Listen and Be Still

His Resurrection and Ours

He who raised Christ from the dead will also give life to your mortal bodies through his Spirit.
ROMANS 8:11

ROMANS 8:9-11

It is sometimes observed that part of the sadness that is expressed at a wake is caused by the mourners being reminded that soon they too will die. "Never send to know for whom the bell tolls; it tolls for thee," writes the seventeenth-century poet John Donne.

If this is true, it should also be true that part of the joy for Christians is celebrating not only Jesus' resurrection but also their own.

Romans 8 makes clear that Christians may celebrate this way. The passage we have read for today tells believers that the presence of the Holy Spirit in their hearts is a guarantee that just as Jesus rose from the dead, someday they will rise too.

Jesus exhibited the power of the Holy Spirit continuously when he was with us, and when he died, the Holy Spirit touched him yet again with the reality of eternal life. In the same way Christians live with the power of the Holy Spirit during their lives. And when they die, the Holy Spirit will touch them too with the reality of eternal life.

Every day is a great day of celebrating Jesus' resurrection and our own. Let today be a day of renewal and strengthening of faith, a day of opening our hearts once more to the influence of God's life-giving Spirit. May God bless you with courage and joy this glorious day.

PRAYER

O God, we rejoice because of the living hope you have placed in our hearts by touching us with your Spirit. Use us to share this good news and bring many to faith. Amen.

Listen and Be Still

391

The Sign of the Grain

"A kernel of wheat falls to the ground and dies. . . .
but if it dies, it produces many seeds."
JOHN 12:24

JOHN 12:20-26

As we think about the crucifixion and the resurrection of Jesus, let's return again to the cross and think about its role in our lives. So long as we are in this world, we live beneath the sign of the cross, and this sign colors everything we are called to do.

We know this because God wants us to be imitators of Jesus, who gave up his own life to make life possible again for us. And Jesus has shown that for him and for us the glory of real living is received along the way of suffering. The sign of the grain makes this clear.

John 12 records Jesus' anticipation of glory—"The hour has come for the Son of Man to be glorified." Indeed, some Greek people (Gentiles) had just come to seek out the Lord, and they represented the coming of his worldwide kingdom. But Jesus announced that he would achieve his glory in the same way a grain of wheat achieves its purpose. He would die, as the grain must die, and as it then grows and bears much fruit, Jesus would rise again and usher in his kingdom.

In this passage Jesus declares that those who follow him must walk the road of suffering, as he did; they, too, must learn the lesson of the grain of wheat. Following Jesus involves suffering, humiliation, and sorrow. That's the way it is. And yet this is the way God uses us mightily.

PRAYER

Master, make us willing to be planted and to die to ourselves in your service. Teach us the sign of the grain, and help us to walk the road you walked. For your sake, Amen.

Listen and Be Still

Sure Enough

"Did I not tell you that if you believed,
you would see the glory of God?"
JOHN 11:40

JOHN 11:28-44

Often pastors are privileged to ride along on someone else's journey of faith. Bill and Nancy (not their real names) welcomed me aboard their faith ship several years ago. It was a wild ride!

Slowly they realized that their business wasn't going to support them. They had to make some tough decisions. Could they sell their business? Would they have to move? Could Bill get a job? Would Nancy have to work? How would this affect their child?

The process of change was unbelievably stressful. It was all Bill and Nancy thought about—and sometimes fought about. I encouraged them to believe that God could do more than they dared to expect. I even said miracles might happen. We prayed.

Those days seemed so dark. Sometimes Bill and Nancy had more faith than I did. Sometimes their child had more faith than any of us. But things looked as bleak as they did at Lazarus's tomb. Yet we knew that if we believed, we would see God's glory.

A strong buyer appeared. Creditors settled debts on good terms. Someone offered Bill a new career. Housing worked out. Nancy found a good job too. A marvelous little miracle took place right in front of our eyes.

PRAYER

In our dark days, Lord, help us to remember your promises and to believe that the power of the resurrection is there for us in life's ordinary calamities. In Jesus' name, Amen.

Listen and Be Still

Christ and the Children

People were also bringing babies to
Jesus to have him touch them.
LUKE 18:15

LUKE 18:9-17

Sometimes we forget that our Savior came to call children also. We, in our shortsightedness, suppose that because they are too immature to grasp all the mysteries of salvation with their minds, Christ has neither a message nor a blessing for them. Yet our Savior took the little ones in his arms and blessed them. Of them he said, "The kingdom of God belongs to such as these."

How necessary it is for Christian parents to learn this lesson. When we take our children to church, we teach them the meaning of worship, explain the prayers and sacraments to them, and teach them the songs that are sung. We show them that Sunday is a day of joy for the whole family because we enter the presence of our God.

In our homes, family worship can be made meaningful and attractive. Bible reading and prayers can be regarded not as necessary chores but as spiritual privileges. Christian homes are meant to be happy places.

The calling of our Christian communities is to bring our children daily to Jesus, who alone can bless their lives. May you seek and find occasion to touch a child's life for Jesus today—whether that child is yours or a child of a friend, acquaintance or fellow church member.

PRAYER

God of the covenant, we thank you for sending Jesus to our children too. Help us to teach them in the way of salvation. And may we love you with childlike faith. Amen

Listen and Be Still

The Poor

"You will always have the poor among you. . . ."
JOHN 12:8

JOHN 12:1-8

In the once-popular book *Diary of a Country Priest*, George Bernanos talks about "the saddest saying in the gospels." He's referring to this saying of Jesus: "You will always have the poor among you."

This saying does seem to be one of the saddest. It also seems, at first glance, to be callous and uncaring, as if Jesus is saying, "The poor? You are concerned about the poor? Well, you always have some of them around." Is this Scrooge or Jesus? But we must note the context. Judas had objected to the honor Mary showed Jesus by pouring perfume on his feet. Judas used the plight of the poor to further his own ends. Like many modern politicians and social planners, he used the poor.

Let us not misunderstand our Lord. There are several things here which must be—and sometimes are—pointed out. The main point is that this is not a prescription but a prediction. This is no warrant to ignore or to induce poverty. Someone has rightly observed that we always have the ignorant with us too. Must we shut down our schools? We have the sick. Shall we close our hospitals? We have the unbelieving. Is this a license to quit preaching the gospel?

Never! Always we have the poor. Yes. And always, as our Lord elsewhere told us, we are called upon to help them. Let us do so in his name.

PRAYER

Father in heaven, give our daily bread this day to the poor, and your presence to the poor in spirit. Open our eyes to see poverty and to give as we have been given. Amen.

Listen and Be Still

Believe and Receive

*"Whatever you ask for in prayer, believe that
you have received it, and it will be yours."*
MARK 11:24

MARK 11:20-25

C.S. Lewis and other readers of the New Testament have remarked that our Lord really presents two patterns of prayer. One of them is found in the Lord's Prayer ("Your will be done,") and in the model of prayer in Gethsemane ("Not my will, but *yours* be done"). This is the pattern we usually follow, deliberately subordinating our wills to God's. After all, our wills are tarnished, shortsighted, and heavily biased in favor of ourselves.

The other pattern we find is this remarkable statement of Jesus: "Whatever you ask for in prayer, believe that you have received it, and it will be yours." This seems to say that what counts is not so much what God wills, but what we believe, and that as long as we believe, we will get whatever we want.

"But how are we to pray this very night?" asked Lewis. This much can be said. Belief is always a gift of God. It is never something we crank up on our own. We are not told here to grit our teeth, bear down, and try to create believing feelings within ourselves.

Instead, as always, we are to place ourselves and those whom we love in God's keeping. It may be God's will to grant us the mountain-moving kind of belief. The resurrection of Jesus is the evidence that our God can move mountains, for the power that raised Jesus from the dead is exercised by our prayer-hearing God.

PRAYER

Lord, we believe. Help us in our unbelief. Teach us to pray in line with your will, O Lord. And by your Spirit give us insight to ask for what you want us to receive.

Listen and Be Still

The Golden Rule

"In everything, do to others what you would have them do to you."
MATTHEW 7:12

MATTHEW 7:7-14

Does this rule always apply? Suppose a person wishes to be paid for political favors. Or let's say a person wishes to be ordered around like a slave. Suppose that what a person wants others to do to him or her is actually evil.

As Wallace Alston has pointed out, if you take the golden rule out of the life and off the lips of Christ, it could be understood in quite peculiar ways. When a whole society goes bad, what people wish others to do to them is often perverse. If, then, they do the same to others, the situation is not improved. Taken on its own, the golden rule is not enough.

A story is told about a theologian and an astronomer who were talking together. The astronomer said that after reading widely in the field of religion, he had concluded that all religion could be summed up in the words: "Do unto others as you would have them do unto you." After a brief pause, the theologian replied that after reading widely in the area of astronomy he had concluded that all of it could be summed up in the words: "Twinkle, twinkle, little star; how I wonder what you are!"

Neither, however, is enough! "Whatever you *ought* to wish others to do to you, do to them." All of our wishes must be formed by the perfect will of God.

PRAYER

Instruct us thoroughly, O Lord, in that central part of our lives where desires and wishes are formed. Then make our wishes like yours, we pray. In Jesus' name, Amen.

Living Memory

"This is my body given for you;
do this in remembrance of me."
LUKE 22:19

LUKE 22:7-23

Memories are important. Whether positive or negative, they teach both wisdom for the present and insight for the future.

The Christian faith is rooted in memories. Jesus gave us a feast, the Lord's Supper, which calls us to remember the greatest event in history—the broken body and poured-out blood of Christ!

Yet what exactly is the character of remembering? Well, first, there is the remembrance of facts—Jesus was betrayed, mocked, and crucified. We remember that history. Second, the facts call us to remember the message: we remember hurt and Jesus' healing; we remember despair and the Spirit's comfort; we remember sin and God's response to it in Christ—he will remember it no more (Jeremiah 31:34).

Finally, through God's message of kindness we hear the call to accept his forgiveness. To those who repent and believe, Jesus gives this great promise: "I will never blot out his name from the book of life, but will acknowledge his name before my Father and his angels" (Revelation 3:1-6).

In the Lord's Supper, Jesus calls us to remember him until he comes again. May you have courage to accept his call, for in remembering the gospel you will find wisdom for today and insight for the future.

PRAYER

Father, we remember your kindness displayed in the suffering and death of Jesus Christ. Teach us wisdom for today and give us insight for tomorrow. In Jesus, Amen.

Listen and Be Still

Second Fiddle

He brought him to Jesus.
JOHN 1:42

JOHN 1:35-42

For many years, a large Christian organization has regularly sponsored "Andrew dinners." Christians invite their non-Christian friends or neighbors to be guests at a banquet. Along with good food there is excellent music and a good speaker. At the end of the banquet, the speaker invites the guests to commit their lives to Jesus Christ as their Savior and Lord. Many respond joyfully and begin a new life of freedom in Jesus.

It was Andrew who introduced Peter, his brother, to Jesus. Later, Andrew, along with Philip, brought some Greeks to Jesus (John 12:20-22). Andrew was also the one who told Jesus about a young lad who had five loaves of bread and two fish (John 6:8-9).

Most people, however, don't remember much about Andrew. Although he was the one who brought Peter to Jesus, we tend to remember Peter and forget Andrew. We forget Andrew's role in the other events as well.

But Andrew probably wouldn't mind. He recognized that Jesus didn't choose him to play first chair in his "orchestra." His task was to be "second fiddle," and he played his role well. He knew that playing second fiddle for Jesus is far more wonderful than playing first for anyone else! Few of us are "first chair" players. But, like Andrew, each of us can bring one person at a time to meet Jesus. Whom is God leading you to bring to Jesus?

PRAYER

Lord, we do not ask for a position of prestige and honor. We pray simply that you will help us to do all you want us to and to be faithful in every situation. In your name, Amen.

Listen and Be Still

Hope in God

Everything that was written. . . was written
to teach us, so that. . . we might have hope.
ROMANS 15:4

REVELATION 21:1-7

The psalmist once asked the question, "How long must I wrestle with my thoughts and every day have sorrow in my heart?" (13:2). These words represent our cry for hope. How long must the innocent victim of HIV despair? How long must sorrow rule the hearts of the parents whose son became the innocent casualty of gang warfare? How long must death make a mockery of life? "How long…?"—this is the daily cry for a better life.

The Bible is not silent on this matter. According to Paul, history teaches us hope for tomorrow! Jesus became like us in order to create hope (Hebrews 2:14-17). Like us, he shed tears (John 11:35), experienced rejection (Matthew 26:47-67), and faced death's hellish mockery of life (Matthew 27:45-50). And for us he rose from the dead to open a new world of hope (1 Corinthians 15).

These events of the past paint a hopeful future. Jesus will return, take up residence with his followers, tend to their tears, and nurture gladness of heart. Jesus himself promised a bright tomorrow when he said, "I am making everything new!" (Revelation 21:5).

We may wrestle with our thoughts and have sorrow in our hearts. But we also have God's promises and his Holy Spirit. Therefore we can endure, be encouraged, and yearn for the day when God will turn our mourning into dancing (Psalm 30:11). Put your hope in God!

PRAYER

Father, our lives are vulnerable, and events unpredictable.
Encourage us with your Word, and help us to endure on our
journey with hope. In Jesus' name we pray. Amen.

Listen and Be Still

Peace?

"Peace I leave with you; my peace I give you.
I do not give to you as the world gives."
John 14:27

Romans 5:1-5

Peace is rare in today's world. The media relentlessly confront us with stories of child abuse, sexual harassment, the threat of AIDS, racial conflict, and global economic uncertainty. When peace is established, it usually occurs under strange conditions. Ceasefires are achieved with "neutral" tanks, marriages are "saved" through contracts; both are extremely vulnerable to a lack of trust. All desire peace, but few possess it.

Christians, however, can have peace. What humanity cannot achieve, Jesus has freely given: "Peace I leave with you; my peace I give you." The goal of the gospel has become the believer's birthright. In Christ we are children of the kingdom of peace (Colossians 1:18-20).

But what kind of peace do we receive? While hope yearns for the renewal of creation, peace is the confidence of being held in the strong and forgiving hands of God. What used to be a relationship of hostility has become one of friendship with God because of the suffering and death of Christ (Ephesians 2:15-16; Colossians 1:21-22). In the spirit of true friendship, God's peace protects faith, hope, and love in Jesus (Philippians 4:4-7).

Though peace is indeed rare in our hate-filled, violent world, those who trust in Jesus Christ can have peace in their hearts. May "the Lord turn his face toward you and give you peace"(Numbers 6:26).

Prayer

Father, we see the restlessness, pain, and disease of our day. In grace grant us your peace, and protect our hearts and lives as we await the great day of your salvation. Amen.

Listen and Be Still

Life's Biggest Question

"What about you?" he asked.
"Who do you say I am?"
MATTHEW 16:15

MATTHEW 16:13-20

Today Jesus stands before us, asking each of us this question. He asks it every day.

In a way, it's like a wife asking her husband, "Do you love me?" Every day a husband expresses an answer to that question.

Perhaps years ago you accepted Jesus as the Christ. Perhaps, like Peter, you decided to follow him; you said, "Jesus is the Christ! He is my Savior and Lord."

But today (and every day) he repeats the question. Answering it once for all doesn't answer it all at once.

Perhaps today you are very worried about something. Picture Jesus standing before you. "Now, again, WHO do you say I am?" he asks with a smile. "Oh yes," you say, "I'm forgetting! You are the Christ. You control everything. Help me to learn to trust you." Only very slowly does Jesus become fully all that he is in our lives.

Perhaps someone has deeply hurt you, and you resist forgiving that person. "WHO do you say I am?" he repeats. Or perhaps you're confused as you face a hard decision. Or maybe you face a daunting project and worry about its outcome. Again he stands up before you and asks, "WHO do you say I am?" He repeats his question again and again.

Jesus never stops asking until we acknowledge his lordship with every fiber of our being. Each day we must answer him anew.

PRAYER

Today, Lord Jesus, may I trust you more deeply, follow you more completely, rest in you more sweetly. You are Lord and Christ. Be that in my life today. In your name, Amen.

Listen and Be Still